ON THIS

GW00538083

VOLUME TWO

STORIES OF WATERFORD CITY, COUNTY & NEARBY

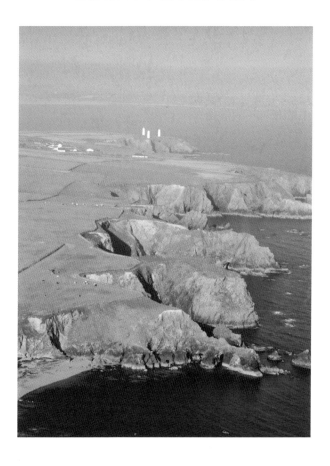

JULIAN WALTON

WITH FRANK O'DONOGHUE

Published by Frank O'Donoghue in association with Julian Walton

Copyright 2014 Frank O'Donoghue and Julian Walton

ISBN 978-0-9574484-2-1

Printed in Ireland

Design by

Cover picture: Fáilte Ireland

Frontispiece picture: Ivan Power

Chapter divider images and other great help from Andrew Kelly:

1. Séipéal San Nioclás, An Rinn
2. Dunhill Castle
3. The Salmon Leap, Colligan Falls
4. The Vee
5. The *Dunbrody*
6. Mahon Falls
7. The Barrow Bridge

SPECIAL ASSISTANCE FROM

CONTENTS

CALENDAR OF EVENTS *ON CD

CD CONTENTS

Narrator: Julian Walton
Pianist: Des Manahan
Editor: Wayne Brown
Recorded at WLRFM studios

INTRODUCTION

Throughout 2014 Waterford City has been celebrating eleven hundred years of history, and so the first volume of *On This Day* was mainly – but not entirely – city based. In our second volume we reverse the process, giving pride of place to the county outside the city. 2014 has also seen the amalgamation of our two local authorities, so we are all one now for the first time since Queen Elizabeth's charter of 1574 established a separate County of the City of Waterford. Citizens of the Urbs Intacta will just have to get to know their rural brethren in such exotic places as Knockanore, Ballymacarbery, Aglish and Touraneena.

However, county boundaries, though convenient for the GAA, are at best an artificial concoction. "On This Day" aired for nearly nineteen years on WLRFM, and as the airwaves tend to ignore lines on a map the programme included items from adjacent counties within the catchment area, and some of these also feature in this volume.

Several points made in the introduction to Volume One need to be made again here. First of all, this is not a history of Waterford but a series of stories about people, places and events. It is not primarily intended for academics, though I hope they will find it useful, but for readers with a general interest in Waterford's past. Much modern history writing is overbearingly solemn and pompous; there is no reason why it cannot be fun as well.

Secondly, the items in this volume were all broadcast originally on WLRFM and were intended for a radio listenership. They were compiled over nearly twenty years, and since the series started there has been an explosion of fresh source material, and this process will continue into the future thanks to the wonders of the Internet. When the series began I was confined to sources that were readily available, and the unrelenting pressure to keep the series going limited the time available for in-depth research. That is why some obvious subjects were not included and other rather peculiar ones were.

Waterford has been fortunate in the number and calibre of its past historians, and I owe a particular debt to Charles Smith (1746), R.H. Ryland (1824) and P.M. Egan (1894) for their county histories, as to Canon Power for his wonderful gazetteer of our placenames and his history of our diocese. The journal of the

|₁₁₁₁|₁₁₁₁|₁₁₁₁|₁₁₁₁|₁₁₁₁|₁₁₁₁|₁₁₁₁|₁₁₁₁|₁₁₁₁|₁₁₁₁|₁₁₁₁|₁₁₁₁|₁₁₁₁|₁₁₁₁|₁₁₁₁|₁₁₁₁|₁₁₁₁|₁₁₁₁|₁₁₁₁|₁₁₁₁|

Waterford and South East of Ireland Archaeological Society (1894-1920) and its modern successor *Decies* have provided invaluable material. Among other modern publications, the appearance of Tom Fewer's *Waterford People* was especially welcome, supplemented on a broader field by *The Oxford Dictionary of National Biography* (2004) and *The Dictionary of Irish Biography* (2009):

"Lives of great men [and women] oft remind us

We can make our lives sublime..."

John Young has generously allowed me to use material from his *Maritime & General History of Dungarvan 1690 - 1978,* which is particularly useful for local ship wrecks. Newspapers provide a bottomless well for the local historian, but they are cumbersome and time consuming to use, and I could never have managed to avail of them without the conscientious burrowings of my two Transition Year students of the mid-nineties, Deirdre McGrath and Ciara O'Shea.

Some of the items in Volume Two, as in Volume One, are based on topics that I have researched extensively myself, but in many cases I have relied on the labours of others; the accuracy of what appears in these pages depends on what they have written, but the interpretations and value judgements are my own. In a work such as this it is not possible to acknowledge sources, except in a few cases where it seemed necessary to state the authority for what is written. Most of the stories appear much the same as when they were first heard on air; a few have been updated in the light of later revelations. None of them could have appeared without the generous help of a number of people and institutions; they are listed at the end of the book.

In selecting the material, I have tried to include as broad a mix as possible, ranging across the political, religious and social spectrum. If the "decade of commemoration" is to teach us anything, the lesson should be that we are a very diverse people and that we should glory in that diversity. No one tradition or set of beliefs has the sole right to interpret Ireland, let alone the Déise; through our involvement with Ireland we can all rejoice in what Wolfe Tone called "the common name of Irishman".

I hope that the stories in this book will enrich the readers' knowledge of our history, engender a pride in our past, and encourage awareness of the need to preserve the heritage of which we are merely the temporary custodians.

Julian C. Walton

THE FIRST
CENTURIES

THE GLAS GAIBHNEACH

Uair amháin, fadó fadó, many centuries before the invention of milking machines and quotas, there roamed through the lush pastures of Munster a cow. She was called the Glas Gaibhneach – and she was no ordinary cow. So capacious was her udder that it was said that any vessel she was milked into would be filled to the brim before it ran dry. Fortunately, neither supertankers nor cold storage were known in those days, or who knows to what indignities this generous animal might have been subjected.

The Glas Gaibhneach paid many visits to the Déise. There are traditions of her presence at Ballycommera in the parish of Grange, whence she wandered to Ardmore and thence to Ferry Point. At Seafield near Bunmahon is Gleann an Earbaill - the glen of the tail - a stream channel that was scooped out by her long trailing tail as she munched her way towards Carrigcastle. Another time she spent a night in the little parish of Lickoran, a second night at Newcastle, and a third at Glenanore, departing thence via the Gap to Rathgormack. Sheegouna in the parish of Garrangibbon is named after her. And so fertile did she find Páirc an Iarla in the townland of Killune near Tramore that she patronised it for several nights.

Indeed, this remarkable beast might still be with us today had it not been for the ungrateful cynicism of a farmer's wife in Ballylaneen, who devised an ingenious method of testing the tradition that the Glas Gaibhneach's udder would never run dry. So long did the milking take that, having submitted patiently for several hours, the Glas Gaibhneach looked round to see what was happening, only to find that she was being milked into a sieve! Is there no end to the curiosity of a woman?

Now, if there is one thing a lady can't stand, it's the feeling that another lady is taking the mickey out of her. With one belt of her hind legs the Glas Gaibhneach sent the sieve and its owner flying into the nearest slurry pit. She then stalked out of the milking parlour with her eyes blazing and her voice rising from her usual gentle lowing to an ominous bellow. As a sign of further displeasure she stuck her horns in the ground and left a trench behind her that bore an uncanny resemblance to the R675 (though with fewer potholes). The grinding of her teeth left a trail of loose chippings. Nor did she stop till she reached Bunmahon, where she plunged into the sea, leaving a wake after her that swamped a thousand holiday caravans.

And from that day to this there has been no sign of the Glas Gaibhneach. Nach mór an trua é!

Main source: P. Canon Power, Place names of Decies (1952 edition),
pp 92, 119, 160, 259, 351, 368.

DÉISE MAN DISCOVERED

On this day in 2002 the accidental discovery of ancient human remains on the lower slopes of the Comeragh Mountains caused a flurry of excitement among archaeologists. The turfy nature of the soil has ensured excellent preservation. This makes Déise Man every bit as important as the Bog Bodies of Denmark. What can scientists tell us about him?

Well, the remains are those of a large, strongly built male in his mid-twenties. The fact that so much care was taken over his burial – the spectacular mountain site, for instance – suggests that he was a mighty warrior, perhaps even a chieftain. This is confirmed by the nature of the objects interred with him. The largest is his weapon, a long wooden cudgel made apparently of native ash, and with a curiously flattened edge obviously intended for a series of rapid and deadly strikes at the bodies of his foes. Close by was a small round object, its surface apparently made of skin. Most experts believe that the innards were the brains of a slain enemy, and which in turn would be thrown at the head of a future foe – readers will remember that such was the custom in the time of Cuchulainn, and that King Conor Mac Nessa actually lived for several years with such an object lodged in his forehead.

Admittedly, one eccentric scholar has suggested that the cudgel was actually used for hitting the round object back and forth between opposing armies, probably as part of a religious ceremony or even a pastime. But this theory has been universally ridiculed: with the perpetual need to procure food for his wives and children, Déise Man would hardly have had time for such an absurd pursuit.

The peat has preserved several shreds of the man's clothing. From these we may deduce that the upper garment of Déise Man was made of white woven cloth, decorated in places with the blue dye known as woad. Above the left breast is the crude depiction of a shield, on which are drawn a number of what look like boats, currachs taken in tribute from a defeated enemy, no doubt. On the opposite side is a runic inscription, the letters of which appear to be G L A N B I A – probably a magic incantation to ensure the continued supply of food. Close by were a number of silver goblets, used no doubt for carousing after victory in battle – "one for the woad," so to speak.

But the most exciting news is that scientists have succeeded in extracting from the body some small amounts of DNA. It should now be possible to compare these with the DNA of present inhabitants of the county. So who knows who may prove to be directly descended from Déise Man, discovered in the Comeragh Mountains in 2002.

And if the date hasn't already made you suspicious, please note that it happened – on this day!

ST DECLAN AND ST PATRICK

|᠎᠎|

St Declan's Way is the name given to a long-distance walking route from Ardmore to Cashel. It's 86 kilometres long, and as far as possible it follows the ancient pathways that would have been used by traders and pilgrims travelling between the two places. For most of the way the countryside is gently undulating, but the main natural obstacle, the Knockmealdown Mountains, has to be crossed by a high pass, the Bearna Cloch an Bhuidéil. May St Declan's Way prove a source of pleasure, refreshment and inspiration to both natives and visitors for many years to come.

"Ok Pat, I surrender - you don't have to nail me to the ground."

Dave Moore

According to the biography of Declan, the saint himself plodded along this route in order to preach to the King of Cashel, Aongus mac Natfrioch, whom he hoped to convert to Christianity. The King was pleased with Declan's preaching and allowed him to wander round his kingdom baptising his subjects. However, he himself refused baptism at the hands of St Declan, the reason being that Declan belonged to the tribe of Déisí, who had been expelled from their original homeland in County Meath, whereas Aongus belonged to the Eoghanacht of Cashel, their traditional enemies. Aongus did not become a Christian until the arrival of St Patrick, and you'll probably remember the story of what happened during the baptism ceremony. Patrick intended to drive the sharp end of his crozier into the ground, but in the process stuck it through Aongus' foot, neatly skewering the King to the ground - you know how careless saints can be.

Patrick and Declan had known each other for a long time. For when Declan was on his way back from Rome to Ireland after being blessed by the Pope, he met Patrick going in the opposite direction and they had a long chat. They were destined to meet again when Patrick came to Cashel, for here the news reached him that although Declan's missionary work in the Déise had been pretty successful there was one obstinate chieftain named Ledban who refused to be converted.

Now Patrick had been appointed the chief bishop of all the Irish, and if there was one thing he couldn't abide it was obstinate chieftains. So off he went to the plain of Inneoin, where the Kings of Déise were traditionally inaugurated. Learned scholars have identified it as the townland of Mullaghmoney in the parish of Newchapel, four miles north of Clonmel. Here St Patrick prepared to lay a curse, not only on Ledban, but on all the people and territory of Déise for all eternity. And to make the curse all the more effective, he preceded it with a fast. Luckily, Declan was informed of what was going on by an angel, so he set off at top speed, and arrived just in time, for Patrick was working himself up into a fine cursing mode. Declan managed to get a brief moratorium put on the cursing, and hurried off to make a frantic plea to Ledban. The latter, however, remained obdurate, whereupon Declan deposed him and appointed in his stead a young man named Fergal Mac Cormac who, in the best tradition of Irish politics, just happened to be the saint's cousin. He then managed to pacify Patrick with the gift of a large tract of land west of Clonmel in which there was a great pool of clear water. To this very day it's called St Patrick's Well.

Impressed with the generosity of Declan, Patrick made some rapid last-minute alterations to his curse, changing it into a blessing. And to show that he was now in a good mood, when Declan carelessly ripped his foot open by walking on an iron spike, Patrick cured the wound instantly with a lofty wave of his hand.

So you see that but for the intervention of St Declan, Patrick would undoubtedly have turned our beloved Déise into a blackened desert. The feast of Declan, patron saint of Ardmore, to whom we should all be so grateful, occurs on this day.

Main source: Rev. P. Power (ed.), Life of St Declan of Ardmore and Life of St Mochuda of Lismore, London, Irish Texts Society, 1914.

ST CARTHAGE AND THE APPLES

There's no doubt about it, St Carthage, also known as St Mochuda, was a powerful man. Although he's remembered today as the founder of Lismore, he in fact spent most of his life as abbot of Rahan, a great monastery he founded near Tullamore. Many and great are the miracles attributed to him, and every word is guaranteed true.

He seems to have had a special thing about apples. One fine day in early spring a pagan druid came to him and said: "OK, Mochuda, if you're so great put leaves on this apple tree."

Now that kind of thing was no bother to Mochuda at all. A quick sign of the cross and the tree sprouted leaves.

The druid merely raised his eyebrows. "That was easy," he scoffed. "Now how about some blossom?" A quick flick of the fingers, and behold, there was blossom.

"Huh, very impressive," snarled the druid sarcastically, though a little uneasily. "But what use is an apple tree without fruit?"

Hey presto, a few seconds later the apple tree was bursting with fruit which fell to the ground fully ripe. One particularly large apple hit the druid on the head as it fell.

The druid picked it up and greedily sank his teeth into it. Instantly he spat it out in disgust. "This bloody apple's sour!" he yelled triumphantly. "What use is fruit that you can't eat?"

Not to be outdone, Mochuda blessed the apples so that they instantly became sweet as honey. And to punish the druid for his uncouth behaviour, he very properly struck him blind for a whole year.

On another occasion Mochuda and his followers were on their travels when they came to an orchard full of ripe juicy apples. They begged the owner to give them some, but he gruffly told them to clear off. "OK," said Mochuda, "but if we go the apples go too." And not one apple ever grew in that orchard again.

One day Mochuda and his merry monks were crossing the Blackwater at a ford when they saw a large apple floating in the river. Mochuda grabbed it and took it away with him, and to this very day the spot is called Baile Átha na hUalla,, or in English Ballyhooly.

One of the monks asked Mochuda to give the apple to him, but Mochuda refused, saying he was keeping it for a special purpose. Soon afterwards they came to a lios in which a group of little girls were playing, among whom was Flanad the daughter of Cuana Mac Cailcin. The poor girl had lost the use of her right arm.

"Here, child," coaxed Mochuda, "have an apple." Flanad had very properly been taught by her mother not to speak to strangers, but the sight of the rosy apple was too much for her and she reached out her left hand. "Other hand please," said Mochuda sternly, and she stretched out her right arm, which was instantly cured.

Flanad could now have had her choice of all the warriors of Erin for her husband, but she chose instead to follow Mochuda and live in holy chastity for the rest of her days.

On another occasion Mochuda performed a similar miracle on a pregnant woman named Brigh. Not only was her withered hand healed as soon as she touched the apple, but the moment she bit into it she gave birth painlessly to her child.

An apple a day keeps the druid away
Dave Moore

It wasn't just with apples that Mochuda could work miracles. For a long time he refused to allow his monks keep cows. One day a neighbouring abbot, Lachten of Freshford, brought him a present of thirty cows, a bull, some cattlemen, and two lovely maids. But to make sure Mochuda would accept them, he decided to play a trick on the saint. Coming near Rahan, he hid the cattle, then went on to Rahan by himself.

On arrival at the monastery he pretended to be ill and asked for a drink of milk. Mochuda, having no cows, had of course no milk, but that was no problem to him. He had a pitcher filled with water, which he blessed and turned into milk.

Lachten, of course, realising it was magic milk, promptly changed it back into water, and sent it back to Mochuda with bitter complaints. "I'm not going to eat or drink in this house," he said, "until you promise to accept the present I've brought you."

Mochuda naturally had to agree, and Lachten sent for the cattle. Never again was Mochuda's monastery short of milk.

There's no doubt that St Mochuda was a powerful man; and his feast is celebrated in Lismore - on this day.

Main source: Rev. P. Power (ed.), Life of St Declan of Ardmore and Life of St Mochuda of Lismore, London, Irish Texts Society, 1914.

THE SPEAKING STONE

The story of the elderly husband, the pretty young wife, and the ardent lover, is one of the great themes of folklore. It is found in all cultures, ancient and modern. It forms the basis of the great epics of Diarmuid and Gráinne, of Deirdre and the Sons of Uisneach, of Tristan and Isolde, of King Arthur, Queen Guinevere and Sir Lancelot.

Many and ingenious are the devices by which the lovers seek to conceal their adultery. In some versions of the Tristan saga, a "speaking stone" vouches for their apparent innocence.

In the Déise we have our own Speaking Stone. It stands beside a small tributary of the River Tay, in the townland of Durrow near Stradbally, and is probably Ireland's largest glacial erratic boulder. Its name in Irish is An Cloch Labhrais, and in ancient times it possessed magical powers, for it could determine whether or not a person denying a crime of which he or she had been accused was telling the truth.

But is there no limit to the wiles of the fair sex? One day a woman accused of having committed adultery announced that she would swear to her innocence upon this stone. As the party approached the stone, the woman's lover appeared in the guise of a poor hermit, who humbly offered to carry the woman on his shoulders across the raging torrent to take her oath at the stone. When they had struggled through the stream, the woman laid her hand upon the stone and swore that no man had ever been between her legs apart from her husband – and of course, the poor hermit who had just carried her there.

Thus the Speaking Stone was forced to declare that she had told the truth, but so enraged was it at such trickery that it cried out in a loud voice: "Bíonn an fhírinne féin searbh" – Truth itself is bitter – and split in two with a crack like thunder. Since then, not one word has it uttered, in either of the national languages.

Go there and try it out for yourself!

Main source: Account of Co. Waterford written by Sir Richard Cox, c. 1685.
Published in Decies, no. 36 (1987).

Dave Moore

EPIPHANY AT ARDMORE

Kings in ancient times were expected to be judges as well as rulers of their people. Solomon son of David, King of the Jews about three thousand years ago, was especially renowned for his wisdom. One day two quarrelling women were brought before him. The first had a sorry tale to tell. They lived in the same house, she said, and they each had a baby son, but one night her neighbour lay on her child and accidentally smothered it. Ingeniously, the other woman swapped the babies, so that in the morning the neighbour had the speaker's living child and she had the dead one. "Lies, all lies!" shrieked the neighbour. "The living child is mine."

How could the King find out which of the women was telling the truth? His solution was effective, if somewhat crude. "Bring me my sword of burning gold!" he commanded. "I shall now chop the child in two, so you can have half each." "Suits me," shrugged the smother mother. But the real mother cried out in alarm: "No, no, my lord, give her the baby!" "That sorts that," snapped the King. "You are the one who really cared for the child, so you must be the real mother."

The Judgement of Solomon is carved in dramatic detail on the arcading of the ruined cathedral of Ardmore. But there is a surprise in store. For underneath we see depicted the tender Virgin with the infant Jesus being visited by the three Magi bearing their gifts. Why has the sculptor (uniquely) placed these two scenes together? Father Donal O'Connor, in his booklet *The Pilgrim's Ardmore*, explains. A child is at the center of both stories. In the first, the King uses his God-given wisdom to discern the truth. In the second, the Wise Men lay their symbolic gifts before the baby Jesus, for he being God is the seat of all wisdom.

Though the carvings are now somewhat battered after a thousand years' exposure to the elements, the skill of the ancient stonecutter is still plain to see. Both scenes are alive with movement – the tension

of the quest for truth, and the resolution of that quest in Jesus. Today we celebrate the final act of the Christmas liturgy – indeed for the Eastern churches it *is* Christmas.

The feast of the Epiphany is celebrated – on this day.

Main source: Rev. Donal O'Connor, The Pilgrim's Ardmore (2000).

INISLOUNAGHT – THE LAND OF COCKAYNE?

The Normans never completed the conquest of Ireland. Their westward advance ground to a halt in the 13th century, leaving the country divided between Gael and Saxon. Even the Irish Church was divided. There were English monasteries in the Pale and the larger towns, and Irish monasteries in the countryside.

The two groups of monks did not like each other. In particular, the English-speaking monks claimed that, while they observed the rule of their order to the very letter, the Irish monks had a far more laidback approach to monastic discipline. One day in the mid-14th century, an English-speaking monk in a Kildare monastery, with gall in his heart as well as in his inkpot, took up his quill and wrote a poem 190 lines long in which he bitterly satirised the goings-on at an Irish monastery in what he called the Land of Cockayne. There, he claimed, the monks had zealously dedicated themselves to a life, not of prayer, hard work and abstinence, but of sloth, gluttony and lust.

Admittedly, Cockayne was not an easy monastery to get into. The novice's training included wading up to his chin in pig-dung for seven years. Once he had qualified, however, life was pretty good. To medieval man, domestic animals meant work and filth, so they were banned from Cockayne. However, there was food in plenty, and if you felt peckish between meals all you had to do was to break off a piece of the monastery and eat it, for the walls were made of pastry and meat, the shingles of cake, and the timbers of fat puddings. There was no kitchen, for there was no cooking - at mealtimes geese and larks flew to the table ready cooked and spiced with garlic.

Every time the monks went to Mass, a miracle took place - the windows filled with the purest crystal glass. The trees in the cloister produced delicious spices such as ginger and cinnamon, and their branches were populated with beautiful singing-birds. The monks' daily routine consisted entirely of play. No trudging around the monastic lands - they simply extended their sleeves like wings and flew. On sunny afternoons they betook themselves to the river, where they joined the nuns from the nearby convent boating and skinny-dipping. This could be thirsty work, but refreshment was all around, for the river was a river of fresh milk. Finally, after yet another meal, each monk staggered off to his cell, where his wife lay waiting - and by the way everyone was allowed twelve wives per year.

The Cockayne poem provides historians with an invaluable guide to the kind of English spoken in the Pale in the age of Chaucer. But is it merely the outpouring of the jaundiced imagination of some frustrated monk, or does it have some basis in reality?

Dave Moore

Well, the poem does contain some clues as to the whereabouts of Cockayne. The monks are grey monks, and that means Cistercians, not Franciscans. Their abbey is situated beside a river of fresh milk and not far from a convent. Various possible locations have been suggested, but there is one, and only one, major Irish-speaking Cistercian monastery that fits the bill exactly. It was called Sancta Maria de Surio (Our Lady of the River Suir) and it was situated upriver of Clonmel, not far from the convent of Molough, at a place called Inis Leunachta - the island of fresh milk.

What do we know of the lives of its monks? Well, in 1537 the jurors of Clonmel reported that the abbot of Inislounaght kept a harlot "openly by day and night to his pleasure, and every monk of his having his harlot and household"; and the Waterford City jurors found that James Butler, abbot of Inislounaght, "is a man of odious life, taking yearly and daily men's wives and burgesses' daughters, and keepeth no divine service but spendeth the goods of his church in voluptuosity".

Well, whether or not Inislounaght was indeed the abbey of Cockayne, there is nothing left of it now, and more's the pity. Its life came to an end with the arrival of the grim-faced commissioners of King Henry VIII in 1536.

THE BATTLE OF PILTOWN

The word Pottlerath (that's Rath an Photaire - the Potter's Fort) is hardly one to conjure with in Irish history. And indeed there's little left now at Pottlerath (halfway between Callan and Urlingford) to show that in the Middle Ages it was one of the chief strongholds of the mighty Butlers. Yet so it was, for it was built in the mid-15th century by the worthy Edmund mac Richard Butler.

Edmund was a cousin of the Earl of Ormond, and as the Earl spent most of his time living it up at the English court, he placed Edmund in charge of his vast domains. Edmund was both a warrior and a builder. As Seneschal of the Earl's town of Carrick, he built there the castle and the great stone bridge. In the year 1453 alone he built the bawn of Dunmore, two castles at Thurles, and the castle at Boolick. He obtained from the Pope a bull authorising the foundation of a convent for the Augustinians at Callan, and this convent was indeed built by his son.

Edmund was also a scholar. In his castle at Pottlerath he had a copy made of one of the great old Irish manuscripts, the Psalter of Cashel (it's now in the Bodleian Library at Oxford). It was made in December 1453, and the scribe added various notes as he went along, such as (I translate freely from the Irish): "This is the Friday before Christmas. Night has fallen and it's raining cats and dogs. The son of the house went off this morning. I hope to God he gets back safely." And again: "We are at Rath an Photaire and there's only five days left till Christmas."

All went well with Edmund mac Richard until the end of the year 1461, when his lord and master returned from England. He did not return alone, for he brought with him a whole army of English soldiers. And he was out to make trouble. At this time the Wars of the Roses were in full swing, and the noble earl seems to have thought it would be a shame for the Emerald Isle not to have its own Wars of the Roses as well. The Butlers backed the house of Lancaster, which in 1461 was overthrown by the house of York. In these wars the victors devoted much time and care to lopping off the heads of their defeated cousins, and the earl was lucky to get away with his life. On arrival in Ireland, he proceeded to raise the Lancastrian flag and instigate a revolt against the Yorkists.

He got off to a good start: Waterford City gave him its full support, and so did Kilkenny and the Butler lordships thereabouts. His main problem was with the Fitzgerald Earls of Kildare and Desmond. Not only did the Geraldines back the house of York, but they also had the impudence to claim lordship of the Butler manors of Kilsheelan, Clonmel and Kilfeacle. In the height of the summer of 1462, the army of Desmond confronted the Yorkist army consisting of Butler levies commanded by Edmund mac Richard and the English soldiers

|ₗₗₗₗ|ₗₗₗₗ|ₗₗₗₗ|ₗₗₗₗ|ₗₗₗₗ|ₗₗₗₗ|ₗₗₗₗ|ₗₗₗₗ|ₗₗₗₗ|ₗₗₗₗ|ₗₗₗₗ|ₗₗₗₗ|ₗₗₗₗ|ₗₗₗₗ|ₗₗₗₗ|ₗₗₗₗ|ₗₗₗₗ|ₗₗₗₗ|

commanded by the earl of Ormond. They met close to the modern village of Piltown in south Kilkenny.

"Sire," reported Edmund to the Earl, "we are ready to start the battle." "Battle??!" wailed the horrified Earl of Ormond. "But you can't have a battle today - it's a Monday. You know it's unlucky to have a battle on a Monday." And he withdrew all his forces to a safe distance.

Poor Edmund was now left to face the Desmond onslaught with just his own men. Battle was joined near Rogerstown Castle, close to the present water-tower west of the village. The Butlers, heavily outnumbered, were driven with much slaughter south-eastwards, over the pill, as far as where the presbytery now stands. The annals record that 410 bodies were buried afterwards, "besides all that was eaten by the dogs and by the fowl of the air". Edmund himself was taken prisoner, and was not released until a huge ransom had been paid, including two of the most precious items in his library, the Book of Carrick and his beloved copy of the Psalter of Cashel.

The battle of Piltown took place in 1462 - on this day.

Originally built in 1805 by the 3rd Earl of Bessborough to commemorate the presumed death of his son in the Peninsular War, but abandoned upon his safe return. The upper floor was added in 1950 when converted to a water tower. It marks the approximate site of the battle of Piltown.

Photo by Donal Sheerin

THE 1500s

THE BATTLE OF AFFANE

Amid the chaos that was Ireland in the early 16th century, one of the few unchanging features was the hatred that existed between the two most powerful families in Munster – the FitzGeralds Earls of Desmond and the Butlers Earls of Ormond. In 1565 matters came to a head with a pitched battle to the south of Cappoquin, on the banks of the little River Finisk, a tributary of the Blackwater

The cause of the battle was Desmond's claim to rule over the territory of FitzGerald of Decies (that's roughly the land between Dungarvan and Cappoquin). The Lord of Decies was Sir Maurice FitzGerald, and his chief castle was at Dromana on the Blackwater. For generations the Decies family, although they were FitzGeralds, had resisted the claim of the Earls of Desmond to be their overlords, and on the principle that my enemy's enemy is my friend they were generally in alliance with the Butlers of Ormond.

In late January 1565 Sir Maurice got a tip-off that Desmond was about to raid his territory and make off with some cattle in lieu of the dues to which he claimed he was entitled. He sent an urgent message for help to the Earl of Ormond, and when Desmond reached the ford of Affane he got a very nasty shock indeed - his raiding party, looking forward to a pleasant day's cattle-rustling, found themselves faced by a much larger force commanded by Ormond and equipped for battle. Lord Power, who was related to all three leaders, begged him not to fight, but Desmond was headstrong and stupid and launched his little force straight at the enemy earl. It was cut to pieces.

Desmond himself was shot in the thigh by one of the Butlers and taken prisoner. As he was being carried off the field on a stretcher, he was taunted with the words: "And where is the mighty Earl of Desmond now?" to which he retorted defiantly: "Where but in his rightful place – on the necks of the Butlers!"

Ormond paraded his stricken foe through the streets of Waterford, then took him off to England to face the wrath of Queen Elizabeth.

The Battle of Affane, the last battle to be fought in these islands between two private armies commanded by noblemen, took place in 1565 – on this day.

Main source: George Butler, "The Battle of Affane",
Irish Sword, VIII, no. 30 (1967), pp 33-47.

THE TRIAL OF ALICE THE ABBESS

I am quite sure that in modern times the holy nuns of Ferrybank have led lives of irreproachable respectability. Unfortunately, the same could not be said of some of their medieval predecessors.

The Augustinian abbey of St Mary's of Kilculliheen was founded in 1151 by Dermot MacMurrough King of Leinster – he who brought over the Normans and married off his beautiful daughter Aoife to Strongbow. Its status was confirmed by a charter of Prince John, granted when he was Lord of Ireland and before becoming King of England. It was a sizeable establishment. Nothing is left of it now. It stood more or less on the site of the Protestant church known from it as The Abbey.

Abbey Church Ferrybank, Waterford circa 1950

There were some very odd goings-on in that convent during the Middle Ages. In 1427 the Earl of Ormond sent a petition to the Pope, accusing the nuns of leading "a dissolute, irreligious and immodest life," and applying for a licence to convert the convent into a secular church. His Holiness instructed the Bishop of Ossory to hold an inquiry, and to suppress the abbey if the accusations were found to be true. But nothing was done.

|٠٠٠٠|٠٠٠٠|٠٠٠٠|٠٠٠٠|٠٠٠٠|٠٠٠٠|٠٠٠٠|٠٠٠٠|٠٠٠٠|٠٠٠٠|٠٠٠٠|٠٠٠٠|٠٠٠٠|٠٠٠٠|٠٠٠٠|٠٠٠٠|٠٠٠٠|٠٠٠٠|٠٠٠٠|

A hundred years later, the nuns were in trouble again. In 1532 the abbess, Alice Butler, was summoned to appear in St Canice's Cathedral, Kilkenny, before the bishop, Milo Barron, to answer some rather startling accusations. It was said that she had "squandered, used up and frittered away divers goods, rights, rents, incomes and finances of the convent, for her own profane and wicked uses". The convent itself she had "allowed to decline outrageously into virtually irreparable ruin and decay in its internal walls, fittings, windows, doors, roof, halls, houses and outhouses". She had wretchedly and impiously stolen from her fellow sisters items which had been granted to the convent, as a result of which they had been compelled to depart from the cloister and move into the houses of powerful lords and other friends, contrary to the rules of their order. Their only alternative was to remain there in penury and poverty without food or clothing.

She had committed various other crimes, vices and misdemeanours by which she had proved herself unworthy to govern or administer the convent. She had committed fornication with a member of another monastic house and had given birth to his child. At the instigation of the devil she had laid violent hands on her fellow nuns, even to the shedding of blood. She had mutilated a young man named John MacOdo (Cody), for which heinous behaviour she could only be absolved by the Pope. And, perhaps worst of all in the eyes of the Ossory clergy, she had left the convent without permission and accepted the garb of another religious order from the Bishop of Waterford.

This was quite a catalogue of crime, and it's not surprising to learn that she was dismissed from her office of abbess. Yet in the following year she was pardoned, and when a few years later the abbeys were suppressed by order of Henry VIII Alice Butler was one of the six nuns apparently living contentedly in the convent and who were granted pensions for life to compensate them for the loss of their home. If there were any basis for the accusations made against her, she was lucky to get away virtually scot-free. How did she manage it? Could it be more than coincidence that she was a Butler and had a useful relation in the mighty Earl of Ormond? We shall probably never know.

Throughout her trial, Alice showed no sign of repentance. She was ceremonially deposed by the Bishop of Ossory in 1532 – on this day.

*Main source: John Mulholland, "The Trial of Alice Butler, Abbess of Kilculliheen",
Decies, no. 25 (1984), pp 45-46.*

LAW AND ORDER IN THE 16TH CENTURY PAORACH

Early modern Irish history is generally reckoned to have started in 1534, the year in which, upon the rebellion of Silken Thomas FitzGerald, Henry VIII decided to govern Ireland by direct rule instead of relying on powerful lords such as Garret Mór, the Great Earl of Kildare. It was a bit like the United Nations deciding to take over Afghanistan. Outside a 30-mile radius round Dublin, Drogheda and Dundalk, power was in the hands of a complex network of Gaelic chiefs and Norman lords who made peace and war with each other as the spirit moved them. Life for their subjects was far too exciting for comfort. They spent most of their time either being plundered by the lord's enemies or being exploited by a series of feudal exactions summed up in the phrase "Spend me and defend me".

In the 1530s life in County Waterford was a bit like the world of the Magnificent Seven, but without the Magnificent Seven. The eastern half of the county was controlled by Sir Richard Power of Curraghmore. Law and order was supposed to be maintained by the county sheriff. But the Sheriff of County Waterford was – you've guessed it – Sir Richard Power of Curraghmore. Moreover, the Curraghmore Powers were now in their fourth generation as sheriffs, an office that was supposed to be subject to annual election. And this in spite of an act of parliament made as far back as 1476 barring the Powers from being sheriff and giving the nomination to Waterford Corporation.

Now, the King's policy was to woo the loyalty of the Irish lords by granting titles to those who supported him. Sir Richard Power, resenting the domination of the Earls of Kildare, opposed the rebellion of Silken Thomas, and his reward was to be created Baron "le Power and Coroghmore" in September 1535. He did not, however, live long to enjoy the title. A few years later, allegedly on service for the crown but actually enjoying a nice plundering trip in O'Callaghan country, he was killed.

As his son was still a child, east Waterford was ruled by his widow, the Lady Katherine. She was a daughter of the Earl of Ormond, who had also died leaving an heir who was a minor. So County Kilkenny was ruled by the mother and the Paorach by the daughter. You might think the ladies would exert a gentler hand than their menfolk. You'd be very wrong. A report compiled in 1537 shows that the Lady Katherine missed no opportunity of oppressing her unfortunate subjects. Her taxation system was delightfully simple, the rules being as follows:

|ₗₗₗₗ|ₗₗₗₗ|ₗₗₗₗ|ₗₗₗₗ|ₗₗₗₗ|ₗₗₗₗ|ₗₗₗₗ|ₗₗₗₗ|ₗₗₗₗ|ₗₗₗₗ|ₗₗₗₗ|ₗₗₗₗ|ₗₗₗₗ|ₗₗₗₗ|ₗₗₗₗ|ₗₗₗₗ|ₗₗₗₗ|ₗₗₗₗ|

- Everyone paid taxes – except the Lady Katherine and her followers.
- Taxes consisted of all that could be removed: money, stock, crops, etc.
- Special occasions, such as junkets to Dublin, visits by the Lord Deputy, and massive rave-ups at Christmas and Easter, were taxed separately.
- When Lady Katherine came visiting, there must be free meat and drink for her family and servants, free fodder for her horses, and even free bread and milk for her dogs – and these were wolfhounds, not chihuahuas.

Justice was dispensed with admirable efficiency. Anyone accused of a crime (and note the word *accused*, not *convicted*) was subject to a system of fines, carefully means-tested and index-linked of course. That's to say, if you were rich you paid a lot, if you were poor you paid less, and if you had nothing you were hanged.

I wonder if Lady Katherine's unfortunate subjects dreamed of the joys of paying some light taxes like domestic rates or service charges. Maybe they even wished back from the dead her late husband, Sir Richard the first Lord Power, whose title had been created in 1535 – on this day.

Farm being plundered in a raid by soldiers of a Norman/Gaelic chieftain
From John Derricke's Image of Irelande (1581)

LORD POWER AND
THE SIEGE OF BOULOGNE

The portly figure of Henry VIII is familiar to all from the famous portrait by Holbein, and he is no doubt one of the most memorable figures in the history of these islands, with his many wives, his break with the Church of Rome, and his plundering of the monasteries. One of the least remembered events of his reign was his campaign in France which culminated in the capture of Boulogne by the English army on 30 September 1544.

On the outbreak of war, the King wrote to his deputy in Ireland, Sir Anthony St Leger, ordering him to produce some Irish soldiers and send them to England – fast. In selecting the local VIPs who could raise such a force, St Leger cast round for Irish lords who had gallowglass and kerne at their command but who were not in rebellion against the crown. Inevitably, his eye fell on the Powers' Country of east Waterford, whose late chief, Sir Richard Power, had recently been ennobled under the title Baron le Power and Coroghmore for his refusal to join the rebellion of Silken Thomas. Sir Richard had come to a sticky end in a local skirmish, and it was his son and successor Sir Piers Power, the second lord, who was given overall command of the Irish force. His second-in-command was Patrick Sherlock, a Waterford merchant whose wealth and prestige had been greatly increased by acquiring the lands of the dissolved priories of St Catherine's (on the site of the present courthouse) and Mothel (near Rathgormack). With such commanders, it's very likely that many of the 700 kerne who were reviewed by the King at St James's Park in London before departing for France were men of the Déise.

If you think warfare in Tudor times just consisted of heavily armoured knights jousting with each other, well, forget it. That was OK for the VIPs, but for the ordinary soldier – and civilian – it was … quite a bit rougher. The Dublin historian Richard Stanihurst, never a man to miss out on a good yarn, wrote of the Irish contingent thirty years after the event:

"In the siege of Boulogne they stood the army in very good stead. For they were not only contented to burn and spoil all the villages thereto adjoining, but also they would ravage twenty or thirty miles into the mainland, and having taken a bull, they used to tie him to a stake, and scorching him with faggots they would force him to roar, so as all the cattle in the country would make towards the bull, all which they would lightly lead away, and furnish the camp with store of beef.

"If they took any Frenchman prisoner, lest they should be accounted covetous in snatching with them his entire body, his only ransom would be no more than his head.

| | | | | | | | | | | | | | | | | | | | | | | | | | | | | | | | | | | | |

"The French, with this extraordinary kind of warfare astonished, sent an ambassador to King Henry, to learn whether he brought men with him or devils, that could neither be won with rewards nor pacified by pity. Which, when the King had turned to a jest, the Frenchmen ever after, if they could take any of the Irish scattering from the company, used first cut off their genitals, and after to torment them with as great and as lingering pain as they could devise."

After the surrender of Boulogne, as the two armies faced each other, a French warrior offered to fight any of the English in single combat, whereupon an Irishman from Kildare named Nicholas Walsh swam across the harbour, killed the Frenchman, and swam back again - with the challenger's head in his mouth.

Lord Power was buried at Mothel Abbey

Lord Power, who at least in name commanded this bunch of desperadoes, fought with distinction at the siege of Boulogne and was badly wounded. His body was eventually brought back to Waterford (suitably pickled, one hopes) and buried in the ancestral tomb of the Powers at Mothel Abbey. We know that a requiem mass for his soul was celebrated there early in the New Year, at the behest of his mother and her brother the Earl of Ormond, and that "much devotion of meat and drink is prepared there".

Piers 2nd Lord Power died in 1544 – on this day.

WATERFORD'S FIRST PRINTED BOOK?

The little book entitled *The Acquital or Purgation of the Mooste Catholyke Christen Prince Edward the VI* is hardly everyone's idea of bedtime reading. But turn to the last words on the last page and your interest may well be aroused. These inform us that it was "emprinted at Waterford the 7 daye of November 1555". If this statement is true, then this is one of the first books to be printed in Ireland, and the earliest Irish printing outside Dublin by nearly ninety years. You note the ominous word "if". Yes, those nasty revisionists have been casting nasturtiums on our heritage again. Lets have a look at the circumstances in which *The Acquital or Purgation* was written.

Edward VI was the boy-king who succeeded Henry VIII, ruled for six years, and died at the age of fifteen. He was a Catholic in the sense that he belonged to the Catholic (i.e. universal) Church, but he was not a *Roman* Catholic. In fact he was a convinced Protestant, and during his reign England became a Protestant country. There was a flowering of Protestant scholarship, and Calvinist theologians from Geneva were encouraged to settle in England. This was good news for printers, and in particular for the London printer Hugh Singleton and for one Thomas Powell, who in 1550 set up business in Dublin and thereby became the first printer in Ireland.

Then in 1553 the young king died and was succeeded by his half-sister the uncompromisingly Catholic Queen Mary and her Spanish husband King Philip II. The filthy foreign heretics were requested to leave, and the country shook with the stampeding of scholarly feet as they headed for the channel ports. The native Protestants were less fortunate. During the next 3¾ years Mary burned 280 of them.

It doesn't seem to be much fun being burned at the stake. When Bishops Latimer and Ridley were executed at Oxford, the wood was damp and burned very slowly; Latimer was lucky and suffocated almost immediately in the smoke, but Ridley suffered horribly despite the efforts of his family who piled on more equally damp wood. Sometimes your friends were allowed to speed you on your way by giving you a gunpowder necklace, but this could go messily wrong as well. All in all, being burned at the stake was not an experience to be recommended.

Then in November 1558 Bloody Mary died of cancer and was succeeded by her half-sister Elizabeth, under whom the religious pendulum swung back in favour of the Protestants.

During Mary's mercifully brief reign the printing presses of Singleton in London and Powell in Dublin fell silent. And yet Protestant literature continued to be printed, emanating from secret presses somewhere in England, or on the Continent, or in Ireland. This is the context in which the little Waterford book appeared.

For there was no persecution of Protestants in this country. The Renaissance, with its beauty and its learning and its ruthless pursuit of power, had not yet reached us. We know that some Protestant refugees from England in fact found shelter here. What could be more appropriate than for a printer to set up in Waterford, the second city in Ireland and having strong links with Bristol and London?

Moreover, there is a clue as to the printer's identity. For its typeface is identical to that of eleven other books of the period, and some of these have a little woodcut with the motto "God is my helper", the initials "H.S.", and a barrel. Why a barrel? Well, another word for a barrel is a "tun", and the fact that there is only one barrel makes it a "single-tun". The printer, in other words, was Hugh Singleton.

Did he arrive in Waterford in 1555, the stink of burning flesh still haunting his nightmares, to set up Ireland's first provincial printing press? Or was the word "Waterford" simply intended to put the authorities off the track of a press that was actually located in the Netherlands, or in the safety of Calvinist Geneva? This, alas, is what most scholars maintain. But personally I believe that it was right here in the Urbs Intacta that Hugh Singleton's little book was printed, in 1555 - on this day.

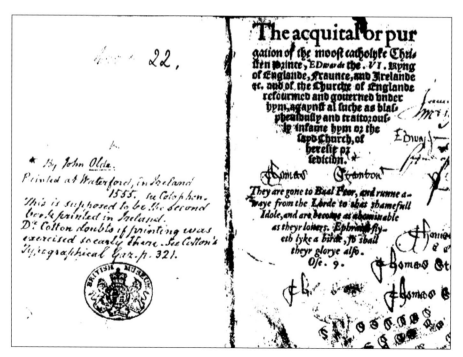

ELIZABETH I: AN IRISH QUEEN?

The long reign of Queen Elizabeth I is not remembered with affection in this country. Yet it's sometimes said that Elizabeth was partly Irish and that her mother, Anne Boleyn the second wife of Henry VIII, was born in the Ormond Castle at Carrick-on-Suir. How true is this? Let's see.

During the Middle Ages, Carrick was one of the manors belonging to the Butlers, Earls of Ormond. In the second half of the 15th century, three brothers succeeded in turn to the earldom. When they were in Ireland their favourite pastime was fighting the FitzGeralds, Earls of Desmond. But they spent most of their time in England, where they joined cheerfully in the series of dreary battles known as the Wars of the Roses. The first brother even succeeded in getting his head chopped off after being on the losing side at one of these battles.

Now the third brother signally failed to provide a male heir, and died leaving only two daughters, both of whom had taken English husbands. The younger one, Margaret, married a certain Sir William Boleyn of Blickling in Norfolk, by whom she had a son Thomas. When Margaret's father died in 1515, Henry VIII granted the title Earl of Ormond to this Sir Thomas Boleyn. Queen Anne Boleyn was his daughter. So it is true that Queen Elizabeth was partly Irish - hence perhaps the red wig she wore when she started going bald.

Unfortunately, there isn't the slightest evidence that Sir Thomas Boleyn and his wife ever even set foot in Ireland, so it's out of the question for Anne Boleyn to have been born in Carrick. In fact we know she was born in Norfolk, probably at Blickling which was after all the family home.

As things turned out, the Boleyn bubble didn't last long. Anne married Henry VIII in 1532, she and her brother got the chop only four years later, and her father Sir Thomas died in the following year. The King then granted the earldom of Ormond to a Butler cousin, the famous Black Tom.

Anne Boleyn

But although we have to debunk Carrick's claim to Anne Boleyn, there is evidence for a far more startling Irish connection with her illustrious daughter. Black Tom Butler and Queen Elizabeth were after all cousins, Black Tom grew up at the royal court, and he and the Queen were lifelong friends. She even referred to him as her "black husband". In the 1560s he built a fine mansion onto the old castle at Carrick, perhaps expecting that she would visit Ireland and stay with him there. Their portraits and monograms may be seen in the stucco work.

Now the year 1553 was the start of a hard time for Elizabeth. Her Catholic half-sister Mary ascended the throne, and she was banished from court, put under house arrest, spied on, and at one stage likely to be executed. Early in 1554 she was said to be pregnant. When offered physicians, she retorted: "I am not minded to make any stranger privy to the state of my body but commit it to God."

At about this time Black Tom fathered an illegitimate child (the first of twelve, incidentally). But who was the mother? From the great favour with which Black Tom treated the lad (Piers of Duiske, father of the first Viscount Galmoy), he was obviously someone of great importance. Could it possibly have been the Virgin Queen herself? This is not my invention but a hypothesis put forward by the recently deceased historian of the Butlers, His Honour Judge the Lord Dunboyne.

After five years of danger for Elizabeth, her unfortunate half-sister Bloody Mary, inventor of the famous cocktail, died, to the ecstatic joy of her English subjects. Elizabeth, whether virgin or otherwise, became Queen of England and Ireland in 1558 - on this day.

SIR PETER CAREW

Engraved portrait of Sir Peter

Studying your family history is no doubt a worthy undertaking, but it can also give a fellow notions. Few who have done so can have made a more startling impact than Sir Peter Carew, a Devonshire man who landed at Waterford in 1568. Sir Peter had not only studied his family history, he had rewritten it so as to prove that he was the heir to Robert Fitz Stephen, the knight who had led the first Norman invasion back in 1169. This, he claimed, entitled him to Fitz Stephen's lands in Counties Cork, Waterford, Meath, Carlow – in fact, all over the place.

Sir Peter was a persuasive man, and the government backed his claim. He was given unrestricted access to the records, and a seat in parliament, and appointed governor of Leighlin. His County Carlow neighbour, Sir Edmund Butler, was not the only local landowner to be underwhelmed at the prospect of being booted off the lands his ancestors had held for 400 years; he was merely the first to launch into revolt. Sir Peter promptly besieged and captured the Butler castle of Clogrenan. The local Kavanaghs were also singularly unamused by Sir Peter's arrival. Very sensibly, they made several attempts to assassinate him. And in Munster, his preposterous claims to lands in County Cork were one of the factors that led to the first Desmond revolt.

The rebellion took years to crush, but Sir Peter was still around when it fizzled out. Then, at the end of November 1575, on the verge of triumph, he died suddenly in New Ross. The government decided to give him a magnificent send-off – in Waterford Cathedral. Sir Peter's legal adviser and hagiographer, the somewhat unfortunately named John Hooker, has obligingly left us a detailed account of the proceedings.

Sir Peter was disembowelled, embalmed, and put into his coffin, which remained at Ross until the preparations were complete. Then, on 15 December, he was taken by boat down the Barrow and up the Suir to Waterford. The funeral was attended by the Lord Deputy, his retinue and guards, the mayor and corporation, and "an infinite number of people". The cathedral was entered in formal

|ıııı|ıııı|ıııı|ıııı|ıııı|ıııı|ıııı|ıııı|ıııı|ıııı|ıııı|ıııı|ıııı|ıııı|ıııı|ıııı|ıııı|ıııı|ıııı|ıııı|

procession, the great man's arms and armour being carried before him while a trumpeter in black "sounded the dead sound".

"As soon as the corpse was brought into the church," wrote Hooker, "it was placed in the middle, next before the pulpit, and all the aforesaid ensigns placed around the same, during the time of the sermon. After the same was ended the corpse was carried, in the like order to the grave, which was in the south side of the chancel, next to the altar.

"As soon as the earth began to be cast in, all the trumpeters being six in number sounded the whole time of his burial, being almost the space of a quarter of an hour. Then, as they had ended, the drums struck up, and therewith all the soldiers discharged their muskets four or five times together, wherewith the church was so full of smoke that one could scarce discern another. Lastly, a number of cannons that were in the churchyard, and all the great ordnance in the town, and in the ships in the river at the quay, were also discharged.

Monument to Sir Peter in Exeter Cathedral

"All these things being performed, they returned all to the house from which they brought the corpse in the like order as before they went" – where I hope they were suitably refreshed with liberal draughts of the Uisce Beatha for which Waterford was famed.

Hooker concludes by telling us that the Lord Deputy, Sir Henry Sydney, when he saw the corpse put into the grave, remarked: "Here lieth now, in his last rest, a most worthy and noble, gentle knight, whose faith to his prince was never yet stained, his truth to his country never spotted, and his valiantness in service never doubted. A better subject a prince never had." A curious verdict on a man whose intervention in Irish history was selfish, destructive, totally negative, and mercifully brief.

Sir Peter Carew died in 1575 - on this day.

Main source: John Hooker, The dyscourse and dyscoverye of the lyffe of Sir Peter Carew, edited by John Maclean (London, 1857).

MUENCHHAUSEN AND THE ISLAND OF LIFE

On this day in 1590 Ludolf von Muenchhausen embarked at Bristol for Waterford. The first leg of the voyage only got him as far as Milford Haven. It was not a pleasant journey. "That night," he wrote in his diary, "there was a storm and a lot of wind, and because we were low on ballast we had to reef sail. The women and children cried, some prayed, others yelled, nearly all of them were so ill that some were vomiting and some suffering from diarrhea. I was disgusted by the stench and the howling, and frightened by the roughness and danger of the sea."

However, they reached Milford safely the next day, and set sail at six in the evening so as not to arrive in Ireland at night. The following morning they got their first sight of the Emerald Isle and sailed along the coast until they saw a white tower, presumably the Hook Lighthouse. "There," he wrote, "we sailed into a river, and having a good tide arrived in Waterford around midday." He lodged with a German woman from Cologne, and spent the next few days exploring the town and its hinterland.

"Waterford," he reports, "is situated in a good position, because it has a wonderful river (the sea is ten miles from town), into which large ships can go right up to town, and were this country rich enough this would be a distinguished city for trade. But even now, ships are leaving for France and Spain and other places, most of them carrying fish such as herring (which is widely caught here) and cow-skins, which are the income and wealth of this country. In return they bring iron, wine and other things.

"Waterford is the most distinguished trading town in Ireland, for this is where the richest merchants live. The houses in Waterford, as elsewhere in Ireland, though built mostly of stone, are bad rustic buildings. The towns of Ireland, including Waterford, are surrounded by walls. In former times, in this as in all other Irish towns, there were all sorts of monasteries, but they are mostly now destroyed. The churches now belong to the reformed religion, but the people still cling to the papal religion, which surprises me.

"The island of Ireland is a wonderful country. It has all sorts of good meat, fish and birds, not only for their need but for admiration and in abundance. There are falcons and eagles and pheasants and goats, there are salmon, game and venison, several kinds of duck, different birds, many otters and martens. Pearls are found in Irish oysters, some of which I bought cheaply – they are not of the best quality. The soil is fertile, though hilly and with many valleys, and there are many plains. I wonder that so much beautiful land is lying fallow, just shrubs and wild grass growing there."

But Muenchhausen did not come to Ireland primarily to admire our wildlife and to sneer at our rustic habits. After ten days spent sampling the delights of 16th century Waterford night-life, he assembled a small safari party consisting of

Dining arrangements of the local nobility
Engraving from John Derricke's Image of Irelande (1581)

an interpreter, a guide and a bearer, and set off upriver rather as if the Suir had been the Amazon. The little group passed through Carrick and came eventually to Cahir. Here they took to their feet and trudged through the trackless wastes of Tipperary, listening apprehensively to the tomtom beats in "Fidden" (which I take to be Fethard) and "Fraglach" (wherever that is).

They spent the following night at the castle of an Irish nobleman, whom the author (alas) declines to name. Here, like other tourists unused to Irish customs of the time, they were shocked by the casual way their host and hostess warmed their bare buttocks at the fire. Then, after a simple meal of herring, bread, leeks and salt, and having carefully washed their feet as custom demanded, they all dossed down together on the straw, covering themselves with their coats against the cold.

Next day they resumed their journey and at last arrived at their destination, which Muenchhausen calls Lan Nimmeo. It is undoubtedly Mona Incha near Roscrea, also known as Oileán na mBeo, the Island of Life. Virtually forgotten today, a haven of peace undisturbed save by the chirping of birds and mooing of cattle, Mona Incha was one of the four chief places of pilgrimage in medieval Ireland. The Book of Ballymote calls it the 31st Wonder of the World. Its Romanesque church has been described as "one of the most delightful gems of 12th century architecture in Ireland".

In Muenchhausen's day it was, as its name suggests, an island in the middle of a bog, rather like Derrynaflan. It was visited by fifteen thousand pilgrims a year. It was renowned throughout Europe for an astonishing quality: it was not called the Island of Life for nothing – no one ever died there, except, of course, women, who would die instantly if they dared enter the monastic enclosure. Muenchhausen had come to see if the story was true.

To begin with, all went well. He was suitably impressed by the sight of some obviously geriatric monks. The chief hermit in particular looked positively decrepit, and when Muenchhausen asked him how long he had been living there the old man began to mutter the years to himself but gave up when he reached a hundred. He could never die there, he announced, nor had he ever seen any of his monks die there. If any of them grew tired of life, they had to return to the mainland to die.

Muenchhausen was less impressed by the penance of walking barefoot eight times around the island, and having tried it once he sat under a tree to nurse his wounds and listen to the groans of his comrades as they did the rounds. There was a little stone crucifix, and if you could stand with your back to it and get your arms around it you would be absolved from all sins, however grave. The interpreter, who was old and arthritic, couldn't quite manage it, but Muenchhausen caught his arms and twisted them backwards until they joined around the cross. The old josser was so overjoyed to be thus liberated from the burden of sin that he failed to notice that his arms were practically dislocated.

Their fellow pilgrims assumed that Muenchhausen was either very holy or very sinful to have made such a long pilgrimage from Germany, a place of which they had never even heard, so to humour them he assured them cheerfully that he had come to be absolved of incest committed with his sister.

He was shown a stone in the bog that had once been a woman who had tried to swim onto the island, but by now he was becoming a little skeptical of the legends associated with the place. Was it really true that even a female animal would die as soon as it reached the island? He announced his intention of trying out a few experiments by bringing over a few female sheep and dogs from the mainland.

His guide and interpreter, however, knew trouble when they saw it and insisted that it was time to move on. And so Leopold von Muenchhausen continued his visit to the Emerald Isle, which had begun in 1590 – on this day.

Main source: The MS of Leopold von Muenchhausen was communicated to me by Pat Nolan of Kilkenny, to whom I am most grateful.

THE 1600s

MILER MAGRATH VISITS LISMORE

| ·   ·   · | ·   ·   · | ·   ·   · | ·   ·   · | ·   ·   · | ·   ·   · | ·   ·   · | ·   ·   · | ·   ·   · | ·   ·   · | ·   ·   · | ·   ·   · | ·   ·   · | ·   ·   · |

In the spring of the year 1601, Miler Magrath, Protestant Archbishop of Cashel and Bishop of Waterford and Lismore, was a little worried about his unfavourable image. Nasty people were reporting to the government that he made no provision for religious services in his diocese or even for clergy to be appointed to the parishes. Church lands were being milked of their income for the profit of himself and his children, and as for the buildings, they were so tumbledown as to be no better than hog sties.

It was time Miler spoke up for himself, so he sent Queen Elizabeth's chief minister, Sir Robert Cecil, a long letter setting forth in detail the tribulations of a bishop in these hard times. If it was true that his churches were like hog sties, well, the country was in the middle of a rebellion and even a bishop could do nothing against the depredations of three classes of people: rebels, Romanists and English soldiers. The worst of the lot were the soldiers. They didn't actually pull down the roofs and walls, but they did plunder everything they could remove - doors, vestments, even bones out of monuments. Miler was now aged 79. What was he supposed to do?

As an instance of the kind of thing he had to put up with, Miler recounted a little incident that had taken place at Lismore the previous Sunday. The castle and manor of Lismore had been sold by Miler's predecessor, Bishop Wetherhead, to Sir Walter Raleigh. Miler had been considerably miffed at losing such a valuable property, but being a resourceful chap he managed to lease it back off Raleigh at a very reasonable rent. He was now in the process of renting it out at considerable profit to a wealthy but gullible tenant, Lord Power of Curraghmore.

It was unfortunate that Lismore Castle had been wrecked and left a smouldering ruin by the soldiers of Edmund FitzGibbon the White Knight, but that did not deter Miler. "Could do with a spot of renovation ... a lick of paint here and there perhaps, but nothing to worry about," he breezily assured his lordship as they rode along to view the property.

On the road between Dungarvan and Lismore, to the bishop's surprise, they met a detachment of soldiers from the garrison of Youghal under the command of a Captain Nuse. The captain greeted them in friendly fashion, and even talked airily of buying Magrath's interest in the estate. But when they reached Lismore, Miler found to his horror that the broken walls were occupied by even more of Captain Nuse's soldiers.

|᾿᾿᾿᾿|᾿᾿᾿᾿|᾿᾿᾿᾿|᾿᾿᾿᾿|᾿᾿᾿᾿|᾿᾿᾿᾿|᾿᾿᾿᾿|᾿᾿᾿᾿|᾿᾿᾿᾿|᾿᾿᾿᾿|᾿᾿᾿᾿|᾿᾿᾿᾿|᾿᾿᾿᾿|᾿᾿᾿᾿|᾿᾿᾿᾿|᾿᾿᾿᾿|᾿᾿᾿᾿|

"Get off my property and back to Youghal where you belong," he blustered uneasily. Nuse retorted that he was there to defend the place and had no intention of leaving.

Miler turned to Lord Power. "You're a justice of the peace - do something," he pleaded.

"Um ...perhaps we ought to send for the sheriff," urged Lord Power weakly.

At the very sound of the word sheriff, Captain Nuse gave a yell of rage, grabbed a pike off one of the soldiers and began to beat the bishop with it.

"Lads, lads, hold on now!" cried Lord Power, despairingly holding up his white wand of a justice of the peace. An enraged poke of the pike in his direction was Nuse's only response. Then turning abruptly to his soldiers, Nuse ordered them to shoot down the intruders.

But by now Miler and his party were running for their horses, and soon they were galloping over the horizon, hotly pursued by Nuse's men and with bullets whizzing about their ears. When they thought they had shaken off their pursuers, they stopped for a breather, and Lord Power panted that it had been a very pleasant ride but he really must be getting home now. Suddenly Nuse's men came galloping round a corner still screeching abuse and firing in all directions, and the hunt was on again.

The last that Miler heard of Captain Nuse was that he had said he was sorry he hadn't killed the bishop stone dead, and if he had only known Miler's sons were in the party he'd have killed them as well.

"So there," Miler ended his letter to Cecil. "That's what a 79-year-old bishop has to put up with these days. What are you going to do about it?" Cecil did nothing.

This extraordinary encounter took place at Lismore in 1601 - on this day.

Main source: Calendar of State Papers, Ireland, 1600-1601, pp 242-3.

"BLACK TOM" BUTLER, EARL OF ORMOND

Throughout the long reign of Queen Elizabeth I, the dominant figure in Irish history is surely Thomas Butler, 10th Earl of Ormond, nicknamed on account of his complexion "Black Tom". Nationalist historians have portrayed him as a renegade because he sided with the English, yet it's hard to see what else he could have done: he had been brought up as a Protestant at the English court, where he had been a companion to the little prince, later Edward VI. He remained intensely loyal to Queen Elizabeth, who was after all his cousin, and he was the only one of all her favourites to remain in her good books virtually throughout her reign.

The battle of Affane in 1565 between the Earls of Ormond and Desmond infuriated the Queen, who locked both earls up in the Tower of London. Ormond was lucky – he was released soon after so that he could keep his rebellious Catholic relations under control. During the two great Desmond rebellions that followed, he commanded English armies in Munster, and the campaigns were fought with savagery on both sides. Black Tom was rewarded for his "contribution to the war effort" with the grant of thousands of acres of confiscated land.

Ormond Castle, Carrick on Suir

|᠁᠁|᠁᠁|᠁᠁|᠁᠁|᠁᠁|᠁᠁|᠁᠁|᠁᠁|᠁᠁|᠁᠁|᠁᠁|᠁᠁|

During the rebellion of Hugh O'Neill, Earl of Tyrone, he again took the field. Then in 1600, at the age of seventy, he was dramatically kidnapped near Kilkenny by a rebel leader named Owney O'More. It was a shameful episode, for the two sides had met in order to parley. After being led from cabin to cabin in great discomfort, he was eventually confined in a castle in Queen's County, where he was allowed his own cooks. O'More threatened to kill him if a rescue were attempted. Eventually some Jesuit priests intervened to secure his release, but even so he had to hand over a number of hostages as security against his taking revenge. However, Ormond had the last laugh, for shortly afterwards O'More was killed in a skirmish and Ormond got the hostages back.

The English historian Cyril Falls passes the following verdict on Black Tom: "Ormond must be accounted a great man ... In a generation of dishonesty and intrigue he kept his hands clean, though certainly not neglecting his own interests. Stern and merciless in civil war, he yet sought opportunities to avoid it and to bring it to an end as early as possible, after which he would beseech the Queen to show her clemency by granting pardons to those who had not committed themselves too deeply. If the viceroys had adopted his policy, Ireland would have been happier and much English blood and treasure would have been spared. The northern lords, the uncouth Shane O'Neill as well as the courtly Earl of Tyrone, treated him with profound respect even when they were in the full course of rebellion. They never had a hard word for him, however bitter their mood, and neither had other Irishmen, always excepting Desmond and his followers."

For the last twelve years of his life, Black Tom was a pathetic blind old man. He died aged 82 in 1614, having allegedly converted to Catholicism, at Carrick Castle, the Tudor mansion he had built in the hope (perhaps) that Queen Elizabeth would one day be his guest. He was buried in St Canice's Cathedral, Kilkenny.

Black Tom Butler, 10th Earl of Ormond, died in 1614 – on this day.

Main source: Cyril Falls, Elizabeth's Irish Wars (London, 1950).

THE KING'S EVIL – AND ITS CURE

Picture: Waterford County Museum

Blackwater Angel is the title of a play by the Waterford dramatist Jim Nolan, which premiered at the Abbey Theatre in May 2001. But who was this Angel of the Blackwater?

Among the many loathsome ailments that afflicted the long-suffering people of the Middle Ages was Scrofula or Struma. It's a tubercular condition of the neck glands which we now know to be caused by defective nutrition. It was also known as the King's Evil because your only chance of a cure was a touch from the hand of the King himself. This belief died out at the end of the 17th century because the Jacobites unsportingly claimed that the good Lord had not passed on the miraculous power to King Billy. His uncle-in-law Charles II had the record for the largest number of "touches" – 92,107 – though we're not told how many (if any at all) were successful. Imagine, then, King Charles's astonishment when he learned that there was in faraway County Waterford a man with a highly successful record in curing the King's Evil. His name was Valentine Greatrakes.

Valentine's father, William Greatrakes, had come to Ireland during the Munster Plantation that followed the rebellion of the Earl of Desmond. He had been granted a small estate of confiscated land at Affane, on the eastern bank of the Blackwater, two miles south of Cappoquin. The future healer was born at Norrisland in 1629, allegedly on Saint Valentine's Day. His first thirty years were spent in the turbulent period of the Great Rebellion and the Cromwellian Settlement, and he even served for a time in the regiment commanded by the infamous Lord Broghill. But in 1662 he was living the life of a country gentleman and devoting much of his time to study and religion. Then one day he received the inner conviction that he had the power to cure the King's Evil. When he mentioned this to his wife she just laughed, and suggested that he should go to Salterbridge nearby and try out his powers on a boy named William Maher who was suffering from it.

|₁₁₁₁|₁₁₁₁|₁₁₁₁|₁₁₁₁|₁₁₁₁|₁₁₁₁|₁₁₁₁|₁₁₁₁|₁₁₁₁|₁₁₁₁|₁₁₁₁|₁₁₁₁|₁₁₁₁|₁₁₁₁|₁₁₁₁|₁₁₁₁|₁₁₁₁|₁₁₁₁|₁₁₁₁|₁₁₁₁|

Greatrakes went with a heavy heart. He must have realised that if he succeeded he'd never have another day's peace in his life. But he laid his hands on the boy's head and called out: "God Almighty heal thee for His mercy's sake!" He stroked the afflicted parts, and the boy was cured.

Four years and many cures later, he was battling for his honour with the greatest scholars in the land at the court of Charles II. Among his supporters was his fellow-countyman Robert Boyle, and Greatrakes wrote an account of his life addressed specifically to him. It was published in London in 1666, together with testimonials from 53 of his supporters. A woodcut was included showing Greatrakes curing the young William Maher.

Greatrakes soon found that he could cure other diseases as well as the King's Evil – aches, pains, rheumatic fevers and so on. His method was to stroke the afflicted parts, forcing the pain outwards to the extremities of the body such as fingers and toes, which then became ice-cold. Eventually the pain was forced out of the body altogether.

As you can imagine, Greatrakes was harried by invalids wherever he went. Even at home, his barns and outhouses were thronged by poor people seeking relief. He used to devote three days every week to healing, took no money for his work, and gave away whatever money he was given to the poor. He made many enemies. Doctors attacked him for healing without a licence. Ministers attacked him because of the prayers he said over the invalids. He was said to be a fake, a money-grabber. His enemies even claimed that he was a Valentine in more senses than one to his rich lady patients, and that the stroking was more in the nature of foreplay. A bawdy ballad was printed, recounting in explicit detail his alleged misbehaviour with Lady Conway. But Greatrakes carried on regardless, fortified by the firm conviction that he was doing the will of God.

He died in 1683. In his will he directed that he should be buried in Lismore Cathedral, and that's where his mortal remains await the sound of the Last Trumpet, when all pain and sickness shall be no more.

He had been born in 1629 – on this day.

For a modern study, see Peter Elmer, The Miraculous Conformist: Valentine Greatrakes, the Body Politic, and the Politics of Healing in Restoration Britain (Oxford 2013)

THE CRIME OF BISHOP ATHERTON

On this day in 1640 an Englishman named John Atherton was hanged in Dublin. His execution caused a storm whose waves were to be felt for over a century. For Atherton was no ordinary felon: he was the Church of Ireland Bishop of Waterford and Lismore. His crime? Sir James Ware coyly recorded in his history of the Irish bishops that Atherton was "condemned and degraded for a crime not to be named". But he was less reticent in his private journal; Atherton, he wrote, was hanged for sexual offences, including buggery committed on his manservant.

At first sight, it's hard to see why there was such a furore. After all, the King's father, James I, had been openly homosexual, many of Shakespeare's sonnets explore the poet's relationship with a young man, and the literature of the time abounds in such allusions. Well, it seems that that sort of thing was OK so long as you didn't do it in the street and frighten the horses! But it was still regarded as an offence "against nature". And the natural world had been set up by God as an integrated unit - damage one part of it, and the whole structure was endangered. Homosexuality was the equivalent of deliberately blowing a hole in the ozone layer – the culprits must be destroyed.

People's ideas had changed little since a thousand years earlier, when the Emperor Justinian had attributed the prevalence of earthquakes in his reign to an outbreak of homosexuality – he had cracked down just in time to prevent the universe from disintegration.

It's hard to believe that in the century that produced scientists such as the Father of Chemistry, Robert Boyle, people still believed such rubbish, but they evidently did, and the legal machinery existed to bring Atherton to the scaffold. All that was needed was an enemy to pull the levers that would set the machines to work, and he was for topping. During his four years in Waterford, Atherton had made many enemies, none more powerful and unscrupulous than the father of the Father of Chemistry, Richard Boyle, the Great Earl of Cork.

King Charles I was chronically short of money, and in 1633 he sent to Ireland a new Lord Lieutenant, Sir Thomas Wentworth. His instructions were to radically reform the Irish economy so as to make it produce as much revenue as possible. One area at which Wentworth looked very closely was the vanishing income of the Church of Ireland, where for several generations corrupt bishops had been selling off church lands and pocketing the proceeds. Few had benefited more from this than the Earl of Cork, whose very home, Lismore Castle, had been bought from the Church.

The Bishop of Waterford at this time was, rather conveniently, one of Boyle's many cousins (he was a man who liked to keep things in the family). In 1635

Bishop Boyle was caught by the new Dean running a scam whereby you could write yourself a pardon for sins you had committed, hand it to the Bishop with something in a brown envelope, and get the pardon back officially stamped and sealed. Not long after, he died. Wentworth seized his chance and replaced him with a tough church lawyer who had already done well in his service, John Atherton.

Atherton set to work with a will. Christ Church Cathedral needed to be repaired, and it had been agreed many years before that, whereas the Dean and Chapter were responsible for the chancel, the Corporation was responsible for the nave. Atherton forced them to keep their part of the agreement. The Mayor, Richard Butler of Knockenattin (now Knockeen), was not pleased.

Way back in 1577 the then bishop had pawned the cathedral silver to the Corporation for £200. The Corporation also had custody of the ancient vestments. Atherton procured an order from Wentworth that the Corporation should either return the silver or honour their bond for £400. They were also to return the vestments. (The silver was later robbed by the Cromwellians; the vestments – and Wentworth's order – are now in Waterford Museum of Treasures.) Once again, Mayor Richard Butler was not pleased.

In 1640 Atherton claimed possession of the lands of Bishopscourt and Kilcaragh, which were formerly owned by the bishops but were now held by a neighbouring landlord, namely the now ex-Mayor Richard Butler. In those days the method of sorting out a boundary dispute was to summon the oldest inhabitants and get them to point out the markers. Accordingly, the commissioners appointed by both sides summoned the local wrinklies, who obligingly disclosed that the lands in dispute had indeed belonged to the bishops.

Ex-Mayor Richard Butler, by now furious, tried to get the judgement disallowed on the grounds of intimidation: "All the inhabitants and dwellers in that barony stand in awe of the Lord Bishop," he declared.

So far, rounds 1, 2, and 3 to Atherton. But nemesis was at hand. He had made too many enemies, and they now joined forces against him. None was more powerful than the Earl of Cork, who was miffed that Atherton was trying to get back from him the former episcopal manor of Ardmore. Back in 1631 he had brought down a rival, the Earl of Castlehaven, by having charges of incest and buggery brought against him. If it had worked once, it might work again – and Atherton's manservant was bribed or threatened into co-operating.

The trial, as you can imagine, caused quite a sensation. Even today a public punch-drunk on clerical scandals would get quite a jolt on seeing the headlines in the tabloids. Whether or not Atherton was guilty as charged (and my guess is that he was) or merely framed, he was not a nice guy. He had been sent to Waterford as hatchet-man for Lord Deputy Wentworth – it was his misfortune to meet an axe-man in the person of the Earl of Cork. Atherton was hanged at Oxmantown Green, and his body buried in a rubbish dump in Fishamble Street. And, by the way, three months later Boyle had the manservant hanged too – on the bridge at Bandon. Wentworth was executed in London in May 1641.

At least Atherton was spared one final indignity. The government, anxious to avoid the scandal of executing one of its own bishops, had arranged to have him deconsecrated – but the Lord Justice died the day before. So it was as Bishop of Waterford and Lismore that John Atherton went to the gallows in 1640 – on this day.

Main sources: Aidan Clarke, "The Atherton File", Decies, no. 11 (May 1979), pp 45-54. Robert Winnett, "The Strange Case of Bishop John Atherton", Decies, no. 31 (1986), pp 4-17. Alan Bray, Homosexuality in Renaissance England (London, 1982). MSS of the Dean and Chapter of Waterford.

THE BALLYANCHOR MASSACRE

In the 17th century the town of Cappoquin marked the eastern limit of the huge estate owned by Sir Richard Boyle, Earl of Cork. Dominating the town was a castle which stood on the site of the present Cappoquin House. When the great rebellion broke out in the autumn of 1641, the Earl realized the importance of having a strong garrison in this castle, so he placed 100 soldiers there under the command of Captain Hugh Croker. Soon the marauding activities of the garrison caused them to be loathed by the local Irish and in February 1642 an Irish force commanded by John Sherlock and Edmond Fennell struck back. They had the element of surprise on their side, and reached the marketplace before encountering the garrison. Then, after a fierce battle, they were driven back, having suffered 200 casualties, including the loss of Captain Sherlock. Licking their wounds, they proceeded westward until they reached a strongly fortified house at Ballyanchor. It was the home of a Mr Edward Croker, the brother of their old enemy at Cappoquin.

Edmond Fennell, the commander who had survived the defeat at Cappoquin, summoned Croker to surrender. But he chose to resist, and with his four English servants kept up a hot fire on the assailants for several hours, wounding several of the Irish. Then, having exhausted their ammunition, they surrendered. But Captain Fennell was not in a merciful mood. Next day he had Croker shot, and the four servants were compelled to hang each other in a field adjoining the house. The house was plundered, but Croker's wife and children were spared.

The slaughter at Ballyanchor was a nasty incident in a brutal war, and played into the hands of propagandists in England, who were determined to whip up a hatred of Irish Catholics by alleging that there had been a wholesale massacre of the Protestant settlers. The Reverend Urban Vigors, chaplain to Lord Broghill, son of the Earl of Cork, denounced it in a letter as "a most barbarous and inhuman act". Even the Irish historian Richard Bellings, who was secretary to the Catholic Confederation, ridiculed Fennell for his elaborate siege of "a little stone house which in truth was not defensible".

Edmond Fennell's later career was equally inglorious. Eight years later, he served as a lieutenant colonel under Hugh Dubh O'Neill at the famous defence of Clonmel against Cromwell, and would have succeeded in betraying the town but for vigilant action by O'Neill. In the following year he served again under O'Neill during the defence of Limerick against General Ireton, and this time he *did* betray the town. Ireton, however, was unimpressed, and after the war Fennell was put on trial by the Cromwellian government for war crimes.

The Ballyanchor "Massacre" was one of the incidents that brought him to the gallows. It took place in 1642 – on this day.

Main sources: T.C.D. Depositions of Murders and Robberies; Carte MSS, Bodleian Library, Oxford, VIII, 29-30.

THE SIEGE OF ARDMORE CASTLE

|ılılılı|ılılılı|ılılılı|ılılılı|ılılılı|ılılılı|ılılılı|ılılılı|ılılılı|ılılılı|ılılılı|ılılılı|ılılılı|

Despite some unfortunate modern development, Ardmore is still one of the most beautiful villages on the Munster coast. It is also one of the most historic, having originated in the monastic foundation of St Declan in the 5th century. Its most spectacular monument is the round tower, which has become virtually a symbol of County Waterford and features on our county coat of arms. Moreover, it is the tallest, latest, and most impressive of the Irish round towers.

The purpose of these graceful buildings has been hotly debated. 18th-century antiquarians believed them to be temples of ancient Phoenician fire-worshippers. Modern scholars reckon that they fulfilled a number of functions – as steeples to the monastic churches, as belfries, as store-houses, and as places of refuge from marauding Vikings. No doubt many of them endured sieges, but the round tower of Ardmore is unique – so far as I know – in being the only one to have been besieged by artillery.

There was also a castle in Ardmore, but not a stone of it now remains above ground and even its site is uncertain. Archeologists reckon that it probably stood on a platform of land to the north-east of the cathedral, just outside the monastic enclosure.

Following the rebellion of 1641, most of the castles in west Waterford were held by the English, and the Irish garrison at Ardmore was a thorn in their flesh. In August 1642 it was decided to take it out. The attacking force consisted of 400 musketeers and 60 horse, commanded by Lords Dungarvan and Broghill, the first and third sons of the "Great" Earl of Cork. Not only did they heavily outnumber the Irish, but they also had a culverin – a type of cannon – which was sent round by sea from Youghal. At three o'clock on the afternoon of 26 August they summoned the Irish to surrender, and on this being refused they settled down to await the arrival of the culverin. In the meantime they captured some outhouses belonging to the castle, and in the evening the Irish burned the rest.

All that night the Irish maintained a determined fire on the besiegers. Nevertheless the English attacked the cathedral and captured it. This was of immense advantage to them, for not only did they find a good quantity of provisions in it, but as it was on higher ground they could now fire down into the bawn of the castle, confining the Irish within the keep. On the other side of the cathedral was the round tower, which contained forty men, well equipped with powder and bullets but with only two guns between them. They were also cut off from their provisions, so that the English were confident they would soon have to surrender.

Next morning a detachment of Irish soldiers tried to approach but was driven off. At noon the badly needed culverin arrived, and the besiegers worked hard to drag it to within half musket shot of the castle. The defenders kept up a steady fire the whole time, but the English protected themselves by carrying woolpacks in front of them. By three o'clock the culverin was in position to demolish one of the flanking towers, but it was obvious that defence was hopeless and the Irish asked for a parley. At first they requested quarter for goods and life, but when this was refused they submitted to the mercy of Lords Dungarvan and Broghill.

Culverin (i.e. a small cannon) similar to that used during the siege of Ardmore Castle
© Antony McCallum Creative Commons

The prisoners consisted of 114 men and 183 women and children taken in the castle, and 40 men taken in the round tower. The women and children were allowed their clothes, lives, and liberty to depart. Such of the prisoners as were English were freed. The more important Irish were kept as hostages. The rest, to the number of 117, were hanged. Such was the "mercy" of the lords.

Lord Dungarvan succeeded his father as Earl of Cork and was also created Earl of Burlington. Lord Broghill was later created Earl of Orrery. Both had distinguished careers ahead of them, but they are not among my favourite characters in Irish history. Nor, I imagine, are they held in much affection in Ardmore, the siege of which began in 1642 – on this day.

Main sources: British Library, Thomason Tracts, E.123 (15); James Buckley, "The siege of Ardmore Castle, 1642", Journal of the Waterford & SE Ireland Archaeological Society, IV (1898), 54-59.

THE "GREAT" EARL OF CORK

The opening a few years ago of a new art gallery in the west wing of Lismore Castle focused attention once more on that magnificent building, so it's fitting to remember today the man who created that castle as we know it, the "Great" Earl of Cork.

Richard Boyle was born at Canterbury in 1566, the younger son of a member of an obscure family of landed gentry. Orphaned as a boy, he drifted to Ireland in 1588, attracted by rumours that it was a desirable field for young adventurers of push, daring and ability. His first job was drawing up land conveyances. Before long he had sussed out the intricacies of the Irish land system and was using his small capital to buy up at nominal prices the vast confiscated estates of the Irish chieftains. In 1595 he married a Limerick heiress, who conveniently died leaving him a large sum in cash and £500 per annum in landed property. This enabled him to buy even more land.

Boyle's big break came in 1602 when he bought (on the cheap, as usual) the whole Irish estate of Sir Walter Raleigh, consisting of 12,000 acres in Counties Cork and Waterford. When the Nine Years War ended in the following year he settled them with English immigrants (a bit tough on the native Irish who were living there already). He built four new towns (Lismore, Tallow, Clonakilty and Bandonbridge), developed iron mines, felled woods to export the timber, and virtually rebuilt Lismore Cathedral and Castle (which he made his home). He was created Lord Boyle, Baron of Youghal, Viscount Dungarvan and Earl of Cork. He was appointed Lord Justice and Lord Treasurer of Ireland, and had a Dublin mansion on the site of the present City Hall.

Boyle built up a complex political power structure, and when Charles I's lord lieutenant, the Earl of Strafford, attempted to smash him, it was Strafford's head, not Boyle's, that ended up on the block. By his second wife he had fifteen children, among them the famous scientist-philosopher Robert Boyle of Boyle's Law. His wives and children are shown on the huge tomb he built for himself in St Mary's Youghal – and in case he died while he was in Dublin he built another one there, in St Patrick's Cathedral.

Boyle was his own best propagandist. In 1632 he wrote a memoir of his life up to that point; a copy of this quite brief document is now in the British Library. In it he recounts how he had come to Ireland at the age of twenty-two in 1588,

|ₗₗₗₗ|ₗₗₗₗ|ₗₗₗₗ|ₗₗₗₗ|ₗₗₗₗ|ₗₗₗₗ|ₗₗₗₗ|ₗₗₗₗ|ₗₗₗₗ|ₗₗₗₗ|ₗₗₗₗ|ₗₗₗₗ|ₗₗₗₗ|ₗₗₗₗ|ₗₗₗₗ|ₗₗₗₗ|ₗₗₗₗ|ₗₗₗₗ|

and by honest industry and devotion to the service of his beloved Queen had risen through the ranks of the Irish government, surviving in the process the filthy machinations of evil men who had plotted his destruction.

The reality was rather different. In an article published in *Irish Historical Studies* half a century ago, historian Terence Ranger dramatically exposed how Boyle had used corruption on a grand scale to rise to the position of the richest and most powerful man in the Ireland of his time.

Boyle is God's own gift to historians, for during the last thirty years of his life he kept a diary, and his personal and business correspondence was kept in meticulous order. And it has survived, for his papers were at his house in Dublin when Lismore was burned by the Irish in 1645. Today, some of the Boyle papers are to be found in Chatsworth (the seat of the Dukes of Devonshire), some are in Dublin in our National Library, and some are still in Lismore.

In the 18th century, our Dungarvan-born historian Charles Smith obtained permission to consult the papers, which were all then at Lismore. His research methods were somewhat drastic by today's standards, for he simply ripped out all the papers he wanted from Boyle's two great letter-books and took them off. Luckily, the missing pages are now in the British Library; one of the letter-books is now at Chatsworth – and the other, alas, is lost.

Tomb of the Great Earl of Cork,
St Mary's Church, Youghal
© *Mike Searl, Creative Commons*

Richard Boyle, the Great Earl of Cork, died in Youghal in 1643 – on this day.

Main source: Terence Ranger, "Richard Boyle and the making of an Irish fortune", Irish Historical Studies, vol. 10, no. 39 (March 1957), pp 257-297.

THE STORMING OF PILTOWN CASTLE

The Irish countryside is studded with ruined square towers which are commonly called castles but are more accurately termed "tower houses". They were built by the local gentry, whether Gaelic, Norman or English, at a time when central government had broken down and every landed gent had to be prepared to defend his property against enemy raids. The earliest tower houses date from the middle of the 15th century, and they were still being built down to the time of Cromwell. Most readers will be familiar with their usual features – the outer walls, flanking towers and moat so often destroyed long ago; the great rectangular tower with its massive walls, spiral staircase, stone vaulted ceilings, mural chambers, and battlemented parapet. They were obviously built with defence in mind, and yet it's disappointingly hard to find any account of the siege of a tower house. Their garrisons seem to have been all too eager to surrender them, and during the wars of the 1640s they changed hands with bewildering rapidity. Tower houses were just no match for artillery.

In County Waterford we do have a detailed account of the siege of a tower house. This was Piltown Castle near Ardmore, which was attacked in August 1646 by the English parliamentary army commanded by the Earl of Inchiquin. A blow-by-blow account of the siege has come down to us from the pen of his second-in-command, Major-General William Jephson. "It was a very strong place," he writes, "and after a serious view thereof I much admired that it proved so feasible."

When the English army had surrounded the place, Inchiquin summoned the garrison to surrender, promising them fair quarter if they gave in before he had discharged three cannon shot against the walls. His offer was refused, but the defenders did send out their women and children, whose lives were apparently spared. The assault then began in earnest. First the attackers had to capture a strong outwork of earth, measuring twenty feet from the bottom of the moat to the top of the wall. Then they had to gain entry to a stone courtyard with walls twelve feet high – and after that another one, before they could even approach the tower. This they accomplished with the loss of several men killed and twenty men wounded.

But, writes Jephson, "when they had taken all of these, they found it a very difficult task to enter the castle itself, and whilst they were endeavouring with bars of iron to force a passage, the rogues from the top of the battlements threw down stones so fast upon the heads of our men below that they hurt many of them. Yet in spite of all these brushes they at last got into the lower rooms. But the rogues still defended it, and brake down the stone stairs to prevent our men getting up to them. We therefore, finding that without much mischief it was impossible to get them down, we were forced to lay powder below, and blow them and the castle up together, which we did last night."

Military convention decreed that when a castle was taken by storm, terms of surrender having been refused, the defenders had no right to quarter. The defenders of Piltown certainly got none, for Inchiquin and his men were infuriated by the stubbornness of the defence. The entire garrison, with the exception of seven men, were put to the sword – the victors gave them no credit for their bravery.

Nothing is left of Piltown Castle today, and we don't know the names of a single one of its heroic defenders. They fell victim to the fury of Murrough the Burner and his merry men in 1646 – on this day.

Main source: Historical MSS Commission, Egmont MSS, I, pp 258, 305-306, 312.

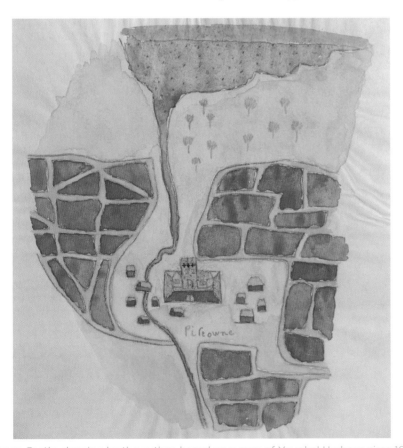

Piltown Castle, drawing by the author, based on a map of Youghal Harbour circa 1600

THE SIEGE OF DUNGARVAN

Angle tower of Dungarvan Castle
Photo: Waterford County Museum

During the wars of the 1640s, the port of Dungarvan was vitally important to the Irish. Waterford was too far upriver; Youghal and Cork remained stubbornly in English hands. From Dungarvan, however, ships could be dispatched to Spain and other friendly countries, whence they returned laden with arms and supplies for the divided and often demoralised forces of the Catholic Confederation. By the beginning of May 1647, Dungarvan had been in Irish hands for five years, and

|˙˙˙˙|˙˙˙˙|˙˙˙˙|˙˙˙˙|˙˙˙˙|˙˙˙˙|˙˙˙˙|˙˙˙˙|˙˙˙˙|˙˙˙˙|˙˙˙˙|˙˙˙˙|˙˙˙˙|˙˙˙˙|˙˙˙˙|˙˙˙˙|˙˙˙˙|˙˙˙˙|˙˙˙˙|˙˙˙˙|

the English commander Lord Inchiquin considered it well worth his attention when he swept through the county with his army.

Attackers and defenders were well matched. The English were better armed and equipped, more experienced, and had an able commander. However, the weather had been foul, they had run out of supplies, and the lack of draught horses obliged them to drag their cannon through the mud. The Irish, on the other hand, were secure behind the walls of town and castle and had sufficient food and arms, but there was no supply of fresh water within the defences. Storms at sea prevented supplies from reaching Inchiquin, but three Parliament ships did manage to shelter within the harbour, forcing a Confederate ship bearing arms and ammunition for the garrison to withdraw.

The fighting was desperate. For four days Inchiquin pounded the walls with his artillery but was unable to make a breach. Nevertheless, he did beat down one of the flanking towers of the town wall, which was lined with earth to a height of fourteen feet, and he took by storm a castle near the town from which the garrison secured their water.

One night the defenders made a sortie and drove the enemy from three of their dugouts near the town. Next day, at about three in the afternoon, Inchiquin attempted to assault the town with scaling ladders, but was beaten back, eighty of his men being killed and a cannon broken. One Irish officer wrote: "The redcoats' dead corpses do lie in the streets as a flock of sheep beside the river."

The siege continued until 9 May. Relief forces failed to materialize. The defenders had exhausted their ammunition and further resistance was impossible. But Inchiquin too had suffered heavy losses and his men were starving. Consequently, when the garrison offered to surrender on condition that they would be allowed to march out with bag and baggage, he was only too glad to accept their terms.

At eleven o'clock on 10 May he entered the town, and on perceiving the strength of its defences he considered himself lucky to have captured it at all. 500 officers and soldiers and 260 women were allowed to march out of the town, leaving behind twelve pieces of artillery.

The stubborn defence of Dungarvan reflected great credit on the Irish forces. Its capture by an English Parliamentary army was to prove of vital importance two years later upon the arrival of the exhausted and hard pressed army of Oliver Cromwell: although Inchiquin had by then changed sides, his garrison in Dungarvan had no stomach for another fight and surrendered without firing a shot.

The five-day siege of Dungarvan by Lord Inchiquin began in 1647 – on this day.

GEOFFREY BARRON

I suppose historians shouldn't think in terms of heroes and villains. Nevertheless, if I were to compile a list of my personal local heroes, somewhere near the top would surely come Geoffrey Barron of Clonmel. He was born in Clonmel in 1607, the eldest son of Laurence Barron, the town's most prosperous merchant, and Mary Wadding of Waterford. Through his mother he was connected by blood to the powerful junta of Waddings, Whites, Comerfords and so on that controlled Waterford's commerce and administration. His uncle was the illustrious Franciscan Luke Wadding, many of his relations were members of religious orders, and he grew up imbued with the uncompromising spirit of Counter-Reformation Catholicism.

When Geoffrey was only fifteen his father died, and even before he came of age the youngster was struggling to deal with the complex network of business interests he had inherited, and to take care of his little brothers and sisters. As was customary for the sons of Irish landowners and merchants, he studied law at one of the London inns of court. References to him, both from this time and later, all stress his attractive character, his popularity, his positive influence on those about him, and his skill as a lawyer.

In 1634 the Earl of Strafford, King Charles I's lord lieutenant of Ireland, summoned a parliament in Dublin, not with any idea of encouraging Irish democracy but simply to screw money out of the country for his master. Geoffrey Barron was elected MP for Clonmel. Strafford made extravagant promises to the Catholics, the money was paid over, and the promises were then broken. The Catholic protest was led by Geoffrey Barron. Strafford was a bully, and enough MPs were leaned on for a vote to be passed which expelled Geoffrey from the house and put him in prison in Dublin Castle for eight days.

With this experience of parliamentary politics under his belt, it's hardly surprising that on the outbreak of the 1641 rising Geoffrey supported the Irish Confederates with enthusiasm. He was assigned a daunting task – to go over to mainland Europe and try to persuade the Catholic powers of France, Spain and the Papal States to back the Irish cause with money, supplies and arms. It was a mission fraught with danger and difficulty – capture by English warships, the indifference or vague promises of the mighty, the shifting complexities of European politics, and even when all did go well the frustration of being upstaged by other Irish delegates. No one could have worked harder for the Catholic Confederation, and it was not Geoffrey Barron's fault that it collapsed.

Seal of the Irish Confederation

When Cromwell arrived before Waterford in November 1649, Geoffrey used all the moral force at his command to persuade the mayor and corporation to resist. In the following year he again urged them to hold out against Ireton. When the city surrendered he went on to Limerick, and when in 1651 Limerick too fell to Ireton he was one of the few Irish leaders singled out for a fair trial and a fair hanging.

At his trial he defended himself with the claim that like the Cromwellians he had only been fighting for the religion and liberty of his country. Ireton replied that Ireland was a conquered country and that the Irish deserved what they got. Before his execution Geoffrey put on his finest clothes and acted with carefree cheerfulness. He explained to his astonished captors that to bestow this last livery upon the body he was about to leave was the least of his duty to so tender a servant.

Geoffrey Barron was hanged in Limerick in 1651 – on this day.

EDWARD WOGAN AND THE DEFENCE OF DUNCANNON

In November 1649 the army of Oliver Cromwell, having wiped the blood of the hapless inhabitants of Wexford off their swords, prepared to march on to New Ross, and thence via Carrick-on-Suir to Waterford. First, however, it was essential to capture the fort at Duncannon so that supplies for the troops could be brought up-river. Duncannon was a strong fort, built in 1590 to resist a possible Spanish invasion, so Cromwell despatched for the task his best general - Michael Jones, victor of the battle of Rathmines, where he had routed an Irish army four times the size of his own.

The commander of Duncannon was a local officer, a Captain Roche, who was understandably jittery about resisting Cromwell after the massacres at Drogheda and Wexford. But Ormonde, the royalist commander-in-chief, had a trick up his sleeve – he appointed as governor of Duncannon Edward Wogan, the colonel of his own regiment of Life Guards.

Aerial view of Duncannon Fort (courtesy of Duncannon Military Fort and Fortifications)

Wogan was an extraordinary man. A member of a historic Irish family of County Kildare, he had been brought up a Protestant, and when rebellion broke out in 1641 the young lad was sent off to relatives in Wales for his own protection. In the following year civil war broke out in England, and Wogan joined the army of parliament. He was rapidly promoted, and fought with distinction in the battles that followed. But as the troubles continued he became more and more uneasy with the behaviour of his own command, broke with the parliamentary army and joined the royalists, and eventually found himself back in Ireland.

Although still a young man and a junior officer, Wogan's handsome appearance caught the attention of his new associates. He had already acquired a reputation as a gallant, charismatic, and energetic leader, and an excellent horseman. He soon put new heart into the demoralised garrison of Duncannon.

Duncannon was regarded by both sides as the key to Waterford. The attackers made several gains: Ballyhack Castle was captured; boats were brought round from Wexford to block the sea approach to Duncannon; Great Island was occupied, and there was talk of bringing the army across to Cheekpoint. Cromwell himself came down to inspect the ground and to deliver a personal summons to surrender upon quarter. But Wogan sent back a defiant answer: "I and those under my command are sensible of your cruel and tyrannical 'quarter'. And this is therefore to let you understand that this place is kept for king and country and the preservation of the people."

Jones found that he was not going to capture the fort simply by making threatening noises. Moreover, the heavy guns had been left behind at New Ross, so he had to make do with what he had. His assaults on the walls of the fort were beaten back with heavy losses, and – worse still – the garrison even sallied out from behind these walls and attacked the besiegers, picking off stragglers and generally making their lives a misery.

Ignominiously, Jones had to call off the siege and rejoin the main army. Wogan had given Cromwellian soldiers their first defeat, beaten their best general, and saved Waterford's bacon – for the moment!

However, when not long after Cromwell's army laid siege to Waterford, Jones was able to recover his reputation by capturing the much smaller fort at Passage East. It was vital that the Irish recapture it, and as the Cromwellian army marched off west towards Dungarvan, a joint attack was planned – the Waterford garrison under General O'Ferrall would lay siege to the fort, and Wogan would ferry his men across the river to help them.

A fierce battle ensued, and the little fort was defended with great spirit. However, unknown to O'Ferrall, the defenders had managed to get word to their comrades further west that they were under attack, and a detachment of cavalry was sent out to relieve them. O'Ferrall failed to keep sentries posted, and in the midst of the fray the enemy cavalry burst down the hill, took the Irish by surprise, and after a bitter battle put them to flight.

O'Ferrall, with much difficulty, managed to rally his men and get them back to Waterford. The garrison of Duncannon were not so lucky. Some tried to escape along the rocks, but were cut off by the incoming tide and drowned. Others were cut down by enemy swords. Eventually, the survivors got back to Duncannon in their boats.

To Cromwell's great delight, Wogan himself was captured. Having originally fought for parliament and then changed sides, he was regarded as a traitor. He was sent off to Cork to get a fair trial and a fair hanging.

But once again, Cromwell had underestimated his man. The following February, Wogan escaped from jail in Cork, and – God knows how – managed to make his way to France where he joined the other royalist exiles. His career was far from over. In 1653 he collected a force of about a hundred volunteers, and brought them swiftly and with great daring through the north of England and into the Scottish highlands, where the Scots were engaged in a small scale, last ditch resistance to what was euphemistically called the "pacification" of the region by the occupying English army. His men were reported to be "gallantly mounted, richly clothed, and well armed", and the following February they defeated an English force.

But in the fighting Wogan received a sword thrust in the shoulder. Due to the incompetence of the surgeon, the wound proved mortal. He was buried at Kenmore Church near Aberfeldy. But his name lives on, not only in Irish history but in the pages of Sir Walter Scott, who included his "short but glorious career" in his novel *Waverley*.

Edward Wogan, the gallant defender of Duncannon, was buried in 1654 – on this day.

SIR ROBERT WALSH – IRELAND'S FIRST GOLD MEDALLIST

The battle of Edgehill, fought on Sunday 23 October 1642, was the first significant engagement of the English Civil War. The royal army was commanded by King Charles I in person, while the parliamentary army was commanded by the Earl of Essex.

In the early stages of the fighting a sudden rush by the parliamentary infantry resulted in the royal standard being captured and its bearer slain. To lose the royal standard in battle was an unbearable disgrace to any army, and gave a corresponding boost to the morale of the enemy. It had to be retaken. Suddenly a royalist captain with the uninspiring name of John Smith plunged into the enemy ranks, fought his way through to the standard, and brought it back in triumph to the King. Smith became the hero of the day. The King knighted him on the field of battle, and a year later presented him with a gold medal bearing the royal head on one side and a banner on the other.

A fact that is not in most history books is that a second royalist officer was involved in the rescue of royal standards that day. His name was Robert Walsh from Ballygunner, County Waterford, Ireland.

Walsh was in command of a troop of royalist horse. Finding themselves behind the enemy lines, they saw approaching them a troop of enemy cavalry that had captured some royal standards. They charged them, put them to flight, and recaptured the royal standards as well as some of the enemy ones and two pieces of cannon and the supply waggon of the Earl of Essex.

Early next morning, as the King's army regrouped on the high ground, Robert Walsh and his troop emerged from the village of Kineton and rode triumphantly to the foot of the hill bearing the captured standards and towing the waggon and two cannon. So pleased was the King that he made Robert Walsh a knight on the spot.

On 1 June following, Charles I issued a warrant to the head of the Royal Mint to make a medal in gold for "our trusty and well-beloved Sir Robert Welch, knight, … and on the reverse thereof to insculp ye form of our royal banner used at the battail of Edge-hill, where he did us acceptable service and received the dignity of knighthood from us".

The day Sir Robert was presented with his medal by the King must have been the proudest of his life. It was the first medal ever awarded by a sovereign for gallantry in action, and is known to experts in such matters as the Welch Medal. He won it in 1642 – on this day.

Main source: An account of the Welch Medal is given in Spink's British battles and medals (London, 1988). However, I am indebted above all to the researches of Spencer Welsh of Rayleigh, Essex, for information on this subject.

THE LOST TREASURES OF WATERFORD CATHEDRAL

The area around Christ Church Cathedral lies in the very heart of medieval Waterford. Men, women and children – and their animals – have lived there for 1100 years. More than a millennium of history lies under our feet as we walk through Cathedral Close. In recent years archaeologists have revealed much of Waterford's Viking and Norman past. For some of our most valuable treasures, alas, they came several centuries too late.

The old cathedral of Waterford, demolished in 1774, had beneath it a secret vault. In 1650, when the soldiers of Cromwell's army were sent to capture the city, the priests and the faithful stored in this vault the treasures of their cathedral, hoping they would be safe there until better times should arrive. When the Church of Ireland was restored in 1660, its officials understandably wished to find out what had happened to these valuables, and commissioners were appointed to look into the matter. They uncovered a sad story.

An Irishwoman (we don't know her name) had incautiously revealed all to a wheelwright from Kilkenny named Nicholas Phary, who had been messenger to the commissioners who governed the town. Mr Phary rushed eagerly to gain favour with his masters hearing news of the hiding-place. When the vault was opened it was found to contain three holy water pots of brass, an eagle, a pelican, several standing candlesticks, one branched candlestick, a censer, "and other things, the names he cannot now remember".

All were taken to the city store, dumped in with plunder taken from

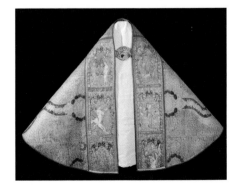

other churches, and eventually put up for auction!

But the crypt was not the only place used to hide sacred treasures from heretical hands. One evening in the early 19th century, a servant at Number 21 Henrietta Street was sent by her employer Mr Henry Ivie to draw beer in the cellar. She rushed back up the stairs, panting excitedly that there was something shining in the ground under the drip of the barrel. A search party descended rapidly, and soon unearthed a cache of chalices, cups, crosses, reliquaries, chains, rings, etc., besides gold and silver coins.

Here (courtesy Waterford Museum of Treasures, Three Museums in the Viking Triangle) are examples of the kinds of treasures that went missing

Many years later, Ivie's daughter – by then an old woman – tried to recall the details of what she had seen brought up when she was a little girl. She described in particular "a gold reliquary, as large as an old-fashioned watch, which opened completely, one side coming out from a groove. The deep side had finely raised figures. The reverse side, which came off like a cover, was richly encrusted with gems, garnets, emeralds, and small diamonds. The reliquary was suspended to a massive gold chain about six inches in length. There was also a gold locket set with blue sapphires and pearls. And there was a small thick gold book, with rubies, emeralds and pearls ornamenting the sides, having a cavity in the centre, supposed to hold a portion of the true cross."

And what happened to these wonderful objects? They were all sold, with the exception of some of the rings, which were given to Mr Ivie's daughter.

The heart of old Waterford has changed beyond recognition since those days. But as you walk through City Square, don't forget that a millennium of history lies beneath your feet - and maybe some treasure too!

The commissioners appointed to discover the whereabouts of the cathedral treasure reported in 1661 – on this day.

Main sources: Depositions re the Cathedral brass, 1661 (parchment roll in Christ Church archives); P.M. Egan, Guide to Waterford (1894).

JOHN BRENAN:
A BISHOP ON THE RUN

When in 1645 Dr Scarampi, the Pope's representative to the Irish Catholic Confederation, returned to Rome, he took with him two gifted young men to be trained for the priesthood. One was Oliver Plunket, the future Archbishop of Armagh, canonized in 1975; the other was a native of Kilkenny named John Brenan. Though chased by an enemy frigate on the high seas and robbed by brigands in Flanders, they reached Rome safely. Plunket and Brenan were brilliant students, and in due course they became priests. In 1669 Plunket was nominated Archbishop of Armagh, and two years later Brenan became Bishop of Waterford and Lismore.

They both returned to an Ireland that had been shattered by years of warfare, plague, confiscation and persecution. However, it was the beginning of a period of hope. Charles II had been on the throne for a decade and he was known to be tolerant in matters of religion. Waterford County was governed by Richard Power of Curraghmore, Earl of Tyrone, a man with a foot in both religious camps, and the Catholic Church in the city was under the control of his kinsman, Dean Robert Power. Catholics were generally free to worship, but they had no churches and their clergy had neither houses nor income. Moreover, there were occasional bouts of persecution when priests, especially bishops, had to take to their heels. For most of his "reign" of twenty-two years as Bishop of Waterford, John Brenan was a homeless wanderer, frequently on the run.

In the winter of 1673-74 Brenan had to flee from his diocese and join his friend Oliver Plunket, also a wanted man, in the Fews Mountains of County Armagh. "The hut in which Dr Brenan and myself have taken refuge," wrote Plunket cheerfully, "is made of straw". When we lie down to rest, through the opening of the roof we can see the stars, and when it rains we are refreshed even at the head of the bed by each successive shower." A little oaten bread was their only food, "yet we choose rather to die of hunger than to abandon our flocks, since it would be shameful for spiritual soldiers who were trained in Rome to become mercenaries."

A few weeks later they were on the move again. "The snow fell heavily," wrote Plunket, "mixed with hailstones very hard and large. Often we were in danger of being lost and suffocated in the snow, till at length we arrived at the house of an impoverished gentleman who had nothing to lose. But, for our misfortune, he had a stranger in the house by whom we did not wish to be recognized. Hence we were placed in a large garret without chimney or fire, where we have been the last eight days. My companion [Bishop Brenan] was attacked by rheumatism in one arm, so that he can scarcely move it."

|¹¹¹¹|¹¹¹¹|¹¹¹¹|¹¹¹¹|¹¹¹¹|¹¹¹¹|¹¹¹¹|¹¹¹¹|¹¹¹¹|¹¹¹¹|¹¹¹¹|¹¹¹¹|¹¹¹¹|¹¹¹¹|¹¹¹¹|¹¹¹¹|¹¹¹¹|¹¹¹¹|¹¹¹¹|¹¹¹¹|

In 1677 Brenan was promoted to the see of Cashel, but it was so impover-ished that he was allowed to keep Waterford as well. He now had a huge area to administer. Cashel had twenty priests and Waterford thirty, many of whom were concentrated in the city, leaving the countryside poorly served. The city priests mostly belonged to religious orders who squabbled among themselves – being a bishop was certainly no picnic in those days. Then in 1678 came the so-called Popish Plot. Brenan's friend Oliver Plunket was martyred at Tyburn, and a simi-lar fate nearly overtook his patron the Earl of Tyrone, who languished for some time in the Tower of London. As for Brenan himself, the Houdini-bishop went on the run again and his hiding-place was never discovered.

The reign of James II brought a res-toration of Catholic power, but it was all too brief. Brenan was one of the Irish team who negotiated the Treaty of Limerick with General Ginkel. It was a civilized business. Brenan was invited to dine with the Dutch com-mander, and Sarsfield brought over a boatload of claret to help them get through the evening.

Brenan lived long enough to see the treaty broken by the English Parlia-ment. He died in 1693 and was buried in the tomb of the great Gaelic scholar Geoffrey Keating in Tubrid. It would be over a century before Waterford got another Catholic bishop as brave and resourceful.

Saint Oliver Plunket

John Brenan was nominated Bishop of Waterford and Lismore in 1671 – on this day.

Main source: P. Canon Power, A Bishop of the Penal Times: Letters and Reports of John Brenan, Bishop of Waterford ... (1932).

UNITING TWO GREAT FAMILIES

In the mid-17th century two of the biggest landowners in County Waterford were Sir John FitzGerald of Dromana, Lord of the Decies, and Lord Power of Curraghmore. Lurking in the wings was Lord Power's son and heir Richard, a shrewd and ambitious man. In 1654 he concluded a very useful marriage with Dorothy, eldest daughter of the Earl of Anglesey, a powerful English nobleman with extensive Irish interests.

Four years later Richard's sister married Sir John FitzGerald of Decies, and when Sir John died in 1663 leaving only one daughter Katherine to succeed him, Richard (who on the death of his father had succeeded him as Lord Power) became the guardian of his little niece, who was now the owner of the vast Dromana estate. As Katherine's guardian it was Richard's duty to find her a suitable husband; who, he reasoned, could be more suitable than his own son and heir John Power? This daring coup would unite under Richard's control both the Dromana and Curraghmore estates, making him rich beyond the dreams of avarice.

Children matured faster in those days than now, but even so the couple was hardly ready for matrimony: Katherine was only twelve and a half and her fiancé not yet eight. Furthermore, Katherine was a willful child and it took a lot of pressure to get her to consent to the match. But at last, thanks to the patronage of Lord Anglesey, Katherine and John were married by none other than the Archbishop of Canterbury himself, in his private chapel at Lambeth Palace in London. After the ceremony they were whisked away to Lord Anglesey's house. Later that same year, Richard Lord Power's

Katherine FitzGerald

career reached a peak of success when he received from Charles II a royal patent granting him two further titles, Earl of Tyrone and Viscount Decies.

But Katherine soon proved that she had a will of her own. She had no intention of hanging around until her husband was old enough to perform his marital duties. Two years after the marriage she made a statement before the Archbishop of Canterbury that she had been forced into it by "immoderate importunity, threats, fear, and the false suggestion of losing her estate".

The following Easter, having now attained the mature age of fifteen, she escaped from Lord Anglesey's house and ran away with a handsome young cavalry officer named Edward Villiers, whom she married shortly after. The Power faction reacted to her defection with furious indignation: jadish viper, fair flirt, wicked urchin, are among the politer terms used about her by Lord Anglesey in a letter to his son-in-law. Of the Villiers faction he says: "Keep up your courage and yield nothing to

Edward Villiers

them till satisfied by their proposals, and this will produce a good issue without the woman, "which is all we aim at", for she is bewrayed [soiled] past touching." In other words – forget about the woman; keep the land.

As you can imagine, the lawyers had a field day. The issue was: in what circumstances can a marriage contracted by minors be repudiated by them when they come of age? For years the case was fought with increasing bitterness through the ecclesiastical and civil courts. The judgement, which was in Katherine's favour, provided a legal precedent for many years to come. The Powers had to give back her lands and she remained married to Villiers, dying at a ripe old age in 1726. Poor John Power, after his horrendous experience, never married again: he died in his late twenties in 1693 and was succeeded by his brother.

The marriage, if that is what it was, between John Power and Katherine Villiers took place in 1673 – on this day.

BISHOP BERKELEY AND THE EXISTENCE OF – NOTHING!

A few miles north of Waterford, the River Nore winds its way through magnificent scenery from Thomastown to Inistiogue and on to its junction with the Barrow. One of the old buildings that enrich this stretch of the river is the little ruined castle of Dysart. In the late 17th century it was the boyhood home of one of the greatest writers and thinkers that Ireland has produced.

George Berkeley was born in 1685, probably on the townland of Kilcrin in St Patrick's parish, Kilkenny. At Dysart the family home was attached to the south-west side of the tower, and an ancient chapel stood adjacent on the south-east side. At the age of ten he was sent to be educated at Kilkenny College, where Dean Swift had been a pupil some years previously.

One schoolboy adventure of which he has left an account is an expedition with some pals to Dunmore Cave. What had begun as a day of sport with guns and dogs turned into an exploration of the cave which left a profound impression on him and encouraged his lifelong interest in natural phenomena. In 1717, when travelling in Italy, he witnessed an eruption of Vesuvius, climbing right up to the crater to record what he saw in more detail, oblivious of the obvious danger.

In 1700 he entered Trinity College, and after graduating was ordained into the Church of Ireland. Already he was writing the works that were to make him famous. He was a tireless traveller (England, France, Italy), an acute observer, and an engaging companion. Soon his attention moved from the Old World to the New. In 1725 he published *A proposal for the better supplying of churches in our foreign plantations, and for converting the savage Americans to Christianity by a college to be erected in the Summer Islands, otherwise called the Isles of Bermuda*.

Over the next few years his charm and his courage were used to persuade influential people to back his ambitious scheme. The British government promised a charter and a grant of £20,000, and Berkeley set off for Rhode Island, where he spent the next three years. He used his time well, but the grant never materialized and he returned to Ireland. He was Bishop of Cloyne for seventeen years, and in addition to continuing his philosophical work he campaigned on behalf of his fellow-countrymen.

|₁₁₁₁|₁₁₁₁|₁₁₁₁|₁₁₁₁|₁₁₁₁|₁₁₁₁|₁₁₁₁|₁₁₁₁|₁₁₁₁|₁₁₁₁|₁₁₁₁|₁₁₁₁|₁₁₁₁|₁₁₁₁|₁₁₁₁|₁₁₁₁|₁₁₁₁|₁₁₁₁|₁₁₁₁|₁₁₁₁|₁₁₁₁|

Berkeley's concern for the well-being of all Ireland can be seen in his tract *A word to the Wise, or an exhortation to the Roman Catholic clergy of Ireland*, which opens: "Be not startled, reverend sirs, to find yourselves addressed by one of a different communion. We are indeed (to our shame be it spoken) more inclined to hate for those articles wherein we differ, than to love one another for those wherein we agree." These were enlightened words indeed at a time when the Penal Laws were at their height.

Berkeley was one of the great influences on world history. He also believed that nothing really exists, and that virtually all ailments can be cured by liberal doses of tar-oil! The existence of a physical thing, he maintained, consists in its being perceived. The great debate over Immaterialism, as this theory is called, was continued in subsequent generations, one of its main inheritors being Lenin, through whom Berkeley's name was well known in the Soviet Union. In America too the impact of Berkeley's scholarship has been enormous – hence Berkeley University, California. In Ireland he influenced men as diverse as John Mitchel, W.B. Yeats, and Eamon de Valera (who spoke at Cloyne on the bicentenary of Berkeley's death in 1953).

So - does an object only exist when we perceive it to be there? The great Oxford-based Catholic theologian Ronald Knox wrote, evidently with Berkeley in mind:

There once was a man who said: God
Must think it exceedingly odd
If He finds that this tree
Continues to be
When there's no one about in the Quad.

To which an anonymous wit replied:

Dear Sir, Your astonishment's odd.
I am always about in the Quad
And that's why the tree
Will continue to be
Since observed by, Yours faithfully, God.

George Berkeley – philosopher, educationist and bishop – was born at Dysart Castle in 1685 – on this day.

SIR NEILL O'NEILL,
A HERO OF THE BOYNE

In 1690 Sir Neill O'Neill of Killyleagh, County Down, was a 32-year-old colonel in the army of King James II. He commanded a regiment of dragoons – soldiers who rode into battle on small, fast-moving horses and then dismounted and fought on foot. There is a magnificent portrait of him in the Tate Gallery in London. He is shown in the traditional dress of an Irish chieftain, but on the ground behind him, surprisingly, is a suit of Japanese armour. The persecution of the Church in Japan was very much in people's minds at the time, and the kendo armour symbolically shows that Sir Neill too was fighting for religious freedom.

|ₗₗₗₗ|ₗₗₗₗ|ₗₗₗₗ|ₗₗₗₗ|ₗₗₗₗ|ₗₗₗₗ|ₗₗₗₗ|ₗₗₗₗ|ₗₗₗₗ|ₗₗₗₗ|ₗₗₗₗ|ₗₗₗₗ|ₗₗₗₗ|ₗₗₗₗ|ₗₗₗₗ|ₗₗₗₗ|ₗₗₗₗ|ₗₗₗₗ|ₗₗₗₗ|

O'Neill served with his regiment in Down and Antrim and at the siege of Derry. As King William's army marched south from Carrickfergus, he helped Sarsfield cover the Jacobite withdrawal to the banks of the fateful Boyne.

Here he was chosen for a vitally important task. Upstream of the main river crossing at Oldbridge, where the armies of William and James faced each other, was a ford named Rossnaree, and James feared that the Williamites might try to put a force across there which would endanger the Jacobite flank. Sir Neill's regiment was dispatched to prevent the Williamites from crossing. His instructions were "to defend the pass as long as he could without exposing his men to the danger of being cut to pieces, and then either to offer battle to King William or to march straight to Dublin".

King William did indeed send a force upstream to Rossnaree, but what the Jacobites didn't know was that it consisted of no fewer than six thousand cavalry under General Count Schomberg, supported by artillery. O'Neill's regiment was hopelessly outnumbered. Nevertheless, for a whole hour they defended the ford against the charges of some of the finest cavalry in Europe. O'Neill was shot through the thigh and was in great pain. Then, when the enemy artillery was brought up, he withdrew his men in good order and with few casualties.

By a cruel irony, when Schomberg's force did get across the river it was unable to attack the main Jacobite army as the ground between the two forces was boggy and full of deep ditches. The bravery of the Irish at Rossnaree had been in vain.

King James has been rightly despised by the Irish for his undignified flight from the Boyne. But one thing does stand to his credit. In his hasty retreat southwards he took care to bring with him the badly wounded defender of Rossnaree. By the time the royal party reached Waterford O'Neill was sinking fast, and when they slipped down the river to Duncannon he had to be left behind. He died here just a week after the battle, and the citizens paid him the signal honour of burying him in the chancel of the old Franciscan friary (now the French Church) and of erecting a fine tomb over the spot.

Sir Neill O'Neill, the defender of Rossnaree, died in Waterford in 1690 – on this day.

Portrait of Sir Neill O'Neill by John Michael Wright c.1680, on display at Tate Britain

ROBERT BOYLE, FATHER OF CHEMISTRY

Robert Boyle was born at Lismore Castle on 25 January 1627. He was the seventh son and fourteenth child of Sir Richard Boyle, the Great Earl of Cork – the "upstart earl" who had risen from obscurity to become one of the wealthiest and most powerful men in these islands - and his second wife Catherine Fenton.

Lismore Castle, where little Robert spent his childhood, had been bought from Sir Walter Raleigh by his father and virtually rebuilt. He saw little of his parents, for his mother died and his father was frequently absent on business. Life at Lismore was not without excitement. At the age of three he was nearly drowned when the horse on which he was being carried fell while crossing a rain-swollen stream; and at the age of seven he was nearly crushed when his bedroom ceiling collapsed.

At the tender age of eight Robert was sent off to school at Eton, an enormous journey for one so young. Flogging and then more flogging was the staple diet of Etonians in those days and for many years to come, but Robert was lucky. His tutor realized he had a child prodigy on his hands and that his problem was not to make him work but to keep him supplied with books. Not surprisingly, Robert soon made himself ill from overwork.

After three years his father removed him from Eton and sent him as a private pupil to the Rector of Stalbridge in Dorsetshire, one of the many properties he owned. Then, after a visit to London, he was sent off to France, then to Geneva where he studied for a year, and then to Italy. He was actually living in Florence studying the works of Galileo when the great scholar died nearby.

In 1643 his father died, leaving him the manor of Stalbridge in his will. Robert settled there and devoted the rest of his life to scientific research. In 1654 he moved to Oxford and in 1668 to London, where he lived in celibate bliss with his sister Lady Ranelagh. In appearance he was tall, slender and emaciated. Abstemious in everything except work, he suffered from chronic ill-health. In character he is described as brilliant in conversation, benevolent and tolerant.

During the 1650s England's puritanical rulers made it dangerous to be a scientist, so Robert and his friends formed what they called the Invisible Society. At the restoration of the monarchy in 1660 King Charles II (who was avidly interested in science) transformed this group into the Royal Society, of which he made himself patron. During the next thirty years Boyle wrote over eighty works. His contribution to science is outstanding. His reputation rests on the law that bears his name, which states that the volume of a gas varies inversely with its pressure. But

|᾿᾿᾿᾿|᾿᾿᾿᾿|᾿᾿᾿᾿|᾿᾿᾿᾿|᾿᾿᾿᾿|᾿᾿᾿᾿|᾿᾿᾿᾿|᾿᾿᾿᾿|᾿᾿᾿᾿|᾿᾿᾿᾿|᾿᾿᾿᾿|᾿᾿᾿᾿|᾿᾿᾿᾿|᾿᾿᾿᾿|᾿᾿᾿᾿|᾿᾿᾿᾿|

he also exerted an important influence over the scientists of his day by his insistence that it is no use having a theory unless you verify it by experiment. Isaac Newton was his contemporary and friend.

Boyle was intensely pious and wrote a number of theological works. With titles like *Occasional Reflections on Several Subjects* you can guess that they're not exactly adrenalin-pumping stuff, and they probably deserved Dean Swift's send-up in his *Pious Meditation on a Broomstick*. More importantly, his zeal for spreading the study of the Bible caused him to fork out £700 to a London type-founder named Joseph Moxon to set up a font of Irish type. This was used to reprint the New Testament, which had been unobtainable for many years. Four years later Boyle paid for the printing of the Old Testament, which had been translated by Irish scholars working under Bishop Bedell but never published. The complete Irish Bible followed in 1690.

Picture: Waterford County Museum

Robert Boyle, the Father of Chemistry, died in 1691 – on this day.

DEATH OF THE EARL OF TYRONE

Richard Power, 6th Baron le Power and Coroghmore, 1st Earl of Tyrone and Viscount Decies, was born in 1630, the eldest son and heir of John, 5th Lord Power, whose family had ruled the Paorach or Power's Country for centuries. Like the other Catholic landowners, Richard's father was deprived of his estate by Cromwell and ordered to transplant to Connacht. Richard, however, was a resourceful chap and managed to have the order cancelled on the grounds that his father was a lunatic and therefore couldn't have taken part in the rebellion. So the huge Curraghmore estate remained in Power hands.

In the same year, 1654, Richard pulled off a very profitable marriage. His bride was Lady Dorothy Annesley, daughter of the Earl of Anglesey. Her family were recent arrivals in Ireland, and they were Protestant and very English-orientated. The restoration of Charles II in 1660 did Richard no harm at all: in the following year he was made Governor of County Waterford, and when in 1662 his father died he inherited his huge estates. He went even further, buying thousands more acres in the county from the new Cromwellian owners. And in 1673 he obtained from the King a patent creating him Earl of Tyrone and Viscount Decies.

Richard seems to have been adept at sitting on the religious fence and keeping in with Protestants and Catholics. However, in 1680 he was caught out by the Popish Plot, an imaginary conspiracy dreamt up by an English con-man named Titus Oates, who alleged that the Catholics were plotting to assassinate the King, bring over the French, and make Catholicism the state religion. It was pure invention, but a number of the leading Catholics were arrested, imprisoned, even executed – St Oliver Plunket was one of the most famous.

On the accession of King James II in 1685, Richard came down openly on the Catholic side. His reward was to be appointed one of his majesty's privy councilors in Ireland. He was also Lieutenant of County Waterford, and raised a regiment of foot to fight in the Jacobite army. It was called Lord Tyrone's Regiment and was probably recruited from among his own tenants.

With his regiment he took part in the battle of the Boyne and later in the defence of Waterford. When the Governor of Waterford cravenly surrendered the city to King William, the defenders were allowed to march off and join the garrison of Cork. Here they soon found themselves under siege and were forced to surrender. Richard was one of the officers who negotiated the terms of the surrender, and they were harsh. The entire garrison were made prisoners of war and shipped off to England. Richard was imprisoned in the Tower of London.

Richard Power, died in the Tower of London in 1690 – on this day.

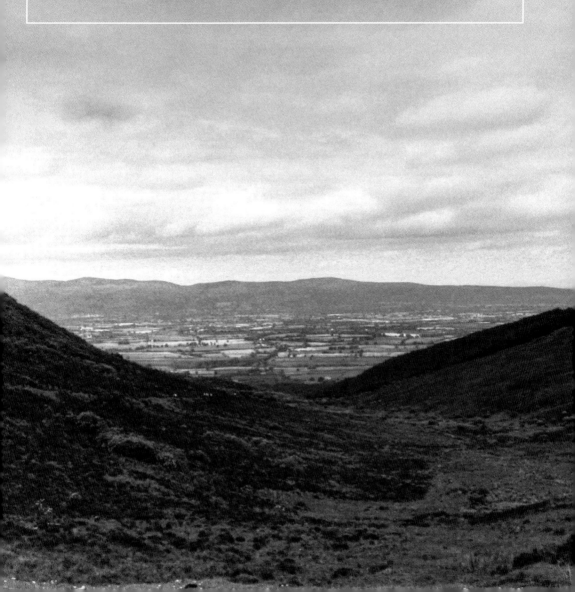

THE 1700s

BISHOP FOY, HIS SCHOOL AND HIS TOMB

The year 1967 saw the closure of one of Waterford's most historic schools, Bishop Foy's. But who was Bishop Foy?

Nathaniel Foy was born in York in 1648. When he was eight years old the family settled in Dublin, as did many other English Protestants during the Cromwellian régime. His father set up as a medical doctor and young Nathaniel was sent to the Dublin Corporation Free School. Foy was no mean scholar. At the age of fifteen he entered Trinity College, where he was soon covered in academic distinctions, and at the age of twenty-one he was ordained a minister of the Church of Ireland. In 1678 he was appointed rector of St Bride's parish, where he soon became known for his extreme anti-Catholic views.

In 1689 King James II – who had lost the throne of England because of his pro-Catholic policies – arrived in Dublin, summoned a parliament, and proceeded to restore the rights and privileges of the Catholic Church. Most of the Protestant bishops and clergy fled the country, but Foy remained and continued to denounce the "errors" of the Church of Rome. Every Sunday the King attended Mass at Christ Church Cathedral, where the sermon was preached by a learned French Catholic professor. Friends of Foy would attend, make notes on the sermon and bring them round to Foy, who in his own sermon the following Sunday would refute what had been said by the Frenchman. Soon Foy's vocal opposition to the régime landed him in prison.

Then came the battle of the Boyne, the flight of James II, and the triumphant entry of King William III into Dublin. The Protestant ascendancy was restored, Foy was among the heroes of the hour, and the grateful monarch rewarded him with the first vacant bishopric – that of Waterford and Lismore. Foy remained Bishop here from 1691 until his death.

In some ways Foy is not an attractive character to us today. He was virulently anti-Catholic. He had no time for the Irish language, nor for the scholars such as Robert Boyle who pioneered the Irish-language Bible. He had a capacity for running headlong into trouble, and was even thrown out of the Irish House of Lords for his intemperate opposition to a bill. And yet he was a good scholar and a genuine reformer – and God knows, the Church of Ireland at that time needed both. He fought hard to improve the moral and educational standards of candidates for the ministry, with a certain amount of success. He was less successful in his opposition to the amalgamation of parishes to make the rich clergy richer at the expense of the poor ones. He was an able and energetic administrator of his diocese.

Like all hyperactive bishops, he had a running fight with his deans – in his case Thomas Wallis in Waterford and William Jephson in Lismore. Wallis was evidently an arch-fixer who had stuck ecclesiastical tentacles into many parts of the diocese and even ensconced himself in the bishop's palace, from which he was only ejected with much difficulty. Jephson proved even harder to shift, even though Foy accused him of excessive drinking, absenteeism, and "a long con-tracted habit of debauchery". He was related to the powerful Jephsons of Mallow Castle and enjoyed the patronage of the Earl of Cork, so he was able to thumb his nose at the Bishop and die with his ecclesiastical boots on.

One of the chief battle-grounds between Catholic and Protestant was the matter of education. Despite the penal laws, courageous Catholics maintained schools in Waterford City, and these attracted also the poorer class of Protestants. Up with this Foy would not put, and he resolved to establish in Waterford a free school for the education of poor Protestant boys.

Foy made elaborate preparations. A site was provided by the Corporation – the old court-house on the corner of Broad Street and Arundel Street. "Bishop Foy's" was to be a staple of Waterford education for over two and a half centuries, until it was eventually subsumed into Newtown School in 1967.

At his death in the final hours of the year 1707, Foy was buried within his own cathedral. A splendid monument was commissioned from the foremost Irish stonemason of his day, William Kidwell. Made of black Kilkenny marble, it is surmounted by a huge headpiece on which the bishop's coat of arms is depicted in glorious technicolor, together with a gruesome skull and crossbones – symbols of the mortality of us all. Having survived the destruction and rebuilding of the cathedral in the 1770s, it stands today in a corner of the vestibule, where other bishops rest too.

Nathaniel Foy died in 1707 – on this day.

[See Declan Grogan, "Bishop Foy and the Cause of Reform", Decies no. 50 (1994), pp 72-84; no. 51 (1995), pp 67-74.]

THE BERESFORD GHOST STORY

If ever a person had a reason for remembering exactly how old she was, it was Nichola Sophia Hamilton – and yet she got it wrong, with fatal consequences, as you shall read.

Nichola was born on 23 February 1666 at Ballygawley in County Tyrone. She was the elder of two daughters and heiresses of Lord Glenawley. As a girl she was sent away from home to be privately educated by a tutor, and among the other children boarding in the house was a boy from County Waterford named John Power. He was the son and heir of Lord Tyrone of Curraghmore.

The two children became close friends. But when at the age of twenty-one Nichola married, her husband was not John Power but a landowner from Coleraine named Sir Tristram Beresford. They had several children and the marriage was a very happy one, until Sir Tristram died in 1701. A few years later, and against her better judgement, Nichola allowed herself to be wooed by a charming but ruffianly general named Richard Gorges. The general, I'm afraid, turned out to be a pretty nasty piece of work and treated her badly.

However, in February 1713 Nichola suddenly cheered up and decided to celebrate her 48th birthday in style. The convivialities were just getting under way when there arrived the old clergyman who had baptized her all those years ago.

"Welcome to my birthday party," cried Nichola, "I'm 48 today."

"Excuse me," replied the aged cleric, "but only this morning I was wondering how old you were and I checked the register. I have some good news for you. You're not 48 – you're only 47."

At this, Lady Nichola turned a whiter shade of pale, muttered a stream of unladylike curses, cancelled the whole party, sent the butler to fetch her son and daughter, stamped off to her bedroom, and slammed the door. When the two youngsters arrived, they found their mother stretched out on the bed with the pallor of death upon her. She then told them the following rather unusual story.

During her schooldays, whatever about the 3 Rs, the religion classes had been a disaster, for her tutor believed in a heresy known as Deism, which he proceeded to impart to his young charges. When this was discovered, every effort was made to drum a bit of orthodox Christian doctrine into their heads. But it was too late – the youngsters ended up in a state of total confusion. So young Nichola and her friend John Power made a pact: the one who died first would return from the dead and tell the other which was the true religion, Deism or Christianity.

Time passed. John Power became Lord Tyrone and Nichola became Lady Tristram Beresford. Then in October 1693 she and her husband went on a visit to her sister who lived at Gill Hall in County Down.

That night Nichola awoke to find Lord Tyrone standing by her bed.

"Remember that pact?" he snapped. "Well, I'm dead, and I came back to tell you that the true religion is - Christianity. And in case you don't believe me, I can tell the future as well. You're going to have a son, and one day he will marry my heiress and unite our two families. Your husband will die, and you'll marry again and be very unhappy. Oh, and by the way you'll die on your 47th birthday. Now, hold out your arm." When she did so, the spirit grasped her wrist and there was a sizzling sound and a smell of scorching sinews. In the morning Nichola found her wrist quite shrivelled. She covered it with a black ribbon and told nobody – until now.

Sure enough, everything the spirit had foretold came to pass: she did have a son, her husband died and she did marry again – unhappily for her. And she did die on her 47th birthday. When her children untied the black ribbon from her lifeless wrist, sure enough – they found it shrivelled, just as she had said.

Four years later, in 1717, the last part of the prophecy came true: her son Sir Marcus Beresford married Lady Catherine Power and came to live at Curraghmore. Their descendants have lived there ever since.

Nichola Hamilton, the central character of the famous Beresford Ghost Story, was born – and died – on this day.

CROTTY OF THE COMERAGHS

William Crotty had his headquarters high up in the Comeraghs where to this day Crotty's Lake is named after him

Photo: Andrew Kelly

Between the Treaty of Limerick in 1691 and the rebellion of 1798 there was no Irish uprising. Many of the old Gaelic aristocracy and their followers – the celebrated Wild Geese – left the country altogether and sought fame and fortune in the armies of Spain and France. But 18th-century Ireland was not a peaceful place to live. There was poverty and there was violence. The new, insecure landlord class attempted to maintain its position by increasingly harsh laws against those who defied it and those who did defy the law successfully, even for a short period, became folk heroes. One of the greatest of was William Crotty.

Records show that Crotty and his gang flourished in the years 1740 and 1741 and that he was captured and executed early in 1742. His henchman was a certain David Norris, who was cleverer than Crotty and planned their daring raids, which Crotty then put into execution. Their arch-enemy was the local magistrate, a Mr Hearn of Shanakill, whose mission it became to capture Crotty and bring him to justice – no easy task, as there was no police force in those days and he had to rely on the co-operation of the military.

Crotty was a hard man to catch. As a last resort he could retreat to his secret cave in the Comeragh Mountains, which he kept stocked with provisions for such an emergency. But Hearn too had a secret weapon – for David Norris was a traitor, and between them they were eventually able to bring the great rapparee's career to an untimely end.

Crotty has survived in local legend for over 250 years. Some of the tales told of him are palpably rubbish but one of my favourites is as follows.

One time the local magistrates were hot on the outlaw's trail and, knowing that he would visit a certain house, they laid an ambush for him. Crotty arrived and the woman of the house knew the soldiers lay in hiding, but how could she warn him in time? Her chance came when he asked for a cup of tea. She gave it to him lukewarm, and when the ungrateful fellow complained she replied: "Caith sé fuar agus teith!" This could mean: "Take it cold and hot" – i.e., lukewarm – or it could mean: "Take it cold and fly". Crotty got the message and bolted out the door.

|₁₁₁₁|₁₁₁₁|₁₁₁₁|₁₁₁₁|₁₁₁₁|₁₁₁₁|₁₁₁₁|₁₁₁₁|₁₁₁₁|₁₁₁₁|₁₁₁₁|₁₁₁₁|₁₁₁₁|₁₁₁₁|₁₁₁₁|₁₁₁₁|₁₁₁₁|₁₁₁₁|₁₁₁₁|₁₁₁₁|

What then is the truth about Crotty? In 1915 our local historian Matthew Butler searched through the affidavits for County Waterford preserved in the Public Record Office in Dublin. They showed clearly that between 1739 and 1742 Waterford and the neighbouring counties were indeed troubled by the depredations of a small gang of robbers led by William Crotty. One of the outlaws, David Norris, was captured and turned King's evidence. The fact that he doesn't seem to have been punished, even though a murder had been committed, supports the tradition that he betrayed his leader.

So far, so good. Matthew Butler now continued his quest by trawling though the national newspapers (no Waterford papers have survived as early as this). The press reports confirmed that Crotty's henchman David Norris had been captured and had informed on his comrades. This led to further captures and more information. In March 1741 six of the outlaws were captured, though Crotty himself escaped into a thick fog. Norris was sentenced to be transported, but escaped from jail – perhaps with the connivance of the authorities.

Finally, Crotty himself was captured and brought into Waterford on 16 February 1742 under a strong guard. He was lodged in the jail where his wife had already been imprisoned before him. He was put on trial at the following assizes, and on St Patrick's Day he was sentenced to be hanged, quartered and beheaded. The sentence was carried out the following day.

Crotty's gun was taken by the triumphant Mr Hearn, the magistrate who had captured him, and remained for many years thereafter at Shanakill House. The outlaw's head was exhibited over the jail gate as a warning to others. Tradition has it that the body was handed over to the Leper Hospital to be dissected for medical research. Some years later, the old hospital was abandoned, and in 1787 a new hospital was erected at the foot of John's Hill – the later County and City Infirmary. In the transition whatever was left of Crotty's body disappeared.

Traditions of Crotty abound in local lore, but it's unlikely that more documentary evidence will turn up. For, only seven years after Matthew Butler had carried out his research, the Public Record Office and virtually all its contents were destroyed at the beginning of the Civil War. He had got there just in time.

William Crotty was executed in Waterford in1742 – on this day.

Main source: Matthew Butler, "Crotty the Robber: Some Original Documents",
Journal of the Waterford and South East of Ireland Archaeological Society,
XVIII (1915), pp 12-20, 56-62, 105-107.

THOMAS SAUTELLE ROBERTS

Dromana by TS Roberts

Of the eight children of John Roberts the architect and his wife Mary Susanna Sautelle who survived to adulthood, no fewer than three were gifted artists. Flora painted landscapes and also did some scenery for the Waterford theatre. Thomas, born in 1748, was also a landscape artist, best known for his four superb views of Carton estate in County Kildare, the home of the Duke of Leinster. Michael Wynne, former Keeper of the National Gallery, described Thomas as "one of the finest landscape painters in Great Britain or Ireland during the third quarter of the 18th century". Alas, his brief career ended in 1777 when he contracted tuberculosis and died in Lisbon, not yet thirty. "What a loss," comments Wynne, "yet what a legacy in work."

Sautelle Roberts, the sixth surviving child of John and Mary Susanna, was born in 1760 and named after his Huguenot grandfather. He was educated in the Dublin Society's Schools, where he trained to become an architect like his father, and was apprenticed to Thomas Ivory, designer of the Blue Coat School and other buildings in Dublin. However, he also had a talent for painting and, upon the death of his gifted elder brother, Sautelle (then aged seventeen) conceived the idea of stepping into his brother's shoes – and his reputation. He changed his name to Thomas Sautelle Roberts, went to London, and trained as an artist.

The style of the two brothers is quite similar. To what extent did the elder influence the younger? Did Thomas perhaps leave some unfinished pictures which Sautelle completed? Unfortunately, we can't be certain, for the earliest dated work of Sautelle's to have survived was painted in 1791, so there is a gap of at least ten years when we don't really know what he was doing.

Although Thomas was by far the better painter, Sautelle's works – generally signed "T.S. Roberts" – are better known. For one thing, as an architect he painted not only landscapes but buildings as well, and that gives him a greater interest for the local historian. Even his trees are said to "resemble the stone fretwork of a Gothic cathedral". Secondly, engravings were often made from his paintings, so his works received a wide circulation.

His earlier works were in water colour, and the engravings (with accompanying text) formed a series entitled "Illustrations of the Chief Cities, Rivers and Picturesque Scenery of Ireland", published between 1795 and 1799. There were twelve illustrations, including several from our area – scenes on the Suir comprised Carrick Castle, views of Waterford City from east and west, Dunbrody Abbey, and the entrance to Waterford Harbour; views on the Blackwater included Dromana (seen from a distance) and the then semi-ruined Lismore Castle.

Sautelle is described as "of somewhat eccentric disposition, sometimes free and communicative in his manner, sometimes sombre and depressed". He was of dark complexion, of middle height, and stoutly built. His dark clothes, grave manner and deep voice made him look rather like a clergyman. In his will he left small annuities to the youngest child of several of his nephews and nieces, considering that he as a younger child had suffered from neglect.

On the foundation of the Royal Hibernian Academy in 1823, Sautelle was one of the three artists chosen to select the members. He contributed to the Academy's first exhibition in 1826. He did not, however, live to exhibit again. A few years previously, while on a journey to London, the coach in which he was travelling was upset and he received an injury to his right shoulder. He was never able to paint again, fell into a state of depression, and took his own life at his house in Portobello, Dublin, in 1826.

In 2009 our National Gallery celebrated the genius of Thomas Roberts with an exhibition and a full length biography. Works by both him and his brother Sautelle feature in the commemoration of the Roberts family in Waterford's Museum of Treasures.

"T.S. Roberts" was baptised in Waterford Cathedral in 1760 – on this day.

Main source: Michael Wynne, "Thomas Roberts 1748-1778 [sic]", in Studies, Winter 1977, pp 299-308. For a recent study see William Laffan and Brendan Rooney, Thomas Roberts 1748-1777 (Tralee, 2009).

DR POCOCKE VISITS WATERFORD

Richard Pococke was born in Southampton, where his father was master of the grammar school, and at the age of fifteen he was sent to further his education at Corpus Christi College, Oxford. He graduated in 1725 and was ordained a priest of the Church of England. In the 18th century it could be very useful if you had an uncle who was a bishop (perhaps it still is), and the Rev. Richard Pococke was a nephew of the Church of Ireland Bishop of Waterford and Lismore, Thomas Milles. Soon after he was ordained he was appointed Precentor of Lismore and given a rake of parishes in the diocese. This brought him a tidy income, with very little work to do, and enabled him to indulge his passion for travel in exotic regions.

In 1737 Pococke set off for the East, and over the next five years he visited Egypt, the Holy Land, Syria, Mesopotamia and other countries. He was no idle tourist: everywhere he went he made copious notes and drawings. In 1746 he was appointed Archdeacon of Dublin, but his travels continued unabated. He has left accounts of journeys in England, Wales and Scotland, and in 1749 he toured the west of Ireland (the manuscript, alas, has been lost). Then, in 1752, he undertook a more detailed journey through the Irish coastal counties, and in September this brought him to County Waterford. His journal provides a fascinating counterbalance to Smith's account, written only six years previously.

He entered the county at Tallow, and then proceeded to Lismore. Here he praised the beauties of town, castle and cathedral. He commented on the rugged beauty of the little river Owenashad. He admired the rock of Kilbree, on the way to Cappoquin, describing it as "a glorious situation for a house". Of Cappoquin he wrote: "The castle over the town is a beautiful situation and commands a fine view of the country every way, and particularly of the rich vale to the east, as far as Dungarvan." This castle would be replaced by Cappoquin House a few years later.

At Dromana he admired the handsome terraces and walks and plantations, and Lord Grandison drove him out in his carriage to see "a new town he has built called Villiers Town". "The design," says Pococke, "is two streets crossing each other with a square in the middle for a market and chapel. There are 24 houses built with a garden to each of them, and his lordship is bringing in about 80 acres of land at great expense for pasturage for the town, for as they are all linen weavers they are not to be diverted by farming. Here are above 20 of the charter boys apprenticed to the weavers, and my lord settles a curate here and intends to build a chapel. One of the streets is to be carried down to the river, at a place where a small rivulet runs into it, on which, above the town, is a very good bleach yard."

|₁₁₁₁|₁₁₁₁|₁₁₁₁|₁₁₁₁|₁₁₁₁|₁₁₁₁|₁₁₁₁|₁₁₁₁|₁₁₁₁|₁₁₁₁|₁₁₁₁|₁₁₁₁|₁₁₁₁|₁₁₁₁|₁₁₁₁|₁₁₁₁|₁₁₁₁|₁₁₁₁|₁₁₁₁|₁₁₁₁|₁₁₁₁|

After spending what was no doubt a convivial night at Dromana, Pococke continued his journey, passing through Affane, Whitechurch, Modeligo, Ballinamult
(where he passed an old fort built to defend the area against rapparees and now an
alehouse) and enjoyed a magnificent view of the Golden Vale before descending to
Fourmilewater and entering Clonmel.

In 1756 Pococke was appointed Bishop of Ossory and in 1765 promoted to
Meath. A few months later (according to a contemporary account) he held a confir-
mation at Tullamore, "returned indisposed, went to his chamber, took a puke, went
to bed about five o'clock, and was found dead at about twelve. He complained of
a pain in his stomach, which he could impute to no other cause than a few mush-
rooms eaten the day before at Ballyboy." A warning there for us all.

Pococke's account of his travels is told in the recently published *Letters from
Abroad*, by Dr Rachel Finnegan of WIT. His death occurred in 1765 – on this day.

Main source: John McVeigh (ed.), Richard Pococke's Irish Tours (Dublin, 1995).

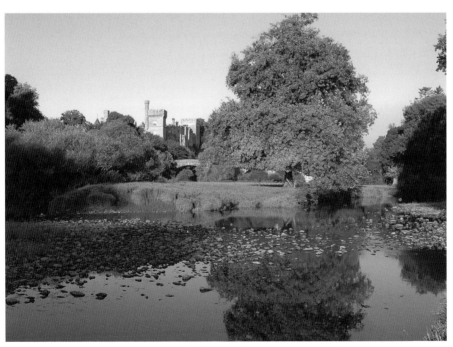

Pococke had an opportunity to take in the beauty of Lismore
Photo courtesy of Failte Ireland

THE DOLLAR BAY PIRATES

On this day in the year 1766 there occurred the grisly end of a sensational episode in our local maritime history.

About the beginning of the previous November, an English brig named the *Earl of Sandwich* left the Canary Islands bound for London. On board were the master Captain Cochrane, the mate and his brother, four other seamen, the cabin boy, and four passengers: a Captain Glass, his wife, his young daughter, and his servant boy Luke. The cargo included wine, Spanish milled dollars, gold dust and jewels – a valuable treasure that was to prove too great a temptation for the four seamen.

On 30 November 1765, after various misadventures caused by bad weather, the *Earl of Sandwich* sighted the Waterford coast. That night Captain Cochrane took a last turn around the deck before descending to his cabin. He never reached it. Two seamen leaped upon him out of the dark, beat him unconscious with an iron bar, and threw his body overboard.

The mate and his brother, roused by the noise, rushed on deck and were attacked in their turn. They put up a stiff fight, but the mate was smashed by the iron bar and his brother stabbed with a sword. Their bodies also went overboard.

Their roars had awoken the passenger, Captain Glass, and he now rushed on deck armed with his sword. After a fierce struggle he was stabbed in the stomach - and was thrown overboard. His wife and daughter rushed screaming from the cabin – and they too went overboard. The cabin boy and young Luke took refuge in the forecastle, where the mutineers very kindly left them.

Three days later, the four pirates lowered one of the ship's boats filled with the treasure and made their getaway. Before abandoning ship they opened the ballast ports to scuttle her. As the vessel began to sink, the two boys begged to be taken off. Luke the servant boy even dived into the water, swam to the boat, and grabbed the gunwale. But one of the pirates seized an axe and hacked off the boy's hands. The cabin boy fared no better, for soon the *Earl of Sandwich* listed and then capsized, and he was washed overboard.

So far, so good – as far as the mutineers were concerned. But now everything began to go wrong. For the *Earl of Sandwich* did not sink – she was washed ashore at Islandkane, and her discovery was reported to the authorities.

The pirates, meanwhile, rowed up Waterford Harbour as far as Broomhill Bay where, by now exhausted, they landed and buried most of the treasure. Next day they rowed on up the Barrow, coming ashore that evening at Fisherstown Quay, four miles below New Ross. The welcoming lights of an alehouse at Ballybrazil beckoned them. Next day, having acquired a monumental hangover and spent

|····|····|····|····|····|····|····|····|····|····|····|····|····|····|····|····|····|····|····|····|····|····|····|····|····|····|····|····|

too many dollars, they proceeded to Dublin, where they lodged at the Black Bull in Thomas Street.

All the authorities had to do to capture them was to follow a trail of Spanish dollars.

Their trial in March 1766 for piracy and murder on the high seas caused sensational excitement in the capital. They were hanged before a huge crowd in St Stephen's Green and, as a warning to others, their bodies were tarred and hung in chains at the mouth of Dublin port, two on the north side and two on the south.

By the way, don't bother going down to Dollar Bay (as it became known) with your metal detector. The local magistrate recovered the treasure, most of it still neatly stored in 250 bags, and sent it all off to the government – at least, that was his story!

There was a brief postscript to these macabre events. The worthy citizens of Dublin, who were in the habit of strolling along the South Wall for their amusement and health, complained of the unpleasant smell from the decomposing corpses – so the bodies were taken down and put into new iron hoops made specially for the purpose. The hoops were then re-erected on Dalkey Island, out of smelling range, in 1766 – on this day.

Waterford harbour with Hook Head on the left and Dunmore East on the right - Broomhill Bay (now called Dollar Bay) is on the right hand side of the Hook peninsula

CATHERINE COUNTESS OF TYRONE AND HER LEGACY AT CURRAGHMORE

Catherine Power was born on 29 November 1702. She was the only child and sole heiress of James, 8th Lord Power and 3rd Earl of Tyrone, and his wife Anne, daughter of Andrew Rickards of Dangan in the parish of Kilmacow.

Her father had inherited Curraghmore in 1693 upon the death of his brother John. The estate had been wasted during the Williamite wars and had narrowly escaped confiscation; the Earl endeavoured to restore some measure of prosperity to his lands, granting new leases to his major tenants on terms which encouraged them to build strong houses, fence their lands, and plant trees and orchards. In 1700, just two years before Catherine was born, he virtually rebuilt Curraghmore, adding a mansion-house to the medieval tower where his ancestors had lived and reigned. The date was carved on a pedestal over the door-case. The present Curraghmore, though radically altered, is still structurally the same.

In August 1704 the Earl died and Catherine, not yet two years old, became sole owner of the vast Power estate in County Waterford, centred on the four manors of Curraghmore, Clonea, Kilmacthomas and Dunmore – not to mention tracts of mountain near Blessington in County Wicklow. The Power Earldom of Tyrone now became extinct; the Barony of Le Poer was claimed by a junior branch of the family, barred from inheriting the estate because the claimant had been outlawed for his loyalty to the Jacobite cause.

Curraghmore courtyard
Picture: W Lawrence, Emerald Isle Album Series, Waterford City & County

In July 1717, four months short of her fifteenth birthday, Catherine was married to Sir Marcus Beresford, Baronet, the owner of a considerable estate at Coleraine in County Derry. The union of two landowning families from opposite ends

|᠁|᠁|᠁|᠁|᠁|᠁|᠁|᠁|᠁|᠁|᠁|᠁|᠁|

of the country created a dynasty that was destined to become the most powerful in Ireland by the end of the 18th century. Marcus and Catherine had thirteen children, and in recognition of the fact that their mother was the Power heiress they were given the surname De la Poer in addition to that of Beresford. Sir Marcus was created Earl of Tyrone in 1746, and his eldest son went a step further up the peerage by becoming Marquess of Waterford in 1789; the present head of the family is his descendant the eighth Marquess. The second son, Commissioner John Beresford, was ruler of Ireland in all but name in the 1790s.

Catherine's long reign at Curraghmore was marked by three significant developments. The first was the building of the huge courtyard, the biggest in Ireland and a rival to that of Blenheim Palace, the seat of the Duke of Marlborough. It is 550 feet long and 192 feet wide, and was the creation of the Waterford architect John Roberts. The flanking ranges of outbuildings form an impressive approach to the front door and entrance hall, which form the ground floor of the medieval tower.

On one wall of this hall is a colossal family group depicting the Earl and Countess of Tyrone and their children. It measures 13 ½ by 8 ½ feet – in the words of their descendant the architectural historian Mark Girouard, "one gets the impression that Lord Tyrone and his wife had determined to have the biggest family portrait, as well as the biggest courtyard, in Ireland".

Shell-house

The second of Catherine's creations is the great room over the entrance hall of the old tower, now the billiard room. Its most beautiful feature is the delicate stucco work, which is probably by the Lafranchini brothers.

Her third legacy is the shell-house, again the finest in Ireland, built to resemble a marine grotto, its interior encrusted with shells of every size, variety and colour. In the centre is a marble statue of the Countess by John Van Nost. In one hand she holds a shell, in the other a scroll stating that she had put up the shells with her own hands in 261 days in the year 1754.

Catherine's husband died in 1763, whereupon she claimed from the Irish House of Lords the Barony of Le Poer in right of her medieval ancestors. Her claim was successful, though being a woman the title she received was Baroness La Poer.

She died in 1769 - on this day.

WILLIAM McCLEVERTY, CIRCUMNAVIGATOR

In 1739 Britain found herself at war with Spain. The conflict has been given the rather disturbing name of the War of Captain Jenkins' Ear, and it was fought mainly at sea. Someone conceived the idea of sending a naval squadron across to South America and round Cape Horn to disrupt the commerce of Spain and attack her colonies of Chile and Peru. It was a brilliant plan, but the preparations were disastrous. The ships were decrepit, the provisions were rotten, and the crews were mainly old Chelsea Pensioners. However, the little fleet did have one major asset – the personality of its commander, George Anson, a man renowned for his diligence and courage, his coolness under pressure, and his humane care for his fellow-men, whether crews or prisoners.

The flotilla of seven ships left England in September 1740 and headed across the Atlantic. In March 1741 they began to round the Horn. The next three months were horrific. The ships were scattered in all directions and Anson had to carry on with just his own flagship, the *Centurion*. A seemingly endless series of storms left the ship battered and broken. Scurvy reduced the crew from nearly five hundred to just under two hundred, and many of these were too ill to man the ship. In June he reached Juan Fernandez, where eventually three more of his ships joined him. For the next eight months they harried the Spanish colonies. Then Anson devised a project of breathtaking audacity – to search out and capture the great Spanish galleon that sailed annually between Acapulco in Mexico and Manila in the Philippines laden with a vast amount of treasure.

In May 1742 he set off across the Pacific. More storms, more scurvy, but at last in November the *Centurion* reached the coast of China. The other ships were lost for want of sufficient men to navigate them. Anson's crew spent the winter on the island of Macao recuperating. Early in 1743 they set off again, tracked down the galleon, and captured her. She was a huge ship, mounted with forty guns, manned by six hundred sailors, and laden with treasure worth about £40,000 (say £50,000,000 in today's money). Anson returned to China to sell her, and then set off home via the Cape of Good Hope. Sailing undetected through the French fleet which lay in the Channel, the *Centurion* arrived in Spithead on 15 June 1744, completing a voyage of three years and nine months. When four years later Anson's chaplain wrote an account of their exploits, it became an immediate best-seller. Anson and the *Centurion* had sailed into history.

Among the survivors of the expedition was a young man from the Glens of Antrim named William McCleverty. His conduct on the voyage had so impressed Anson that, thanks to his patronage, McCleverty was afterwards promoted

through the naval service until he reached the rank of post captain. Three wars and 35 years later McCleverty, now aged 63, was captain of a sloop named the *Hind*, stationed at Waterford. Here in December 1779 he died.

As befitted a veteran of Anson's voyage round the world, he was buried in Christ Church Cathedral and a monument in white marble was erected commemorating his exploits. At the foot of the monument is a beautiful carving of a ship of the line. So intricate is the workmanship that every detail stands out – sails, rigging, gunports, figurehead and so on. Very appropriately, she is shown sailing round a symbolical globe.

William McCleverty, veteran of one of the great voyages of history, died in Waterford in 1779 – on this day.

See Erica Fay, "Captain William McCleverty, 1716-1779",
Decies no. 68 (2012), pp 25-36.

The *Centurion* in action

THE ABDUCTION OF THE MISSES KENNEDY

In 1779 Catherine and Anne Kennedy were the attractive teenage daughters of Richard Kennedy, a gentleman farmer of Rathmaiden in the parish of Fews. Their father was dead and they lived with their mother in much respectability. Under their father's will they were each entitled to £2,000, but their snobbish mother foolishly hinted at an even vaster fortune. The inevitable result was to draw her daughters to the attention of an abduction club.

These clubs were composed of wild young gentlemen who had enough pocket money to keep them away from the farm and get them into trouble. The object of the club was to kidnap and marry young heiresses, the lucky husband being chosen by lot from members of the club. In this case Catherine was drawn by a certain Garrett Byrne of Ballymaun, County Carlow, while Anne was drawn by James Strang of Ullard in County Kilkenny.

In April 1779 the Kennedys came to Kilkenny to enjoy the social season, with its round of race meetings, balls, and evenings at the theatre. This gave Strang and Byrne the chance to chat up their intended victims, to get to know their movements, and to plot the nefarious deed with other members of the club.

One night the Kennedys went to see a play enacted at a house in Graiguenamanagh. Suddenly the house was rushed and the room filled with armed and masked men. Catherine and Anne were dragged from their hiding place, and the members of the club clattered triumphantly off into the night. For the next five weeks they moved from hiding place to hiding place and from shebeen to shebeen.

Dave Moore

|᠂᠂᠂|᠂᠂᠂|᠂᠂᠂|᠂᠂᠂|᠂᠂᠂|᠂᠂᠂|᠂᠂᠂|᠂᠂᠂|᠂᠂᠂|᠂᠂᠂|᠂᠂᠂|᠂᠂᠂|᠂᠂᠂|᠂᠂᠂|᠂᠂᠂|᠂᠂᠂|᠂᠂᠂|᠂᠂᠂|᠂᠂᠂|᠂᠂᠂|᠂᠂᠂|

The brides to be were still virtually children – Catherine, the elder, was aged fifteen. They were terrified by the proceedings, wailing and roaring for their mother. For a while they resisted the entreaties of their suitors, but eventually they caved in and went through a form of marriage. For Byrne and Strang the glamour soon wore off. As the rain poured down, their comrades grew tired of the game and went home, and the forces of law and order kept up a relentless pursuit, the two husbands regretted getting themselves into such a mess. A sort of affection developed between Byrne and Catherine, but Anne Kennedy maintained an implacable hatred towards Strang, and kept up such a hullabaloo that eventually he hit her over the head with a pint mug. It was to prove a fateful blow.

Eventually the party reached the fishing village of Rush in north County Dublin, which was then the smuggling capital of Ireland. Here they boarded a ship for Wicklow town. On arrival the men went ashore. But the vessel's arrival had been noted by the authorities. It was boarded and the girls were rescued. Byrne and Strang fled to Wales, but they must have stood out like a sore thumb, for they were soon arrested and lodged in Carnarvon jail.

In March 1780 Byrne and Strang were put on trial at the Kilkenny assizes. The penalty for abduction was death by hanging, but nobody thought for a moment it would come to that. But Anne had not forgotten that blow with the pint mug, and she was determined to exact vengeance. The defence produced letters from the two girls to their abductors, expressing affection and inviting them to carry them off in the manner of the country. But they were proved to be forgeries made by Byrne's sister. More letters were produced, in which the girls again wrote affectionately of their "dear husbands", but these were proved to have been dictated and written under duress.

The prosecution, led by the Attorney-General, the future Lord Clonmell, declared that if this abduction went unpunished no girl would be safe and no family secure in the whole country. He demanded the death sentence, and the judge, Lord Chief Justice Annaly, gave it. Byrne and Strang were hanged in Kilkenny before a vast crowd.

Catherine and Anne Kennedy were compensated by the government for their sufferings. But the fate of Byrne and Strang had horrified people of all classes. Whenever the two girls appeared in public they were hissed and booed by the mob, and although they both married subsequently they never had another day's happiness.

Their abductors were executed in 1780 – on this day.

Main source: Margery Weiner, Matters of Felony: A Reconstruction (London, 1967).

FUNERAL OF "MAJOR" EELES

People sometimes have pretty strange requests to make about their funerals, but I've come across few more bizarre than that of "Major" Eeles, who in 1781 had himself buried at the top of the Knockmealdown Mountains.

Henry Eeles was born in 1702 in Waterford, where his father was Dean of Christ Church Cathedral. He was also Archdeacon of Lismore, and that was where Henry came to live. As a young man Henry entered the employment of the Boyles at the castle; in 1724 he was appointed Assistant Receiver. These were momentous years for the estate, for in 1753 it passed by marriage from the Boyles to the Cavendishes, Dukes of Devonshire. He seems to have been both popular and efficient (if such a thing is possible in a land agent). But it is not as an agent that his name has come down to posterity.

Eeles invented a wind-powered vehicle which he called the Flying Coach, and gave demonstrations of its prowess in the grounds of Lismore Castle. When these were successful he took out a patent on the machine (it cost him £34.4.4 ½) and gave several exhibitions of its prowess at Lismore, Cappoquin, Youghal and Tourin. Eventually it crashed into a cow – but it and its occupants survived.

Eeles's consuming interest was science, known in those days as philosophy, especially the study of electricity. Scientists at that time were greatly puzzled by the nature of lightning and thunder. Eeles was convinced they were caused by electricity, and carried out experiments in the Knockmealdowns. They were highly successful, though I'm surprised he survived them. He submitted several papers on the subject to the Royal Society for publication in their journal, and when they were rejected he published them himself in 1771 under the title *Philosophical essays in several letters to the Royal Society, containing a discovery of the cause of thunder.* His views caused much controversy, but posterity has shown him to be correct to some extent, and moreover his work pre-dated the more famous achievement of Benjamin Franklin.

He put his interest in electricity to practical use by using electro-therapy to cure ailments and disorders of several kinds: he cured a man sent to him by Christopher Musgrave of Tourin; the Earl of Tyrone, whom he had cured of an ague [fever], wrote to him from Curraghmore saying "Your operation was by much the pleasantest and most effectual I have gone through;" Lord Shannon sent him a person paralysed on one side.

Towards the end of his life, Eeles made up his mind that he wanted to be buried at the top of the Knockmealdowns, not so much for the fine view but so as to be near his beloved lightning. The matter became a sort of standing joke among his friends. Christopher Musgrave invited him to lunch one Sunday in the following words: "Dear Major, Though 'tis an odd kind of subject to address to a gentleman – that of his interment – yet, as we have been at work this week past to facilitate that matter for you, as far as we could, if you take pot-luck here today I make no doubt but we shall continue your *expansion* to the *summit* of your wishes, and at the same time a lasting monument to the memory of Major Eeles."

Six months later Henry Eeles (he was never a major – apparently he just looked like one) died at Lismore, and by the terms of his will was buried on the summit of Knockmealdown. When the funeral cortège reached the foot of the mountain, tents were pitched, food and drink were produced in abundance, and vast crowds spent the night feasting and dancing to the music of pipe and fiddle. Next day, hangover or no hangover, the mourners dragged the coffin up the mountain, and Eeles received, as he had wished, a tomb with a view – though without the addition of horse, dog and gun, as ascribed by legend.

I only hope he didn't meet the same fate as the Earl of Antrim, who had decreed that he was to be buried upright at the top of a hill where he could look down for all eternity on his beloved glen and castle. But alas, by the time the coffin-bearers had got to the top of the mountain they were so exhausted and so intoxicated that they buried him upside down.

Eeles's story is well remembered in Lismore. But how much is truth and how much is colourful embellishment? A few years ago his papers were generously presented to our County Museum, and they confirm his reputation as a serious scientist. Newspaper reports of the time endorse the account of the funeral. The papers even contain specifications for building the Flying Coach - so that a replica could be made today! Henry Eeles was buried in 1781 – on this day.

Stones marking Eeles's grave in the Knockmealdowns
Photo: Andrew Kelly

WILLIAM GRATTAN TYRONE POWER, ACTOR

William Grattan Tyrone Power, one of the most celebrated actors of his generation, was born in Kilmacthomas in 1797 as plain William Power. His early childhood was a succession of disasters. When he was only a year old, his father died. His mother emigrated with her child, and after several mishaps, settled in a cottage in Cardiff where William grew from child to teenager. A steady if uninteresting career seemed to be on the cards for him when a Mr Bird, who was a connection of his mother's, offered to take him into his printing and publishing business. But perhaps his calamitous infancy had given him a taste for adventure. At the age of sixteen he ran away with a troupe of travelling players.

His first years as an actor were not a success, and in 1820 - by now with a wife and young children to support - he began to specialize in Irish roles, and here he gradually made his way. The leading Irish actor in London, Charles O'Connor, died, and Power was able to step into his shoes, adding as he did so two illustrious names from Irish history to his own.

The Irish buffoon was a favourite character on the English stage: hot tempered, hard drinking and reckless, perpetually getting into trouble, and mangling the King's English - the stage Irishman, whether aristocrat or peasant, was always good for a laugh, and Tyrone Power's style of acting was guaranteed to have the audience splitting its sides. It wasn't a very good way of making the name of Irishman respected among the nations, but it certainly established Tyrone's reputation. Even stranger to relate, he proved to be popular in Ireland as well, and in America. By 1838 he had done three American tours and his income was reckoned to be the then huge sum of £7,000 a year.

He left behind him not only his name and reputation but descendants in whom the acting tradition would be sustained with honour. His grandson William Tyrone Power also became a famous actor and transferred successfully to the world of cinema. He died in 1931 while preparing for the title part in *The Middle Man*.

And *his* son Tyrone Power, born in Cincinatti in 1914, became one of the great swashbuckling stars of the thirties, forties and fifties. He was rapturously received when he came to Dublin in 1936 to perform in George Bernard Shaw's play *The Devil's Disciple*. In 1958 he was in Spain filming *Solomon and Sheba* for his own company when he died of a heart attack.

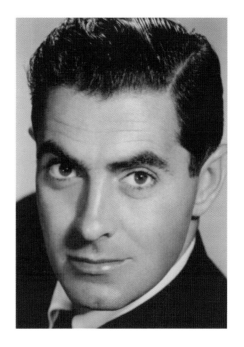

Another great-grandson of the original Tyrone Power was Sir Tyrone Guthrie. Born in Kent in 1900, he had a long and varied career as an actor and theatre producer. He directed plays at the Old Vic and Sadler's Wells theatres in London, and it was he who brought Laurence Olivier to fame in the role of Hamlet. In 1961 he was knighted for his services to the theatre. He made his home near Newbliss in County Monaghan where, concerned at the rate of emigration from the county, he established a jam factory. He died there in 1971. In his will he directed that after the death of his wife their home, Annagh-makerrig House, should pass to the government to be used as a retreat centre for artists and writers.

Tyrone Guthrie's sister Peggy married an old college chum of her brother, the writer Hubert Butler of Maidenhall near Bennettsbridge in County Kilkenny. They played an active part in promoting the cultural life of Kilkenny and in encouraging openness of thought in the ultra-conservative Ireland of the fifties. Her death in 1997 deprived Kilkenny of one of its most vibrant and colourful personalities.

I remember attending in 1957 a film at the Savoy Cinema entitled *The Rising of the Moon*. Directed by John Ford, it actually consisted of three separate stories about Irish life in the earlier part of the century, and starred such stalwarts as Cyril Cusack, Jimmy O'Dea, Noel Purcell, and Maureen Potter. It was introduced by Tyrone Power, who began by stating that his great-grandfather had come from Kilmacthomas, County Waterford, Ireland. Everyone in the cinema cheered and clapped.

The first Tyrone Power was born in 1797 – on this day.

"PRESIDENT" JOHN MOORE DIES IN WATERFORD

The Moores of County Mayo were an English Protestant family who in the 17th century bought a small property at Ashbrooke near Straide. They became Catholic through marriage, and one of them made a small fortune as a merchant at Alicante in Spain, the proceeds of which enabled him to build a stately home which he called, appropriately, Moore Hall. His son John received legal training at

Moore Hall, said to have been designed by John Roberts. Destroyed by anti-Treaty IRA during the Civil War

London and Dublin, as befitted the heir to a landed estate, and his surviving letters show that his spendthrift habits got him into trouble with his father. They certainly don't give the impression that he was a budding republican. In fact he approved of the forming of a militia by the government in 1793, commenting: "I think, besides a defence to the country, it will greatly tend to civilise the lower orders of the peoples".

And yet, when in August 1798 a French force under General Humbert landed at Killala and called upon the Irish to rise against their Saxon oppressors, John Moore was one of the few gentry to join him – probably just for the crack. With his gentry status, legal knowledge and Catholic religion, he was just the kind of person Humbert needed, and when he marched east he left Moore behind to administer the liberated areas, giving him the impressive title "President of the government of the province of Connaught".

His role was to preside over a council that administered the internal affairs of the province, or at least that small section of it that the French controlled. Beyond the issuing of a few tokens in his name, we know nothing of his part in the Rising. Apparently the responsibilities of office were too much for him, and he took to the bottle in a big way.

When the French evacuated Castlebar, Moore was captured by the British. Under interrogation he at first remained silent, but when threatened with instant decapitation by a dragoon he panicked, begged for mercy, and produced his certificate of appointment from Humbert. This crazy action sealed his fate.

If he had kept calm and the certificate had not been found, there would have been no legal case against him.

The fate of the Irish prisoners was pretty grim, and Moore would probably have been executed had not his family used their influence to have his sentence commuted to transportation. His health had already begun to break down, but his attorney managed to secure him the best of medical care during his imprisonment – and then sent the family a bill for the then huge sum of £2,000. Moore's letters from prison are full of complaints, but he has not one word of sympathy for his fellow prisoners, whose condition was far worse than his.

Eventually Moore set off under military escort for Duncannon Fort to await a vessel to take him away, but on the long march his health – never very strong – broke down. When he arrived at Waterford he was lodged at the Royal Oak tavern in George's Street. A plaque marks the spot today. There he died, and his family had him buried privately in the lonely hillside graveyard of Ballygunner Temple.

In August 1959 some men digging a grave for a private burial on this now derelict site accidentally came across a large flat slab on which was inscribed: "Here lies the body of John Moore Esquire of Ashbrook, Co. Mayo, who died in Waterford on 6 December 1799 aged 36."

The discovery caused great excitement, and soon arrangements were being made to have Moore reburied with honour in his native county. The slab was lifted and remains were exhumed and taken to County Mayo under military escort. There, after High Mass, they were conveyed on a gun carriage to be reburied on The Mall in Castlebar. National and local dignitaries, including President de Valera, were in attendance. The monument over the new grave bears an inscription in Irish and English, hailing "Ireland's first President and a descendant of St Thomas More, who gave his life for his country in the Rising of 1798. ..... By the will of the people exhumed and reinterred here with all honours of Church and State."

Half a century later, it is surely possible for us to view John Moore in a less emotional light. There's no evidence that he was descended from St Thomas More [sic]. It's hardly correct to describe him as Ireland's first president. And it's begging the question to assert that he died for Ireland. His sad end certainly deserves our sympathy.

John Moore died in 1799 – on this day.

Main sources: Grattan Freyer and Sheila Mulloy, "The Unfortunate John Moore", Cathair na Mart, IV (1984), 51-68, V (1985), 103-4; Sheila Mulloy, "John Moore of Moore Hall: The general who wasn't", Irish Sword, XVIII, no. 73 (1992), 264-70.

INCIDENT AT BAKER'S BRIDGE, ARAGLIN

The upper reaches of the little river Araglin, a land of hills and moors where the three counties of Waterford, Tipperary and Cork meet, is a desolate spot even today. Two hundred years ago it was a nest of rapparees, Whiteboys and United Irishmen. Understandably, the government showed little inclination to do anything about it. But one man who did intend to take action was a local landlord, Colonel Richard Mansergh St George of Macroney Castle near Kilworth.

The colonel spent most of his time on his other estate at Headford in County Galway, quarrelling with his neighbours and nursing a head wound he had acquired when fighting the American revolutionaries. But in February 1798 he set out for Araglin to do battle with the dragon. In a fit of bravado he let it be known that he would be spending the night without an armed guard in the house of his agent Jasper Uniacke.

That night a group of men with blackened faces entered the house and chopped St George and his agent in pieces with a rusty scythe. They spared Mrs Uniacke and fled from the house, imprudently leaving Uniacke's list of suspected rebels lying on the table. The housemaid very sensibly threw it into the fire.

This time the government had to act, and Lord Mountcashell was sent in with his regiment of militia to nuke the parish. However, it was pointed out to him that if he did so he would in fact be destroying his own estate, since he owned most of it. So he contented himself with rounding up a few bewildered locals and persuading Mrs Uniacke that they were her husband's assassins. Two were hanged on Baker's Bridge at Araglin and a third later in Cork.

We know of these events from a letter written to the government by another local landlord, William Collis of Careysville and Castle Cooke (my maternal great-great-grandfather).

Exactly two hundred years later, on a cold but sunny afternoon, a plaque was unveiled at Baker's Bridge and a tree of liberty planted to commemorate all five victims. Descendants on both sides - including Dr Martin Mansergh and myself - shook hands in a spirit of reconciliation, and then adjourned to the local hostelry. Bizarrely, it was also my fifty-seventh birthday.

Death came to Baker's Bridge, Araglin, in 1798 on this day.

1800-1850

JOHN HOGAN, TALLOW-BORN SCULPTOR

In the year 1795 a west Waterford landlord named Richard Gumbleton had grandiose plans for extending the family mansion, which was named (predictably) Castle Richard. It's on the site of the present Glencairn Abbey. To carry out the work he employed a carpenter and builder of Cove Street, Cork, named John Hogan. While at work on the house, Hogan made the acquaintance of a certain Miss Frances Cox, and it was love at first sight.

The Cox family was horrified at the very thought of a match between their Frances and a common builder. But Frances was a determined girl, and she and John Hogan got married in spite of all. Her punishment was to be cut off without a penny, or to be precise without the handsome dowry of £2,000 she would have received if she had married someone of her own class.

The young couple set up house in Tallow, and soon the children began to arrive. The third child, named John after his father, was born in 1800. He was educated at a local school, but soon the family moved back to Cork, and at the age of 14 young John got a job as clerk in the office of a solicitor named Michael Foote. He did not find the life of a human photocopier very congenial. Soon his employers discovered to their horror that instead of spending his working hours endlessly transcribing legal documents he was carving figures in wood and making architectural designs. After two years Mr Foote gave John the boot, and John's parents found him what they

Picture: Waterford County Museum

hoped would be a more suitable assignment as apprentice to the builder and architect Thomas Deane. Here he worked as a carpenter, but he still spent his spare time drawing and carving.

Before long Deane realized that he had someone rather special on his hands, and he agreed to pay his young apprentice the then sizeable sum of 13 shillings a week to draw plans and carve balusters, capitals and ornamental figures. At the end of 1819, to everyone's astonishment, John carved a full size skeleton in pinewood, finished with extraordinary accuracy. In the following year his apprentice-ship finished and, encouraged by Deane, he applied himself fulltime to sculpture. He attended anatomy lectures. He copied casts of ancient statues. He carved bits of bodies in wood. When Deane built an insurance office on the South Mall, John carved a life size statue of Minerva for it. This brought his work to the great and good of Cork, and in 1821 he was employed by Bishop Murphy to carve 27 wooden statues and a replica of Leonardo da Vinci's "Last Supper" for the North Cathe-dral. It looked as if he had embarked on a steady career.

In August 1823 the writer and engraver William Paulet Carey paid a visit to Cork and was shown, in the Gallery of the Society of Arts, a small torso carved in pine. He was aston-ished at what he saw and sought an interview with its creator. He was introduced to young John, saw more of his work, and realized that he was in the presence of a potential genius. He knew also that, for this potential to be developed, John must be got some-how to Italy. The only way to get him there, and to pay for his maintenance, was by public subscription. Carey's vigorous campaign netted £250, of which £100 was donated by the Royal Dublin Society. In November 1823 John commenced his journey to Italy, and when, early in 1824, he reached her Eternal City, he realized that a new and wonderful world was open-ing before him.

Daniel O'Connell in Dublin City Hall, one of the many statues sculpted by John Hogan from Tallow.

Hogan idolised O'Connell and here (1846) depicted him as a Roman orator wrapped in a long robe. This work of art is 10 feet high and made from finest Italian marble, the transportation of which created its own problems.

Photo: Donal Sheerin

Thus began the career of John Hogan, one of the most brilliant sculptors that Ireland has produced. "The Dead Christ", "The Drunken Faun", "The Sleeping Shepherd" and the statue of Bishop James Doyle in Carlow Cathedral are his mas-terpieces. He was born in Tallow in 1800 – on this day.

BISHOP HUSSEY, A LION IN THE HIERARCHY

No Lions in the Hierarchy is the title of a book on the Irish Catholic bishops by Father Joseph Dunn, published in 1994. It may be true of the Ireland of our days – or it may not. It was certainly true of the diocese of Waterford and Lismore in the 18th century, when our bishops either lived on the continent or in a nice safe part of the diocese, well away from Waterford and making sure to keep on good terms with the local gentry. This mould was abruptly broken with the arrival in 1797 of a new bishop, Thomas Hussey.

Thomas Hussey belonged to a junior branch of one of the old Catholic families of the Pale. Trained for the priesthood in Seville, he was appointed chaplain to the Spanish ambassador in London. This appointment placed him at the centre of a bustling political and intellectual circle. Few failed to be impressed by his intellect and wit, and he was soon on familiar terms with some of the leading politicians of the day, especially his fellow-countryman Edmund Burke, who became his close friend. When Maynooth College was founded in 1795 Hussey became its first president, and when the see of Waterford became vacant not many months later he was appointed bishop.

Given his energy and ability and his experience of life in Spain and London, it is not surprising that this cosmopolitan confidant of statesmen should proceed to live as a bishop might be expected to live. No skulking in Carrick or Clonmel for him – he took up residence in Waterford, in a fine Georgian house on the Grace Dieu Road. No obsequious crawling to the government for him – his outspoken Lenten pastoral of 1797 demanding the lifting of the Penal Laws startled even his friends and terrified his fellow-bishops (was he the *only* lion in the hierarchy?). He encouraged Edmund Rice to persist in his mission of educating the poor, and brought to Waterford its first teaching order of nuns – the Presentation Sisters.

The years have taken their toll on what was a fine Georgian house

Photos: Andrew Kelly

MOST REV. DOCTOR HUSSEY
(1741 – 1803)
LIVED IN THIS HOUSE

The establishment of an Irish militia in 1793 had brought to a head the problem of Catholic soldiers being forced to attend Protestant services. The rank and file of the militia were mostly Catholic, and the punishments inflicted on them for refusing to attend service were sometimes barbaric. Hussey threw himself into battle on their behalf. In one instance a Private Hyland had been sentenced to two hundred lashes at Carrick-on-Suir. Hussey proceeded straight to Carrick and demanded his release. When the officer in command threatened to flog him as well, he found himself on the receiving end of a verbal lashing from the Bishop, who reported the whole affair to the Duke of Portland and secured the soldier's release.

In July 1803 Hussey took a brief holiday in Tramore. No lounging in bed till noon for him – his day commenced with a vigorous 5 a.m. dip in the sea. After a few days of this, perhaps not surprisingly, he collapsed in a fit and died. His funeral procession two days later was disrupted by a group of drunken soldiers returning from an Orange meeting who tried to toss his coffin into the Suir and threatened to "cut up his remains and his friends". The riot was only quelled with the arrival of the local militia, who recovered the remains and escorted the turbulent Bishop Hussey to his last resting place, in his cathedral.

Bishop Hussey died in Tramore in 1803 - on this day.

CAPTAIN MARK ANTHONY,
A HERO OF TRAFALGAR

"It was off Cape Trafalgar in 1805
There was fought a sea-battle with few left alive ....."

At the battle of Trafalgar in 1805 the British fleet commanded by Admirals Nelson and Collingwood utterly defeated the combined fleets of France and Spain. Few battles in history have been so decisive – it would be a hundred years before any country would again threaten the security of these islands. The death of Nelson, the darling of England, in the moment of victory added to the drama of the occasion. London's Trafalgar Square was so named in honour of the occasion, and one of the four bas-reliefs at the foot of Nelson's Column is by Tramore-born sculptor John Edward Carew. In Dublin, Nelson's Pillar was erected in the city's principal street. And at Faithlegg House Cornelius Bolton installed a fine marble fireplace (damaged some years ago when the house lay empty, in a pointless act of vandalism) decorated with the portraits and crests of the two victorious admirals; he also enlisted his younger son in the Royal Navy.

Captain John Conn, who commanded the frigate *Dreadnought* in the battle, is said to have belonged to the Conn family of Mount Ida near Rosbercon – a junior branch settled in Passage East, where there is a fine monument in the old graveyard at Crooke (descendants still live in the area today). Until ten days before the battle, *Dreadnought* had been Collingwood's flagship, and the admiral had trained its guns to such a peak of efficiency that they were reckoned to be the best in the fleet. However, it was some time since *Dreadnought*'s hull had been cleared of barnacles, and she was reckoned to be too slow for a flagship, so Collingwood transferred his flag elsewhere. Coming late into the battle, *Dreadnought* captured after a stiff fight a Spanish ship, the *San Juan*, and then took on another, the *Principe de Asturias*, but her barnacle problem hampered her and the prize escaped. Captain Conn was rewarded for his services with a gold medal and a sword of honour.

Recent researches suggest that perhaps a quarter of Nelson's navy was in fact Irish. Several dozen Waterford men served at Trafalgar, including young Lawrence Power from Tramore who was only fifteen. Mark Anthony from Carrigcastle near Bunmahon was probably even younger. He served

Dave Moore

Painting of battle scene at Trafalgar courtesy of Andrew Kelly

as a midshipman aboard the British frigate *Naiad*. Towards the end of the battle *Naiad* engaged the French ship *Achille*. When *Achille* caught fire, everyone knew that before long she was bound to blow up, but the British sailors took to their boats and at enormous risk to themselves rescued as many survivors as they could, amongst them (surprisingly) a black pig and a naked woman. The lady's excuse was that she was the mate's wife, and that her clothes had been set on fire by blazing tar falling from the rigging – ouch! – so she had stripped off and plunged into the sea. The men under Anthony's command saved 35 officers and men. And in the terrible storm that followed the battle his ship towed the crippled *Bellisle* from a dangerous position near rocky shoals to safety in Gibraltar.

Mark Anthony survived into old age and retired as Harbour Master at Dunmore East. He lies buried with his ancestors in the old graveyard at Ballylaneen. His naval career had been long and arduous. But his proudest moment was surely the part he played in one of the greatest battles in history. It took place in 1805 – on this day.

See Hubert Gallwey, "The Anthony Family of Carrigcastle and Seafield",
Decies, no. 16 (1981), pp 15-22.

COMMISSIONER BERESFORD

The Right Honourable John Claudius Beresford was the second son of Sir Marcus Beresford and Lady Catherine Power, whose marriage in 1717 had united the two great Irish landed estates of the Beresfords of Coleraine and the Powers of Curraghmore. John's father was created Earl of Tyrone, and when in due course his elder brother became head of the family he was created Marquess of Waterford. John was born at the family's Dublin residence in 1738, and was educated at Kilkenny College and TCD, where he studied Law. In 1761 he was elected MP for Waterford County, which he represented without interruption until his death 44 years later.

Beresford was a politician of enormous energy and ability. In 1768 he was made a Privy Councillor, in 1770 a Commissioner of the Revenue, and in 1780 its First Commissioner. At this time Dublin's trade was rapidly expanding and the Revenue Department was quite inadequate to deal with it. Under Beresford's vigorous administration a major overhaul took place and a magnificent new Custom House was built. The architect, James Gandon, was enticed over to Ireland by Beresford, and went on to design the Four Courts as well. Beresford also played an active part in the Wide Streets Commission and was responsible for the creation of the capital's main thoroughfare, Sackville St. – now O'Connell St. At the same time he persuaded Gandon to build him a country pad at a north Dublin village called Kinsealy. He called it after the home town of his first wife, Abbeville in northern France. In later times it was the residence of another famous Irish politician, Charles J. Haughey.

Much has been written of the Irish Volunteer movement of Grattan and Flood. The Volunteers had three principal aims – free trade (which they got), a free parliament (which they got, at least in name), and parliamentary reform – that was trickier, as nobody was inclined to give up the 18th-century mercs and perks. As the reform movement floundered, power fell into the hands of three men – John Foster, John FitzGibbon, and John Beresford.

From 1783 until the passing of the Act of Union in 1800, Ireland was virtually ruled by the three Johns. They worked well together, and they worked well with the man who was Prime Minister throughout the entire period, William Pitt. Their policy was the maintenance of the Protestant ascendancy, and they were implacably opposed to political reform, especially if it involved concessions to Catholics.

In 1795 a temporary weakening of Pitt's power in England caused the arrival in Ireland of a new viceroy pledged to bring about Catholic relief, Lord Fitzwilliam. Almost his first act was to fire Beresford. It was also almost his last. Beresford went over to London, had a few quiet words with Pitt, and Fitzwilliam was on the boat home – his period in office had lasted ten weeks.

Over the next few years Beresford took a hand in the ruthless suppression of the United Irishmen, a role which earned him several impolite nicknames, the most repeatable of which was The Mangler. And when Pitt decided that the best policy for Ireland would be complete union with Britain, it was Beresford who pushed the necessary bill through parliament and obliterated the Irish state, such as it was.

Commissioner Beresford was twice married and fathered seventeen children. His second wife, Barbara Montgomery, was a celebrated beauty. He was a man of enormous wealth and power. Among the many offices he held was that of Taster of Wines in the Port of Dublin, which must have been fun. He has had a bad press from Irish nationalist politicians, and rightly so. Yet he also played a major part in making Dublin one of the finest cities of 18th-century Europe.

Commissioner Beresford died in 1805 – on this day.

DONNCHADH RUADH
MAC CONMARA

|ₗₗₗₗ|ₗₗₗₗ|ₗₗₗₗ|ₗₗₗₗ|ₗₗₗₗ|ₗₗₗₗ|ₗₗₗₗ|ₗₗₗₗ|ₗₗₗₗ|ₗₗₗₗ|ₗₗₗₗ|ₗₗₗₗ|ₗₗₗₗ|ₗₗₗₗ|ₗₗₗₗ|ₗₗₗₗ|ₗₗₗₗ|ₗₗₗₗ|ₗₗₗₗ|

In the year 1747 Europe was, as so often in the 18th century, at war, and as usual the Netherlands were the cockpit. For two months in the blazing summer of that year the French army, foiled in their efforts to capture Maastricht, laid siege to the Dutch fortress of Bergen-op-Zoom. Casualties among the besiegers from disease were horrendous. Then, quite easily, they captured it in a night assault.

Among the French forces was the Irish regiment of Lally, and one of its officers was a major named James Fitzgerald. He was a Waterford man, related to the Fitzgeralds of Kingsmeadow who erected the fine monument in Christ Church Cathedral. During a lull in the fighting he wandered off into the countryside and there, suddenly, he was overwhelmed with homesickness for his native land. When he returned to the camp he had composed a long nostalgic poem celebrating the beauties of Ireland: *Uileacán dubh Ó*.

This poem was recited wherever Irishmen were to be found on the Continent, and some years later it reached the ears of another exile from County Waterford who was drowning his sorrows in a tavern in Hamburg – the Gaelic poet Donnchadh Ruadh Mac Conmara. He revised the poem, brought it home with him, and it became his most famous work:

> *Beir beannacht óm chroí go tír na hÉireann*
> *Bán-chnoic Éireann Ó.*

A century later it reached English speakers in the fine translation by James Clarence Mangan:

> *Take a blessing from my heart to the land of my birth*
> *And the fair hills of Éire O.*

Donnchadh Ruadh was born in about 1715 at Cratloe, on the road from Limerick to Bunratty. Sent to Rome to study for the priesthood, he was thrown out for misconduct. Returning to Ireland, he set up as a schoolmaster in the Sliabh gCua area of County Waterford, where the old traditions of hospitality to Gaelic poets still flourished – Touraneena, Bleach-green of the Wine, didn't get its name for nothing. But soon he was on the move again, this time following the thousands of migrant labourers from the Land of the Three Rivers across the Atlantic to Talamh an Éisc – the fishing ground of Newfoundland. On his return he composed the mock-epic poem *Eachtra Ghiolla an Amaráin* – The Adventures of a Luckless Fellow.

Back in Sliabh gCua once again, he was reduced to such a state of poverty and demoralization that he did the unthinkable – he "took the soup" and turned Protestant. Not that the soup was especially succulent, but as a Protestant he was now able to earn a meagre wage as parish clerk for Rossmire (that's Kilmacthomas).

Here too he was a failure, for having been thrown out of his job for drunkenness he drifted back into the Catholic Church. When he eventually died in 1810, the *Freeman's Journal* recorded his death thus: "At Newtown near Kilmacthomas, in the 95th year of his age, Denis Macnamara, commonly known by the name of Ruadh or Red-haired, the most celebrated of the modern bards."

Remarkably little is known for certain about Donnchadh Ruadh's life, and what is known is disreputable. It has even been questioned whether he ever set foot in Newfoundland. But surely he must have experienced in person the hardships and miseries he

Photo: Andrew Kelly

depicts so vividly. His career and his work have had a huge attraction for scholars. His *Eachtra* was translated and published by Percy Arland Ussher (a Waterford connection there too) in the same volume as *The Midnight Court* in 1926, and his life was the subject of a three-decker novel by Francis McManus.

In addition to the two poems I've mentioned, he composed "satires, humorous verse, and a great song of repentance that places him high among all Irish poets and very high among the poets of the 18th century twilight". He wrote the Latin sonnet that's inscribed on the tomb of his friend Tadhg Gaelach Ó Suilleabhán at Ballylaneen. But my favourite is undoubtedly the poem inspired by what he heard that night in a Hamburg pub:

> *The water-cress and sorrel fill the vales below*
> *The streamlets are hushed till the evening breezes blow*
> *While the waves of the Suir, noble river, ever flow*
> *Neath the fair hills of Éire Ó.*

Donnchadh Ruadh Mac Conmara died in 1810 – on this day.

LORD NORBURY AND THE "WHITEBOY ASSIZES"

Picture by kind permission of The Honorable Society of Kings Inns

John Toler was born at Beechwood in County Tipperary in 1740 and educated at Kilkenny College and TCD. His career in the legal profession was spectacularly successful. He became a judge in 1781 and eventually Chief Justice of the Common Pleas. As a little reward for supporting the Act of Union he was raised to the peerage as Baron Norbury. He's been described as follows: "Short and pursy, with a jovial visage and little grey twinkling laughing eyes, he had the singular habit of inflating his cheeks at the end of every sentence. His court might be distinguished by the bursts of merriment that issued through its portals. There he sat in all his glory, good humour personified, puffing and punning and panting till his ruddy countenance glowed like a full moon."

Well, I doubt if the unfortunate prisoners tried and nearly always condemned by Norbury found him quite so congenial. Their sides were far more likely to be split by the floggings he generously imposed than by his witticisms. At one assize he tried 98 prisoners and sentenced 97 of them to death. Curran, the great County Cork barrister who defended the United Irish leaders – most famously Robert Emmet – once found himself sitting next to Norbury at a public dinner.

Norbury, who liked his meat high, sniffed his plate suspiciously. "Is that hung beef?" he enquired. "It will be if you try it, my lord," was Curran's grim reply.

In February 1811 Waterford was honoured with a visit from Baron Norbury. He presided at three cases of agrarian outrage.

In the first, seven farm labourers who had been taken on at the hiring fair at Kilmacthomas were accused of having assaulted Edmond Flahavan and John Connors of Ballyduff near Kilmeadan. They had heard that Flahavan had taken a small farm from which the tenant had been evicted. To punish him, they had broken into his house one night and beaten him and his nephew severely with sticks. As the victims lay on the floor they had danced on their bodies and forced them to swear they would quit the farms they had taken. They had then departed, taking with them a pistol and a powder horn.

The crime had aroused horror among the local people. Norbury now compounded it by sentencing all seven culprits to death. They were taken out to Ballyduff and hanged on a gallows erected for the purpose at the corner of a field. After the corpses had been removed for burial in Waterford jailyard, it became the custom for passers-by to throw a small stone onto the site of the gallows, until eventually a cairn piled up.

The second case involved four men who had stolen a gun, some money and some whiskey from the house of a Catholic landlord, the famous duellist Pat Power of Tinhalla near Carrickbeg. Norbury sentenced all four to death, but said that only one (a blacksmith named Maurice Quan) was to be hanged. The others were to be kept as hostages for the good behaviour of the people in their district. Ten days later, Quan was accordingly hanged on Carrick Bridge.

The third case involved a sixteen-year-old youth named Thomas Power who had robbed a house at Curraghroche. He too was condemned to death but kept as a hostage for the good behaviour of his neighbours.

Then, having left instructions that if there was any further trouble the hostages were to swing, Lord Norbury passed upon his way, satisfied no doubt that he had restored peace to our beloved county.

Curran's biographer has described Norbury as "one of the most blackhearted and sadistic scoundrels who ever wore scarlet and ermine". Eventually, Daniel O'Connell denounced him for having fallen asleep during a murder trial and only woken up just in time to pass the usual death sentence. But although the government had to fire him, they sugared the pill by making him an earl.

The "Whiteboy Assizes", as they were called, took place in 1811 - on this day.

THE REV. D.A. DOUDNEY: A CLASH OF CULTURES IN BUNMAHON

David Alfred Doudney was born near Portsmouth in 1811 and at the age of thirteen was apprenticed to a printer in Southampton. In 1832 he moved to a firm in Fleet St., London, and three years later he established his own printing business. It must have been a success, for in 1840 he was able to purchase and become editor of a long-established periodical called the *Gospel Magazine*. Its tone was Protestant and Evangelical; its readers showed a passion and concern for the welfare of others; and it was this concern that brought Doudney to Ireland. On the outbreak of the Great Famine, the readers of the *Gospel Magazine* raised £700 for the relief of the victims, and in November 1846 Doudney came to Ireland to distribute these funds in the form of meal to the starving poor of Templemore, County Tipperary. A year later he was ordained a minister in Waterford Cathedral, and after a brief spell as curate of Annestown he was appointed to the parish of Monksland.

His parish included the mining settlements of Bunmahon and Knockmahon, squalid enough at the best of times but then particularly badly hit by the Famine. Doudney set to work with enormous energy to educate and employ the youth of the parish, and established a printing school, an infant school, an agricultural school for the older boys, and a school of embroidery for the older girls.

Sketch of Bunmahon by Rev Doudney showing the copper mines operating

Between 1852 and 1857 no fewer than twenty works were printed by Doudney at Bunmahon, including two periodicals: The *Gospel Magazine* and *Old Jonathan*. He had been urged for some time to produce an abridged version of *Dr Gill's Exposition of the Old and New Testament*, a scholarly work first published in 1766 and unavailable for many years. But Doudney was not a man for half measures: he decided to produce a new edition of the full six volumes. It was a massive undertaking, but the devoted readers of the *Gospel Magazine* were induced to contribute to the costs, and work started in October 1851. The final copies of the sixth volume were despatched in February 1854.

The statistics involved are staggering. In 2½ years, 2,250 sets of six volumes were printed, folded, stitched and covered. Each volume contained at least 900 pages, and some had over 1,000. There were in all 13,500 volumes. 25 tons of paper had been used. There were nearly 47 million letters. And all this was done at the printing school in Bunmahon by four compositors, three pressmen, three girls, and 28 apprentices. When the first volume was shown at the Cork Industrial Exhibition of 1852, those who saw it refused to believe that it had been produced in a remote County Waterford village. The subscribers, as a token of gratitude, presented Doudney with 150 sovereigns and a silver tea and coffee set.

But trouble was also brewing. For Doudney was perceived as poaching converts from the Catholic Church, to which the vast majority of parishioners belonged. He always denied proselytising (as it was called), but what, after all, was being printed in the printing school? An apparently unending stream of vigorously Protestant works, many of them simple stories for the literate poor. To men such as Doudney, Catholicism was a mass of ignorance and superstition. He even managed to convince himself that the Great Famine – the original reason for his coming to Ireland – was itself a manifestation of the errors of Rome and was "among the greatest benefits that could have befallen Ireland", for it would convince the Irish of the superiority of Protestantism.

Eventually, it was announced that the following Sunday the priest would denounced Doudney from the altar. As the people flocked past the rectory on their way to the chapel, they were heard to remark: "Ah, when we come back he'll be *grazing*!" For it was confidently expected that the priest would turn him into an ass, or a goat, or a pig. "Which, dear reader," remarks Doudney, "do you think would have suited best?" But the metamorphosis did not take place, for the mine manager Mr Petherick (not a Catholic but married to one) courageously stood up and forbade the priest to proceed.

But the strain of so much hostility was too great. There were even letters from anonymous "well-wishers" containing messages such as "Mister Doudney have your coffin made and your grave dug, for our hands we will wash in your blood." In 1858 Doudney abruptly resigned his curacy and returned to England, where he spent the rest of his long life ministering to the grateful poor of Bedminster, a particularly unsalubrious suburb of Bristol.

The Rev. David Alfred Doudney was born in 1811 - on this day.

Main source: Thomas Power, "Rev. David Alfred Doudney and educational establishments at Bunmahon", Decies no. 10 (Jan. 1979), pp 6-19; no. 11 (May 1979), pp 26-34. See also Dr Power's recent publication Ministers and Mines: Religious Controversy in an Irish Mining Community 1847-1858.

THE WRECK OF THE *SEAHORSE*

Painting of the *Seahorse* in rough seas by Brian Cleare

On this day in 1816 the *Seahorse* troop transport foundered in Tramore Bay. Out of nearly 400 people crammed onto this ship of only 350 tons – mainly soldiers, their wives and children, on their way to garrison duty in Cork – a mere thirty survived, mainly by chance. The disaster is commemorated today by two fine monuments, a plaque on the Doneraile Walk and an obelisk in the Church of Ireland graveyard. It was the main cause of the erection of the five pillars at the entrance to the bay, two at Brownstown and three at Westown, one of which is crowned by the Metal Man which has become synonymous with Tramore itself. As the bicentenary approaches, preparations are underway to mark the event.

On 25 January 1816 the officers and men of the 2nd Battalion of the 59th Regiment, together with their wives and children, set sail for Ireland. After years of tough campaigning, they no doubt felt that they deserved a rest. They had fought the armies of Napoleon up through Spain and into France under the command of Wellington. They had guarded the rear of the main British force at the battle of Waterloo. They had done three months garrison duty near Paris, and when peace was restored they had marched to Calais and taken ship for England. Now they were setting off for a few years of light duty in Ireland. For most of them, however, it was to be a voyage of disaster.

The regiment embarked from Ramsgate in Kent, bound for Cork, in two transports, the *Seahorse* and the *Lord Melville*. The voyage began well. The weather was good and the wind fair – in fact it was so fine that the regimental band played on deck. On the 29th, four days out, Ballycotton Island was sighted at about 12 miles distance. But then their luck turned. The first omen of disaster was when the mate, John O'Sullivan, fell from the rigging and broke both arms and legs. He was dead within three hours. And he was the only man aboard who had a good knowledge of the coast.

So far the wind had been favourable, but now it veered to the south-west, bringing a thick mist with it. By 5am on the 30th the ship had been blown back to Dungarvan Bay. During all that morning the weather worsened, the foremast went over the side, the mainsail was torn to ribbons, and the vessel continued to drift helplessly before the gale. Captain Gibbs, finding it impossible to weather Brownstown Head, anchored in Tramore Bay, but the storm was now so fierce that the anchors dragged and the ship ran aground.

The mountainous waves soon began to pound her to pieces. The plight of crew and passengers was pitiable, and they were washed overboard in large numbers. The ship's boats had already been lost, but in any case they would only have been smashed against the side by the now rapidly ebbing tide. The doom of the *Seahorse* was watched from the shore by a huge crowd, helpless to intervene. It was impossible for them to launch any boats in the mountainous waves. In all, 13 officers, 264 men, 15 sailors, and all of the 71 women and children were lost in the wreck. Miraculously, 28 managed to reach the shore alive, including Captain Gibbs. They were dragged out of the sea by those on shore, often at great risk to their own lives. A first aid post was set up in a cottage near the shore, where a great fire was made to warm the survivors, dress their injuries, and pour hot drink into them.

The parish register meticulously kept by the rector, the Rev. John Cooke, shows that the bodies were still being washed ashore from the *Seahorse* up to four months later. Most of them were unidentifiable. To begin with, they were buried in the old graveyard at Drumcannon, but from mid-March onwards the wretched remains were simply interred "on the Burrow".

There have been many shipwrecks in Tramore Bay, but the *Seahorse* has maintained a unique place in the folk memory. For one thing, there is the stark horror of so many lives being lost all at once. For another, there is a special mystique about the *Seahorse* as being the headquarters ship of the battalion. When she went down, the regimental equipment was lost too – including the silver from the officers' mess. "By the awful dispensation of an all-wise but inscrutable Providence," the lives of 363 men, women and children were cut short by the wreck of the *Seahorse* in 1816 – on this day.

THE WATERFORD SAVINGS BANK

The early 19th century was the golden age of the small bank in Ireland. The last twenty years of the previous century had brought increasing prosperity to the country, and even after the Act of Union with Britain the good times continued awhile. The Napoleonic Wars lasted for nearly a quarter of a century and engulfed the whole of Europe, spreading devastation and costing hundreds of thousands of lives, but Irish farmers and manufacturers benefited because there was great demand for their products in Britain, and the main consumer was the British war machine.

But what should the successful producer or wage-earner do with his savings? Bank them, obviously – hence the growth of private banks. They had many advantages: they were small, they were local, and their owners were known to all, being men of substance whose fortunes were considered to guarantee the stability of their banks.

And yet disasters could happen, and when they did they spread ruin all around them – the domino effect of the collapse of Newport's Bank in Waterford in 1820 is a case in point. Hence the growth of the savings bank movement, a system whereby the funds of the bank were lodged with the National Debt Commissioners, thereby giving absolute security to the depositors.

The Cork Savings Bank, founded in 1817, is generally credited with being the first. But in point of fact Waterford beat them to it by several months, opening its door to the public on 5 August 1816.

Mind you, opening hours were a little bit shorter in those days, namely from one to three on Mondays *only*! The time when the bank could offer long opening hours as a special facility was way into the future. Nor was there in fact much of a door to open, for the bank didn't even have its own building. It operated merely from a rented room in the Exchange, which stood on the site of the present GPO. Nevertheless, business was brisk, and according to the *Waterford Mirror* in those first two hours 75 depositors lodged a total of £58.3.9. The minimum deposit was 10d.

In the succeeding weeks, business continued to flourish. An important feature of the bank was that it offered savings facilities to *everyone* – rich and poor, young and old, male and female. Manufacturers encouraged their employees, landlords their tenants, and masters and mistresses their servants to invest, and often lodged their savings for them.

On the second Monday of opening, not only did quite a number of people lodge the minimum amount of 10d, but the princely sum of £39 was deposited in the name of a lady in trust for the servants of her house. This won the approval of the *Waterford Mirror*, which commented: "This is a peculiarly useful and gratify-ing example; if followed by the heads of families it will be attended by the most beneficial consequences. It would be every way for their comfort to encourage their servants to lay up their money in this secure and profitable way, and not to spend it in the public houses or in imitating in their dress the idle fashions of those above their sphere." In other words, it would stop them squandering their money on drink or clothes. Well, it was certainly safer than hoarding it in the mattress, it was perfectly secure, it could be withdrawn at any time, and mean-while it earned an interest of 4%.

Over the next twenty years the Waterford Savings Bank went from strength to strength, and by 1834 the deposits exceeded £75,000. It was time for the trus-tees to think about vacating their rented room in the Exchange, buying a site, and building their own premises. A site available in King Street (now O'Connell Street) was selected. Advertisements were placed in the newspapers giving "instructions to architects intending to send in designs for building a new savings bank office". The building was to be in the Grecian, Roman or Italian style, the front to be in hammered or cut granite or limestone. The cost was not to exceed £4,000. There would be a first prize of £40 and a second prize of £10. There was to be a cupola or square architectural erection over the centre of the front to hold an illuminated clock showing the dials on three sides.

There were 27 entries, the lowest tender being that of Cambell & Ross of Bel-fast - £3,300. This was accepted. The elaborate plans for the clock had to be modified; the dials would only be of copper as illuminations would be too expen-sive, and the bell would only be an hour bell as there wasn't enough room for quarter bells or chimes. The work was entrusted to Messrs Ogg of Dublin and the cost was not to exceed £250.

Architecturally, the Savings Bank is reckoned to be the most interesting bank building in Waterford. A survey of our historic buildings carried out in the 1970s drew particular attention to the cash office, the staircase, and above all the board-room, which architectural historian Mark Girouard described as "gigantic and opulently classical – it would not disgrace the Bank of England". The clock tower, alas, turned out to be too big for the structure and was taken down many years ago.

The bank had come a long way since that brief two-hour opening recorded by the *Waterford Mirror* in 1816 – on this day.

Main source: A Short History of the Waterford Savings Bank (Waterford, 1916).

BISHOP ROBERT WALSH AND A PERIOD OF TURBULENCE

It all began with the death in January 1816 of Bishop John Power. During his twelve-year reign the diocese of Waterford and Lismore had emerged from the Penal era and achieved much progress. There were new churches, new religious orders, new schools, a diocesan seminary. But who was to succeed him?

A meeting of the clergy at Carrick proposed the parish priest of Clonmel, Father Thomas Flannery, but this was rejected by the Munster bishops because of Flannery's "serious weaknesses of character". He was asked to stand down but refused to do so; eventually the Bishop of Kerry forced him to withdraw by threatening him with "public exposure and disgrace".

Father Robert Walsh, the parish priest of Dungarvan, was then proposed, whereupon twenty-four priests left the meeting in disgust at the way in which the proceedings had been conducted. They went even further. They sent a letter to Rome stating that Father Walsh was totally unfit to govern the diocese.

The bishops put forward the name of the President of Maynooth, but Father Walsh's supporters then mounted a campaign against the imposition of a "foreign prelate". Astonishingly, Rome disregarded the bishops' advice and appointed Father Walsh bishop! In a rearguard action, the Munster bishops extorted from their new colleague a promise that, whatever else he did, he would not appoint as his successor in Dungarvan his curate, Father Thomas O'Meagher. But no sooner was Dr Walsh securely in office than he broke his promise and appointed O'Meagher PP of Dungarvan.

In November 1818 a synod of the Munster bishops was held at Cashel to investigate charges of immoral conduct against O'Meagher. An enquiry was held in the Presentation Convent, Dungarvan, and despite the testimony on oath of several witnesses who deposed serious moral charges against him he was exonerated. The verdict had obviously been rigged, and several priests who had served on the tribunal resigned in disgust. The Christian Brothers superior spoke of a plot by Fr O'Meagher and his supporters "for the purpose of destroying the character of the nuns of Dungarvan". When the nuns were warned of this, "they were obliged to employ armed men at night for a considerable time both inside and outside their garden".

By this time Rome was being bombarded from both sides by letters, memorials, protests, charges, countercharges, and pleas for intervention. Among Walsh's targets was Edmund Rice, who was especially vulnerable as he was then trying to obtain papal approval of his Christian Brothers. A letter attacking the order, signed by seventeen priests, was sent to Rome – it later proved to have been forged by Fr O'Meagher. The Bishop did not mince his words either. He referred to the Bishop of Cloyne as "an old, wild strange man, ... an imbecile," and to Rice as "a turbulent layman, once a common butcher of the stalls and a public fornicator".

Presentation Convent, Dungarvan - picture Waterford County Museum

A meeting of the Munster bishops held at Fermoy in June 1820 recommended that Walsh be suspended, and at long last Rome reacted. O'Meagher was sacked. Walsh was summoned to Rome, but because of the precarious state of his health he was not deposed. And there in 1821 he died, bringing to an end five years scandal and chaos.

Robert Walsh, Waterford's most turbulent Catholic bishop, was consecrated in 1817 - on this day.

Main sources: M.C. Normoyle, A Tree is Planted: The Life and Times of Edmund Rice (2nd ed., 1976), pp 113-135. Desmond Rushe, A Man Raised Up (Dublin, 1981), pp 76-84.

THOMAS WYSE
MARRIES A PRINCESS

Thomas Wyse

*Picture: Waterford Museum of Treasures,
Three Museums in the Viking Triangle*

Letitia Bonaparte, eldest daughter by his second marriage of Lucien Bonaparte the brother of Napoleon, was born at Milan in 1804. After Napoleon's defeat, Lucien lived with his family near Rome and was given the title Prince of Canino by the Pope. Aristocratic families were perpetually short of cash, and when after the battle of Waterloo wealthy Britons began to resume their visits to Italy the Italians welcomed them literally with open arms. Lucien, with many children to support on a limited income, was particularly interested in getting rid of some of his daughters, and he soon found a gullible victim in a conceited young man from Waterford named Thomas Wyse.

Thomas was heir to the Manor of St John's, a considerable property but much reduced in value because of the Penal Laws. His parents had abandoned Ireland and lived on their rents in Boulogne; the manor (on the site of the Good Shepherd Convent) was demolished. He first visited Lucien in 1815, when Letitia was only eleven. Returning several years later, he found her grown into a young beauty and fell in love with her. The wily Lucien let it be known that he expected him to propose for her, and promised a dowry of £5,000, later increased to £10,000. Thomas's parents were not at all enthusiastic, but the marriage took place in March 1821. Not a penny of the dowry was received, and Thomas's father refused to increase his allowance, so the couple were not exactly well off. Thomas was a cold, scholarly, talented man in his thirtieth year; Letitia a flighty socialite of sixteen. The prospects for a stable marriage were not good.

For a time, all went well. The couple were in love. Letitia produced a son and heir (appropriately named Napoleon) and studied hard under her husband's tuition to improve her education. Before long, however, she grew bored and bad-tempered and – worst of all – irritated her husband by continually making spelling mistakes in her lessons. The last thing Lucien needed was to have his daughter back, and after Letitia had run screaming from the house he encouraged Thomas to

Dave Moore

put manners on his wife by locking her up in a convent. After seven months of imprisonment, deprived of even the sight of her infant son, Letitia's nerve cracked and she promised abjectly to be obedient to her husband – and to make earnest endeavours to improve her spelling.

In 1825 Thomas brought his family to live in Waterford, where they lodged with his brother on the Adelphi (on the site of the Tower Hotel). Here in 1826 Letitia gave birth to her second child, William Charles. Waterford society delighted in being shocked by Letitia, an uninhibited chatterbox who discoursed freely in public about the intimate details of their private life. They were unimpressed by her Bonaparte blood, and if they did not give her the precedence she felt she deserved, she had the habit of screaming her head off until they did – to the great embarrassment of her husband. Thomas was deeply involved in the affairs of the Catholic Association, and during the 1826 election campaigned vigorously for Villiers Stuart against the Beresford faction. In fact he seems to have been even more energetic than Villiers Stuart himself, who found Letitia's company more interesting than politics. Flamboyantly supporting the Catholic cause, she wore orange ribbons on her shoes, so adjusted that as she walked they were trampled into the dirt – to the annoyance of their snooty Protestant neighbours.

In January 1828 Letitia dramatically fled Waterford, but her memory would linger on for many a year. She and Thomas Wyse were married in 1821 – on this day.

Main source: Olga Bonaparte-Wyse, The Spurious Brood: Princess Letitia Bonaparte and her Children (1969).

THE O'SHEA FARMHOUSE MASSACRE

|᠂᠂᠂|᠂᠂᠂|᠂᠂᠂|᠂᠂᠂|᠂᠂᠂|᠂᠂᠂|᠂᠂᠂|᠂᠂᠂|᠂᠂᠂|᠂᠂᠂|᠂᠂᠂|᠂᠂᠂|᠂᠂᠂|᠂᠂᠂|᠂᠂᠂|᠂᠂᠂|᠂᠂᠂|᠂᠂᠂|᠂᠂᠂|

Yet meet him in his cabin rude
Or dancing with his dark-haired Mary
You'd swear they knew no other mood
But mirth and love in Tipperary.

These lines were penned by Thomas Davis, the Young Ireland ideologue who died in the year of the outbreak of the Great Famine. How strange that they should have been chosen by the Fenian novelist Charles Kickham for the title page of his best-selling novel *Knocknagow*. A native of Mullinahone, Kickham well knew that there was a dark side to life in 19th-century Tipperary, punctuated by deeds darker far than even Mary's hair.

Land and Violence is the title of a history of the county written in 1985 by local teacher Denis Marnane. Land and violence were indeed inextricably linked. Violence was inflicted by landlord upon tenant. Tenants cheerfully reciprocated by burning crops, maiming animals, and threatening or killing the landlord and his servants. One landlord was shot at so many times that he was known to all the county as "Woodcock" Carden. Luckily for him, his assailants were not very good shots.

But tensions over land could erupt between other groups, too. The inflation in land prices brought about by the Napoleonic Wars produced conflict between the "Caravats" (mainly labourers and small farmers) and the "Shanavests" (mainly strong farmers). Fairs were the scene of drunken brawling and also of the more formally organized faction fighting. The lawlessness of Tipperary society induced Sir Robert Peel to set up a new police force, and it was in Cashel that the famous "peelers" first went into action in 1814.

In November 1821 even Tipperary people were shocked by a horrific incident at a place called Tobber in the townland of Ballinattin, on the northern slopes of Slievenamon. Severe weather had caused the failure of the potato crop, and famine stalked the fields of Tipperary. A strong farmer named O'Shea was already at loggerheads with his neighbours over some land. Moreover, unwilling to pay the high wages demanded by local men, he imported labourers from Kerry. As the very lives of the newcomers were threatened, they were lodged for their safety in the kitchen of the farmhouse. Matters came to a head when O'Shea evicted a tenant named Gorman, who vowed vengeance, for which he enlisted the help of an agrarian secret society led by a man named Meagher.

Their headquarters were a public house owned by a man named Kelly and his wife. Now Mrs Kelly had a cousin named Kate Mullally who was a servant to the O'Sheas and lived in their house. She had been married some months and was near her time. One day Kate came to the pub to visit her cousin Mary Kelly. Meagher was in a back room melting lead to cast bullets in a mould. He came out to speak to Kate, and with the aid of much plámás and a little whiskey he wormed out of the innocent creature details of the number of men in the O'Shea house and what arms they had.

But if Kate was less than bright, Mrs Kelly was no fool. Well aware that mischief was intended, she got up in the middle of the night, put on her husband's coat, and made her way to the Meagher cottage. She was just in time to see a group of men set out into the night. Eight of them she recognized. All were armed, and one of them was carrying two pieces of turf which he kept alight by blowing on them. Sick with apprehension, Mrs Kelly stumbled through the dark until she found herself on the hill overlooking the glen in which stood the farmhouse of the O'Sheas.

Suddenly a bright light burst from the thatch of the farmhouse. Another flame broke out on the opposite side. The house was soon a sheet of flames and the whole glen was lit up by the glare. Shrieks of terror arose from the inferno within, and yells of triumph from the attackers outside. By the time the neighbours arrived on the scene, it was all over. The blackened corpses of seventeen human beings were found piled against the front door, where they had been crushed together in their panic to escape their gruesome death.

And what of poor Kate Mullally, who had unwittingly betrayed her companions to the vindictive fury of Meagher and his men? The scorching heat and the terror had brought on premature labour. When she felt the first pains she dragged herself to the washroom, where there was a large tub of water. As soon as the child was born she plunged the baby into the tub, holding its head above water so that it might breathe. And there the suffocated child was found, together with the arm that had held it, hanging over the side of the tub.

The crime had obviously been committed by local men, but all attempts to find the culprits were met by a wall of silence. For five years Mary Kelly remained haunted by what she had seen. At last she confessed it to her priest, and he commanded her to do the unthinkable: to tell the authorities what she knew. In trepidation she sought an interview with the magistrate, Captain Despard. Warrants were issued, the culprits were arrested, and after trial they were all hanged in Clonmeen village, not far from the scene of the crime.

But poor Mary Kelly still found no rest. Haunted now with a double burden of guilt, and with her own life in danger, she had to flee from the area and spent the rest of her life in hiding.

The massacre at the O'Shea farmhouse took place in 1821 – on this day.

Main source: "The Burning of the Sheas", MS account written at Gurteen le Poer, 16 November 1862.

PAT POWER OF DARRIGLE, DUELLIST

| . . . . | . . . . | . . . . | . . . . | . . . . | . . . . | . . . . | . . . . | . . . . | . . . . | . . . . | . . . . | . . . . | . . . . | . . . . | . . . . | . . . . | . . . . |

In the graveyard attached to the old church at Kilmeaden is the tomb of an 18th century Catholic gentry farmer named Patrick Power who lived at Darrigle and later Tinhalla.

The surviving Catholic gentry held on by keeping their heads down. Towards the end of the century, however, they plucked up enough courage to send a delegation to George III begging him for some relaxation of the Penal Laws. The secretary to the delegation was a young Protestant lawyer named Wolfe Tone; our Patrick Power was one of its members.

His fame, however, rests not on his political work but on his skill with a duelling pistol. He's described as "a fat, robust man, much distinguished for his intemperance, and generally seen with a glowing red face". He would take up his pistols either against anybody or on behalf of anybody. He even fought a duel with a fire-eating companion and neighbour, Bob Briscoe of Tinvane. When taking aim, he said he still had a friendship for Briscoe, and would show it - so he only shot off his whisker and the top of his ear.

When travelling in England, we are told, he had many encounters with persons who were attracted by his brogue and clumsy appearance. This was the great era of the stage Irishman, and the theatre-going public imagined that Irishmen off the stage committed the same blunders and absurdities as they did on it.

On one occasion he and his servant were staying at an inn. He ordered supper and, while waiting for it, he sat reading the newspaper. After some time the waiter laid two covered dishes on the table, and when Power examined their contents he found they were two dishes of steaming potatoes. They were a present, the waiter informed him, from the two gentlemen sitting opposite – two mounds of spuds for the Paddy Irishman.

Power sent for his servant and quietly gave him instructions in Irish. He then set to work on the potatoes, to the great amusement of the two Englishmen. By the time the servant returned, Power had demolished both dishes of potatoes and his two fellow-diners were laughing fit to burst. But the servant also brought in two covered dishes, one of which he laid before his master and the other before the two Englishmen. When the covers were removed, there was found in each a loaded pistol. Power took up his and cocked it, telling one of the others to pick up the other. "We are at a very proper distance for a close shot," he assured him brightly, "and if one of you should fall I am ready to give satisfaction to the other."

Before you could say "Colt 45" the dining-room was empty and the only sound was the stampeding of panic-stricken feet as his fellow-diners headed for the next county. As they were in too great a hurry to pay their bill, Power paid it for them along with his own.

But there was a more serious side to Pat Power as well. In reporting his death *The Waterford Mirror* said of him: "He maintained through life a high and independent spirit. His private character was marked by a most rigid integrity, and was particularly distinguished for benevolence towards the poor, with whose sufferings he sympathised and upon whose behalf an appeal was never made to him in vain." Helping the poor and standing up for the civil rights of the community is not a bad judgement on anyone.

Pat Power, the Darrigle duellist, died in the 76th year of his age, in 1827 – on this day.

Main source: John Edward Walsh, Sketches of Ireland sixty years ago (Dublin, 1847), pp 25-28.

A typical Irish duel in progress

PÁDRAIG DENN OF CAPPOQUIN

A small plaque in the chapel yard at Cappoquin commemorates Pádraig Denn, who died in 1828, and informs us loftily that "the religious works written by him in the Irish language met with general approval and are proofs of his learning as an Irish scholar and his zeal and piety as a sincere Christian."

Denn was a native of Coolroe in the parish of Modeligo. He is said to have been aged 72 when he died in 1828, and if this is accurate (always a big "if"!) then he was born in 1756. A Pat Dinn who was a farmer in the townland of Graigue in 1772 may have been his grandfather. His father, Laurence Denn, was unsuited to the life of a farmer on account of a physical deformity – he had a club foot – and became instead a schoolmaster. The Penal Laws were then in force and no Catholics were allowed to keep schools, so Laurence Denn became a scoláire bocht, wandering from place to place and teaching in the open air or in a thatched cabin by the side of the road. Pádraig too became a hedge-schoolmaster, and we know that around the year 1800 he had a school at Poulbautia near Affane.

In the early years of the 19th century the Penal Laws were relaxed and he moved into Cappoquin and opened a school in Main Street. On the completion of the new church in 1822 he became parish clerk – an important position in those days. On Sundays he taught Christian doctrine in the church. The parliamentary return of schools in 1824 states that he had a pay school, the building being of lime and stone and thatched. It was attended by 49 boys and 11 girls, all Catholic. His annual income was £21, of which £9 came from the bequest of a Mr Magner of Boston for the education of 24 orphans.

St Mary's Church, Cappoquin
Photo: Waterford County Museum

Like his fellow Gaelic poet Tadhg Gaedhealach Ó Suilleabháin, Denn took to religion in a big way and produced a large amount of sacred verse. Unlike him, however, he was not reared in the scholarly tradition. Denn is not a good poet, but the homely sincerity of his verses gave them a wide appeal. Unfortunately it's pretty grim stuff, and the joy of Christian redemption is virtually absent from his work. His constant theme is the wickedness of sin and its inevitable consequence in the horrors of eternal damnation. In *An Saol meallta*, for instance, he rails against lustfulness, obscenity, scandal-mongering, cursing, boasting, and (of course) drunkenness – a potent recipe for a bellyful of hellfire unless the flames can be quenched by tears of repentance!

He wrote *Comhairleach an Pheacaigh agus Aitheanta Dé Minighthe* (Advice for the sinner and the commandments of God explained), *Stiúratheoir an Pheacaigh* (Advice to the sinner), *Eachtra an bháis* (The adventure of death), *Aighneas an Pheacuig leis an mBás* and many others. He translated into Irish *Think well on't*, a book of meditations for every day of the month written in 1728 by Bishop Challoner of London. And in about 1819 he brought out a new edition of Tadhg Gaedhealach's *Pious Miscellany*, adding some of his own verses as an appendix. It sold like hot cakes, the Irish appetite for hell and damnation being apparently insatiable.

Among Denn's pupils were two brothers named Patrick and John Power. Nothing unusual in that , except that many years later John Power became Bishop of Waterford. His brother Patrick became Parish Priest of Cappoquin and commemorated his old teacher by erecting the plaque over his grave in the chapel yard.

Pádraig Denn, poet and schoolmaster, died in 1828 - on this day.

PHILIP BARRON AND SEAFIELD COLLEGE

Philip Barron was born in about 1802 at Durrow, County Waterford, the eldest child of a local landowner who died leaving young Philip heir to a sizeable estate. He was educated at Trinity College, but left without taking a degree. Then in 1825 he bought a local newspaper, the *Waterford Chronicle*, and used it to support the cause of Catholic Emancipation. In the great electoral contest between Beresford and Villiers-Stuart, the *Chronicle* backed Stuart enthusiastically.

Unfortunately, Barron's career as a newspaper editor came to an abrupt end. During the campaign he published an article denouncing a Cork barrister named Denn for the way in which he treated his tenants at Tallow. Denn sued him for libel and, although Daniel O'Connell himself defended him, Barron was ordered to pay the then huge sum of £1,350 damages. Unable to meet the debt, he fled the country.

Barron spent the next few years in France and Italy, countries in which an oppressive government was being opposed by a resistance movement that was not only political but cultural. Intellectual idealists were beginning to discover the rich culture of the ordinary people in song, story and dialect. The contrast with his native Ireland, where the impoverished masses were being urged to cast off their language and traditions, was painful. During Philip Barron's years of exile, a dream was born: to found a college that would provide the youth of the countryside with a truly rich *Irish* education. There would be night courses for adults, and books and magazines about Ireland and in Irish would be printed so cheaply that even the poor could buy them.

Barron had returned to Ireland by 1830, and for the next four years he studied, contacted scholars from all over the country, and prepared for the great task that lay ahead. Then in 1834 he began to build his college. He describes its location as "in a silent glen, shut in by hills from every storm, a mile from Bunmahon and three from Stradbally". The ordnance survey map of 1841 shows its position not far from Seafield House. It was Gothic in style, having pointed arches and three steeples. It opened on New Year's Day 1835. According to an advertisement in the *Freeman's Journal,* the syllabus included not only Irish but also writing, ciphering, mensuration, navigation, English, grammar, geography, history, Latin, Greek and Hebrew – quite an ambitious curriculum! There were night courses for adults which included a course in agriculture.

On the same day that the college opened, Barron commenced the publication of his booklets with the first issue of his magazine *Ancient Ireland.* Ten thousand copies were printed, and a second printing was made. Two further issues, each of sixteen pages, appeared in the same month. But this was to be only one of twenty-five types of publication, ranging from a twenty-four instalment set of Irish primers, through dictionaries, catechisms, sermons, geographies and histories to a Hebrew grammar. Six of these were issued over the next month. Then in April there appeared number 4 of *Ancient Ireland*, followed in May by number 5 – a grand total of 176 pages. Philip Barron was confident that a Gaelic renaissance had started.

Yet it had also finished. After May 1835, no further publications appeared. The money just wasn't there. Again Philip Barron had to flee the country to avoid his debts. He spent the rest of his life in London under an assumed name, and died there in 1844. And soon not a stone remained of Seafield College, which had opened amid such high hopes in 1835 – on this day.

Main sources: DIB and Dóirín Ó Murchú, "Philip Barron, man of mystery," Decies no. 2 (May 1976), pp 10-15.

Engraving of what Seafield College looked like

EXECUTING A MURDERER

In 1827 Daniel and Peggy Savage lived in their home beside the Blackwater. It was not, by all accounts, a happy marriage, for Daniel Savage lived up to his name and was a bad-tempered man given to fits of violence. One day, Peggy's battered body was found in the river a few yards from their home. Her husband had disappeared. For two years there was no sign of him. Then one day Peggy's brother James met him on the mountains; he had grown a beard and was obviously leading a wandering life. When James accused him of having murdered his sister, he snarled back: "And I won't be content until I've murdered more of ye."

In October 1834 Peggy's family learned that Daniel Savage, beard and all, had been arrested in Waterford and charged with the murder of his wife. The case was heard the following March. The first witness was Peggy's brother James, who described the encounter on the mountain. William Savage, a nephew who had lodged with Daniel and Peggy, described what he had seen and heard the night his aunt was killed. Since then, he claimed, he had not seen his uncle, adding enigmatically: "And I do not see him now."

The prisoner seemed quite crushed and bewildered by the whole business. Timidly he denied the charge, denied moreover that he was Daniel Savage and claimed that he was in fact one Edmond Pine, a labourer from Gurranereagh near Cork. He tried to produce a letter written on his behalf by a gentleman from Cork, but the judge would not admit it in evidence. He was positively identified by witnesses as Daniel Savage, found guilty, and hanged.

After the execution the prison chaplains had Daniel's body washed and the beard shaved prior to giving him a Christian burial. They invited his sister to bid him a last goodbye. She looked into the coffin and gasped: "But that's not my brother!"

The hanged man was, in fact, Edmond Pine after all. Alerted by the two priests, Daniel O'Connell MP raised the matter in the House of Commons. But the prime minister blandly replied "that the man hanged in Waterford was the man the jury had found guilty".

Edmond Pine – or Daniel Savage – was hanged in Waterford in 1835 – on this day.

Main source: Article by Patricia Fitzpatrick in Ireland's Own.

THE MURDER OF MRS ROGERS

Two hundred years ago the reading public was as eager for stories of violent crime as it is today. Broadsheets narrating grisly murders sold like hot cakes among a public gasping for gore, to the great profit of printers such as Thomas Duncan of the Saltmarket in Glasgow. The following account is taken almost verbatim from one such production – undated, alas.

In the early years of the 19th century there lived near Waterford a widowed lady of fortune named Mrs Rogers. A woman of the most amiable manners and much beloved by all who had the pleasure of her acquaintance, she resided at a neat country house, situated at the head of a delightful avenue surrounded by trees, about half a mile from Waterford ferry on the Kilkenny side. With her lived in the most tranquil manner her servant Mary Scott, who often received testimonies of the friendly regard of this good and kind mistress.

One night, having dined with her neighbours Alderman and Mrs Bates, Mrs Rogers retired to bed at her usual hour. Next morning, however, the neighbourhood was aroused by the shrieks of the servant crying out that her mistress had been murdered!

Indeed, when neighbours rushed to the house they beheld a terrible sight: Mrs Rogers's throat had been cut in the most shocking manner, one of her breasts nearly off, and her right arm, with which it was evident she had defended herself as long as her strength remained from the repeated stabs of the infernal assailant, was desperately wounded, every finger of the hand just hanging by the skin. The bedclothes, by the number of holes that appeared in them, could only be compared to a sieve.

What monster could have committed such a deed? The finger of suspicion pointed inevitably at the servant Mary Scott. Oh, the wretch played well her part, tearing her hair, beating her breast, and mourning the lamentable fate of her beloved mistress at the hand of a gang of desperadoes who had burst into the house. But she had no convincing answer to certain vital questions. Why was there no sign of any violent entry to the house? Why was the body cold and stiff, the blood on the bedclothes hard and congealed, before she raised the alarm? Why was it that the deceased's dog, hitherto so fond of the servant, could now scarce be restrained from tearing her to pieces?

Mary Scott was put on trial, but in the absence of any positive evidence she was never convicted of this most horrid, cruel and inhuman murder ever heard of.

THACKERAY VISITS WATERFORD

William Makepeace Thackeray was one of the great figures of Victorian literature, but when he visited Waterford in 1842 his life up to then had been pretty disastrous.

Thackeray was born in India in 1811 and educated in England. His father died when he was only four. He trained as a lawyer, but gave up his studies to devote himself to literature. He travelled on the Continent and studied drawing in Paris. He became the proprietor of two newspapers, both of which failed. He invested his money badly and lost most of the fortune he had inherited from his father. In 1836 he married Isabella Shawe, the daughter of a Colonel Shawe and Isabella Creagh who came from Doneraile, north Cork. In the next four years they had three daughters, one of whom died. After the birth of the third, Isabella began to show signs of insanity, and Thackeray took her to Cork in the hope that she would improve in the company of her Irish relations. Her condition continued to deteriorate, and she made two suicide attempts, on one occasion throwing herself into the sea. Finally Thackeray took her over to his mother in France and placed her in a *maison de santé*.

In 1840 Thackeray published his *Paris Sketch Book*, and as it was a moderate success he was able to secure a favourable contract to write a book about Ireland. His motives in coming here, therefore, were to make some money, to further his literary reputation, and to take his mind off his domestic tragedy.

He arrived in Dublin on 4 July 1842, spent the next four months travelling round the country, and departed for England – again from Dublin – on 1 November. Like all foreign visitors at this period, Thackeray was appalled by Irish poverty – overpopulation, swarms of idle beggars, hardship, rural and urban slums, and so on. He was also shocked by Irish Catholicism: the power of the priests, the devotion of the people, and the elaborate and mysterious rituals were all quite alien to his liberal Protestant upbringing, and he just couldn't come to terms with them. However, he got an even bigger shock when he went to Ulster and observed the ranting and raving of Evangelical Protestant preachers.

On the other hand, he admired the beauty of the countryside and the liveliness, intelligence and hospitality of the people of all classes. He enjoyed company, was a keen observer, and illustrated his travels with amusing sketches made on the spot. You get the impression that it would have been fun travelling round Ireland with Thackeray, in spite of his prejudices.

After spending a few days in the capital, Thackeray set off via Carlow and Waterford for Cork, where a friend had invited him to see an agricultural show. His description of Ballyhale is not very complimentary: "A dirty, old, contented, decrepit idler was lolling in the sun at a shop door, and hundreds of the population of the dirty, old, decrepit, contented place were employed in the like way. A dozen of boys were playing at pitch and toss; other male and female beggars were sitting on a wall looking into a stream; scores of ragamuffins, of course, round the carriage; and beggars galore at the door of the little alehouse or hotel."

"Will your honour like to come and see a big pig?" he was asked. "We all went to see the big pig, not very fat as yet, but upon my word it is as big as a pony. The country round is, it appears, famous for the breeding of such, especially a district called the Welsh Mountains, through which we had to pass on our road to Waterford.

"This is a curious country to see, and has curious inhabitants. For twenty miles there is no gentleman's house; gentlemen dare not live there. The place was originally tenanted by a clan of Welshes, whence its name. And they maintain themselves in the occupancy of the farms in Tipperary fashion, by simply putting a bullet into the body of any man who would come to take a farm over any one of them.

"Presently we caught sight of the valley through which the Suir flows, and descended the hill towards it, and went over the thundering old wooden bridge to Waterford."

He was impressed by the appearance of the tall red warehouses along The Quay, but surprised by the complete lack of commercial activity, even of anything to buy, in the shops. Of Reginald's Tower he says: "Opposite the town is a tower of questionable antiquity and undeniable ugliness. For though the inscription says it was built in the year one thousand and something, the same document adds that it was rebuilt in 1819, to either of which dates the traveller is thus welcomed.

The Catholic Cathedral he dismissed as "a large dingy Catholic chapel, of some pretensions within". But he admired "the piety – stern, simple and unaffected – of the people within. Their whole soul seemed to be in their prayers, as rich and poor knelt indifferently on the flags. There is of course an Episcopal cathedral, well and neatly kept, and a handsome bishop's palace. Near it was a convent of nuns, and a little chapel-bell clinking melodiously."

He has an amusing description of the assizes held in the courthouse, which was then at Ballybricken ("as beggarly and ruinous as the rest of the neighbourhood"). "A considerable poorhouse has been erected at Waterford," he continues, "but the beggars of the place as yet prefer their liberty." When he asked one old

The beauty of the Blackwater that so impressed Thackeray
as caught on camera by Andrew Kelly

woman why she wouldn't enter it, she replied grandly: "They owe £200 at that house, and faith, an honest woman can't go there."

Leaving Waterford the next day, Thackeray proceeded by coach via Kilmacthomas towards Dungarvan. At Cushcam they were delayed by the turnpike man, who took ages to write out a ticket. "I think he must be writing a book," remarked the coachman, a comment which provoked a spate of further abuse from the passengers.

They entered Dungarvan via the £80,000 causeway and bridge erected by the Duke of Devonshire. The male inhabitants of the town seem to have been singularly ungrateful to His Grace, who had thereby deprived them of what was known as the "Dungarvan Prospect" – "because," as Thackeray explains somewhat prudishly, "the ladies of the country, walking over the river at low water, took off their shoes and stockings (such as had them) and, tucking up their clothes, exhibited – what I have never seen and cannot therefore be expected to describe."

At Cappoquin Thackeray did not visit Mount Melleray, the very thought of which was enough to give him an attack of the Protestant horrors. "I was very glad we had not time to see the grovelling place," he writes, "and as for seeing shoes made or fields tilled by reverend amateurs, we can find cobblers and ploughboys to do the work better." To be fair, he was equally critical of the White Quaker community he found at Carlow.

But meanwhile: "While these reflections were going on, the beautiful Blackwater River suddenly opened up before us, and driving along it for three miles through some of the most beautiful rich country ever seen, we came to Lismore. Nothing can be certainly more magnificent than this drive."

Thackeray loved Lismore – its castle, and especially its cathedral. "The church with the handsome spire, that looks so graceful among the trees, is a cathedral church, and one of the neatest-kept and prettiest edifices I have seen in Ireland. In the old graveyard, Protestants and Catholics lie together – that is, not together, for each has a side of the ground, where they sleep, and, so occupied, do not quarrel. The sun was shining down upon the brilliant grass – and I don't think the shadows of the Protestant graves were any longer or shorter than those of the Catholics. Is it the right or the left side of the graveyard that is nearest Heaven, I wonder? Look, the sun shines upon both alike, and the blue sky bends over all."

From Lismore Thackeray continued his journey through pelting rain via Fermoy, Rathcormac and Watergasshill to Cork. His journey through County Waterford took place in 1842 – [roughly] on this day.

THE AMAZING SAMPSON TOWGOOD ROCH

If we want to know what people looked like in former times – say, the decades just before the Great Famine – there's no shortage of works of art to show us the likenesses of the great and the good. But what about the ordinary working-class people from whom most of us are descended? There are plenty of unflattering descriptions of these miserably poor people from the pens of foreign travellers who often had their own agendas – the backwardness of Ireland, the iniquities of the Catholic Church, and so on.

But can we actually visualize them as real people? In this respect Waterford, Dungarvan and Youghal are uniquely lucky, for the Ulster Folk & Transport Museum possesses a collection of beautiful little paintings depicting their inhabitants in the 1820s and 1830s. Just for once, the artist was more interested in people than places.

He shows us ordinary townspeople at work or at play. A pair of tough looking old women are weighing out huge sacks of potatoes on scales. Two younger women, their hair elaborately done up and kept in place with Spanish combs, are ogling a gauger or revenue official. A long suffering coal porter endures the nagging of his wife. The butter man and his wife sell butter from a churn on a donkey cart. A rather apprehensive lady sells milk from a gigantic urn balanced precariously on her head.

Other working couples include the wool gatherers, who rake sheep's wool off the hedges onto a cart, and the seaweed gatherers, who carry on their backs huge kreels of kelp. A handsome young pedlar cajoles a market woman into buying ribbons. We see a cobbler and a basket maker at work. A man sells fish to two women. A well dressed man is buying a lobster, and from the way he's about to grasp it I'd say he could lose a finger or two.

These are all real people, painted with care, skill and humour, evidently from sketches that had been made on the spot. Old or young, ugly or beautiful, they are ancestors of whom any of us could be proud. But who on earth was the artist?

Sampson Towgood Roch was born in 1759 at Glen Castle near Carrickbeg in County Waterford. The estate had been granted by William III to his ancestor as a reward for swimming the Foyle with a message to the defenders of Derry. To be the son of a Protestant landowner, even a minor one, suggests a life of privilege. Sampson, alas, was born deaf and dumb.

At the age of fourteen, while on a visit to some relations at Cashel, he astonished his hosts by drawing sketches of scenery and small portraits of his friends. His father realized that Sampson had a gift that must be developed, and sent him

Dancing merrily to the music of an uilleann piper.
© National Museums Northern Ireland. Collection Ulster Folk & Transport Museum

to Dublin to be trained. The young man, however, was determined to make his own way in the world, and with admirable independence of spirit refused to be apprenticed to a master, studying instead the techniques of the painters then practising in Dublin. By the time he was twenty-five he was in business as a portrait painter. His first studio was in Capel Street and he later moved to Grafton Street.

In 1792 he left Dublin and went to practise in Bath. His career was spectacularly successful. He became renowned as one of the most skilful miniature portrait painters in Britain, and his clients included several members of the royal family. It is said that he was offered a knighthood, but declined because he felt that his handicap might embarrass the other knights. Indeed, he had nothing to be ashamed of.

When he was about sixty he returned to Ireland and lived with his relations at Woodbine Hill near Youghal. It was at this period that he made the wonderful series of little paintings of local people. He died a couple of years short of his ninetieth birthday, and was buried in the family burial place at Ardmore in 1847 – on this day.

Main source: Rosemary ffolliott, "Provincial Town Life in Munster", in The Irish Ancestor, V, no. 1 (1973), pp 34-37.

THE TOWERS OF BALLYSAGGART

Photo: Andrew Kelly

One of my favourite spots in west Waterford is the old demesne of Ballysaggartmore. Two miles west of Lismore on the Ballyduff road, a sign stating simply "Towers" mysteriously invites you to park your car and ascend the hillside. Trees of many kinds - larch, Spanish chestnut, rhododendron - engulf you as you climb. You pass under a little bridge, follow the avenue as it bears right, and then suddenly, breathtakingly, there stands before you one of the most magnificent - and absurd - structures in Ireland: a huge fortified bridge over a tiny mountain stream. Cross the bridge, turn right through more rhododendron, pass through the fortified gate lodge, and descend the hill to your car. As abruptly as you entered it, you have left the world of the Gothic novel and are back to reality.

What of the mansion for which these magnificent approaches were designed? Because it no longer exists, many people assume it was never built. But indeed it was, and it was not only sumptuous but the last word in early Victorian technology:

"On the ground floor there are two drawing rooms opening into each other and terminated by a handsome conservatory which opens into the pleasure grounds. The dining-room is 40 feet by 20 feet, with billiard, morning room and study. Upstairs are 11 good bedrooms with nursery and school rooms and several well appointed water closets and baths. The court comprises servants' quarters, laundry, coach house, etc., with fruit and vegetable gardens plus peach houses, vinery, etc. which with their connecting vestibules extend 300 feet in length."

The creator of all this finery was Arthur Keily, born in 1777, the younger son of John Keily of Lismore, owner of a large amount of property in west Waterford. To his elder son John he bequeathed Strancally, and John employed the Pain brothers of Cork to build him an imposing imitation-Gothic castle. To Arthur he left Ballysaggart. Here Arthur made his home, and hither in 1824 he brought his bride, Elizabeth, one of the great Martin tribe of Ross in County Galway. They had eleven children, and in 1843 Arthur added the word Ussher to his surname in honour of his grandmother Sarah, daughter of Captain Arthur Ussher of Camphire.

'Tis well for some. The tenants on Keily Ussher's 8,500-acre estate lived in thatched cabins. If, that is, they were lucky – and many of them were not. For only about 1,500 acres were farmable, and that was just where Arthur laid out his mansion and demesne – forty tenant families being evicted in the process. The rest of the estate consisted of the flood-plain of the Blackwater and moorland plateau good only for turf and summer grazing.

Then came the Famine – an ideal opportunity for an improving landlord to clear his estate. In 1847 there were about seven hundred people living at Ballysaggart, and most of them were under threat of eviction. In desperation the tenants sought help from their parish priest, Father Fogarty, who referred them to a rather shady solicitor named Dennehy. Dennehy implied that they had a case, and that if they gave him lots of money he would see what he could do about it. However, the tenants very sensibly decided that it would be much cheaper to shoot the landlord instead.

A business meeting was held at the house of one John Liddy, at which funds were collected to hire a "hit man", John Keeffe of Mountain Barrack. Over the next three days Keeffe made careful preparations. He chose the best spot for his purpose. He borrowed a file from the local smithy to ensure the smooth working of his gun. Then he placed himself in ambush near the grand lodge to await the return of Keily Ussher. As the carriage drew level with him he took careful aim at its occupant and pulled the trigger. The gun misfired.

Liddy and Keeffe were tried in Waterford County Court and sentenced to transportation for life. Five other conspirators were subsequently run to earth, put on trial the following spring, and given a similar sentence. All seven were packed off to Van Diemen's Land.

But Keily Ussher had overspent himself, and in 1853 the Ballysaggart estate, developed at the cost of so much human misery, was put up for sale in the Incumbered Estates Court. There was no buyer. It was divided into eight lots and put up for sale again, but again there were no bidders. It was offered a third time, at greatly reduced price, in 1861, and this time it was sold. A year later Keily Ussher was dead.

Today, his mansion is no more and his demesne is a forest. All that remains of its former magnificence is the preposterous fortified bridge and the Grand Lodge – follies indeed. *Sic transit gloria mundi.*

The first trial of Keily Ussher's would-be murderers took place in 1847 – on this day.

Main source: Patrick Feeney, 'Ballysaggart estate: eviction, famine and conspiracy,' in Decies no. 27 (Autumn 1984), pp 4-12.

THE ATTACK ON PORTLAW

1848 was a year of famine and political turmoil in Ireland. Much of the political action took place around Waterford City and south Tipperary, but at first glance you wouldn't think of Portlaw as being a major target of discontent. After all, it was a newly built model village, centred on the Malcomson cotton mill which was then in full swing and employing 1,800 hands.

The lands around belonged to the well-run Curraghmore estate, which had a resident landlord the third Marquess of Waterford. His Lordship had formerly been renowned for his wild practical jokes, but his beautiful and artistic wife, the Marchioness Louisa, had transferred his energies into care for their tenantry. Cottages were improved, a woollen manufactory employing thirty local women was started in a disused forge, a Curraghmore Clothing Fund was set up – and when famine struck, soup kitchens were organized. Portlaw's famine problem was mainly caused by its being *too* well run, which encouraged starving cottiers from other parts of the county to pour into the village hoping for relief.

But Curraghmore had also inherited an ugly political legacy, and memories of the 1826 evictions were still strong. There were menacing reports of gatherings of rebels at nearby Carrick, where they were addressed by Young Ireland leaders such as Meagher and William Smith O'Brien. Rumours of a planned attack on Portlaw grew ever stronger, and Curraghmore was put into a state of defence.

The architect William Tinsley was commissioned to fortify the mansion. Walking to Curraghmore from his home in Clonmel, Tinsley was surprised to meet crowds of peasants armed with pikes converging on Portlaw. They cheerfully informed him they were going to attack the place, and disclosed the details of their tactics, news which Tinsley equally generously passed on to the defenders.

With battle apparently imminent, Lord Waterford decided that his spouse would be safer in England, and the indomitable Louisa was removed, protesting. She did, however, insist on being informed of developments, and the letters she received from the housekeeper Mary Smith help to keep us in the picture too.

On 2 August she wrote: "We are still going on with barricading the windows. There is now a watchword for every night, so we have it all soldier like. I think my Lord only came home just in time to protect us."

At the end of August Louisa insisted on coming home, and in September she wrote: "We live in a state of siege, 25 soldiers quartered in the house, 16 or 18 specials also watching day and night on the housetop." But siege or no siege, she continued her painting undaunted. "I have been busy colouring and correcting for publication my Babes in the Wood. As for coming over to England again, I cannot think of it till I hear of real peace."

Her kinsman General Charles Stuart, who was staying at Curraghmore at this time wrote: "A detachment of troops was quartered in the outhouses of Curraghmore for its defence, and a six-pounder gun has, through the energy of Lord Waterford, been hoisted up to a commanding position in the house."

Curraghmore, however, was not attacked. As for the siege of Portlaw police barracks, it was a fiasco. General Stuart reported that "it had been defended by a gallant old clergyman and his son against an armed rabble." Other accounts are equally vague. According to one, the police shot one man dead and wounded two teenagers; the attackers, led by Thomas D'Arcy Magee, then marched off towards Kilmacthomas. According to another, they were led by a Dubliner named Fitz-Maurice who marched them back to Tipperary.

Lady Waterford criticised the newspapers for treating the whole episode as a bad joke. Those on the spot realised that Curraghmore and Portlaw had had a very lucky escape. Her letter recounting these events was written in 1848 – on this day.

The 19 indoor staff at Curraghmore circa 1900
From the Poole collection courtesy of National Library

JOHN HORN AND THE NEPTUNE SHIPYARD

When the Malcomson Brothers opened an iron works in Waterford at Canada Street and the Park Road in 1843, what they had in mind principally was to have a repair yard for the company's large fleet of steamships (they controlled both the Waterford and Cork steamship companies and were also shareholders in the P & O Line). But Joseph Malcomson possessed vision as well as business acumen and found it impossible to resist the temptation to launch out into shipbuilding as well. In 1847 the company produced its first paddle-steamer, appropriately named the *Neptune*. By 1882 they had built forty ships.

Joseph Malcomson – the owner's house on the Canada St. / Park Road corner and now containing offices of Kenny Stephenson Chapman, Solicitors
Picture: Bill Irish Collection

John Horn, courtesy of Brian Horn (grandson)
Picture: Bill Irish Collection

The company's first manager was D.R. Anderson. However, in 1849 he was replaced by a Scotsman of considerable experience and talent named John Horn. A skilled engineer and shipbuilder, Horn was destined to run the company for over twenty years. He, his wife Isabella and their children lived in the manager's house which later became St Philomena's Guest House and Park Shop, much frequented by Waterpark boys and operated by four eccentric Murphy sisters from Kerry. In June 1859 tragedy struck the family when their eldest son James, who was aged eighteen and also worked in the shipyard, was drowned while bathing near the Rhineshark in Tramore Bay.

During John Horn's time the technique of shipbuilding was advancing fast, and Malcomson's were among the leaders of innovation. They were the first firm to introduce watertight compartments, the procedure which (had it been properly applied) really would have made the *Titanic* virtually unsinkable. Harland & Wolff claimed to be the first to use Portland cement for the inside bottom of the hull to prevent rusting, but Horn had used this on the *SS Cuba* the year before. And independently of Harland's, he developed the use of iron for the main and tween decks.

St Philomena's Guest House just before it was knocked
Picture: Bill Irish Collection

At this period steamships were still being built with sails, so that when the wind was favourable they could save on fuel. In 1861 Horn fitted the steam ice-breaker *SS Avoca* with a device for lifting the propeller clear of the water, thus preventing underwater drag when under sail. In the following year he fitted the *SS Cella* with a device for steering the vessel from midships or aft. He developed and patented an engine steam condenser. And he was several years ahead of Harland & Wolff in replacing the bowsprit and figurehead with a straight bow.

The *SS William Penn* on the slipway at Neptune Ironworks and ready for launching in June 1865. The Neptune yard comprised 3.3 acres running from the river to where Canada St. meets Park Road and along Park Road to what was Graves timber yard (now carved up into sundry businesses). It later was the location for McDonnell's margarine factory and Gold Crust bakery, both of which have also moved on.
Picture courtesy of F McQuillian - Bill Irish Collection

John Horn retired in 1870 and was succeeded as manager by his son Andrew, then aged twenty-five. Andrew too had his personal tragedy – his wife Emily died in 1879 aged only thirty-three, on a Friday the 13th. Andrew was an exceptionally talented shipbuilder. Among his successes were some fine steam yachts, one of which – named *Maritana* from the heroine of Wallace's most successful opera – won a prize for elegance at Cowes Regatta in the Isle of Wight in 1884.

By this time there had been some dramatic changes at the Neptune Ironworks. Joseph Malcomson died in 1858, and under his sons' management the business plummeted – partly through their fault and partly through external circumstances such as the American Civil War. The firm went bankrupt in 1877, but the Neptune struggled on to complete the last orders. *Maritana*, the yacht so admired at Cowes Regatta, was launched in 1882; she was destined to be the last ship launched from the Malcomson works. The yard was taken over by the Limerick Steam Ship Company and in 1883 there were just 32 people employed there.

Andrew Horn's son, who had the rather unfortunate name of Willie Horn, worked for a time at the Neptune and was then Marine Superintendent for the Limerick Steam Ship Company. He then moved across to Liverpool, where he was for a while a marine superintendent and then a consulting engineer. He took with him great rolls of very heavy drawing cloth on which were the outlines of ships built at the Neptune by his father and grandfather. If these survived today they would provide invaluable evidence for the study of Waterford's lost shipbuilding industry. Alas, they were destroyed by German bombs in World War Two.

During nearly forty years the Neptune yard produced a remarkable number of impressive steamships. Nearly all of these were built under the superintendence of the Horn family. So it was a lucky day for Waterford when John Horn took over the management of the Neptune works, in 1849 – on this day.

[See Bill Irish, "John Horn 1814-1895", Decies no. 69 (2013), pp 109-114.]

Steam-yacht *Maritana* built in 1882, the last ship built at Neptune yard
Picture courtesy of National Library of Ireland - Lawrence Collection

SARAH PURSER:
THE DUNGARVAN CONNECTION

Picture: Waterford County Museum

A hundred years ago, Sarah Purser was one of the dominant figures in the Irish art world. Her career was based in Dublin, and she was born in Kingstown / Dún Laoghaire in 1848. But what is often forgotten is that for the first twenty-five years of her life her home was at Abbeyside, Dungarvan. Her father was involved in brewing and flour milling. The family lived initially in the house now occupied by the parish priest and later in the Hermitage. At the age of thirteen she was sent to school in Switzerland for two years.

In the summer of 1873 she settled in Dublin, where she trained at the Metropolitan School of Art and also in Paris and Italy. Soon she made her name as an extremely talented portrait painter. Through her friendship with the Gore-Booths she acquired a list of distinguished clients – "I went through the aristocracy like the measles," she said in later life.

Sarah Purser was no impoverished artist living in a garret. Her work brought her a respectable income which she astutely invested in Guinness's. She lived in a beautiful Georgian house on Mespil Road. In 1903 she founded An Túr Gloine, the first Irish stained glass studio. She drew the attention of the art world to John Yeats and Nathaniel Hone. And she persuaded the new Free State Government to provide Charlemont House as a Modern Art Gallery, where the Hugh Lane Collection could be housed. She was the first woman to be elected to the Royal Hibernian Academy.

When she left Dungarvan in 1873 a friend sent her a poem which included the following lines:

> *Your name we certainly shall yet hear*
> *In Exhibition Catalogue I'll look to see*
> *The known to fame initials S.H.P.*
> *Appended to some 'Gipsy Scene', some 'Lara'*
> *Some 'Peasant Girl', in kind thought of me*
> *A lady artist famed you'll yet be*

How right she was! Sarah Henrietta Purser was born in 1848 – on this day.

THE ATTACK ON CAPPOQUIN BARRACKS

Cappoquin in the 1840s formed part of the recently developed Cappoquin Navigation. It had the benefit of a conscientious resident landlord, Sir Richard Keane. But it was not without its troubles. In September 1846 local farmers and gentry were terrorized by a mob of five or six hundred who marched through the parish. The following January a local baker named Charles O'Connor had his corn cart plundered en route from Clogheen mills; having identified the robber to the police he was "obliged to have an escort to protect him from the vengeance of people proverbially lawless". In December 1847 a land agent had been fired on near the town.

In mid-September 1849 one of the constables at Cappoquin Barracks named John Power received alarming news: the barracks were about to be attacked! Hasty preparations were made to resist, and when the attack was launched it was repulsed. One of the attackers was shot dead, others were taken prisoner, and a quantity of pikes was seized.

Such, in a nutshell, is what seems to have happened, but when we come to examine the details of the incident we find nothing but confusion. Apparently, in spite of the warning (and who exactly was it that tipped off the police?) there were two constables out on foot patrol at the time. They were hunted down by the attackers. According to one account, one was wounded and the other escaped. Yet we're also told that the wounded constable was stabbed to death with 17 pike wounds, and that the other escaped by hiding in bed with a priest. (What would today's tabloids have to say about that?) A large number of pikes was discovered in a dung heap in the yard of the police barracks (!) and another 47 around the town. We're also told that the alleged rebel shot dead was a man named Donovan who had nothing to do with the barrack attack but was killed by someone else outside Sir Richard Keane's house.

There's as much confusion about the motive for the attack, and what on earth it was supposed to achieve. The following Sunday the parish priest of Lismore, Father Fogarty, strongly condemned the participants, who he claimed were "the dupes of outlaws and misguided men". Their motive, he asserted, was to obtain arms with which to plunder the houses of men of property. The attack was also said to be the work of a secret society. It was also alleged to be a rebellion of farmers against landlords caused by the fall in grain prices due to the repeal of the Corn Laws. And it was also supposed to be the beginning of a great socialist revolution being planned by Fintan Lalor. So you pays your money and you takes your choice.

The attack on Cappoquin police barracks took place in 1849 – on this day.

1850-1900

THE WATERFORD GLASS FACTORY

The great Waterford Glass Factory, founded in 1783, is linked in most people's minds with one family – the Penroses. It was indeed the Penroses who founded the firm, but for most of its sixty-eight year existence it was controlled by another family – the Gatchells. The Penroses were a prolific and active Quaker family with many irons in the fire besides the glass works, and after the deaths of George and William Penrose in 1796 and 1799 the family lost interest in the operation.

Jonathan Gatchell came to work for the Penroses as a clerk in 1781. He became a friend and colleague of John Hill, the technician whose expertise got the glass factory on its feet two years later. When Hill left Waterford after a dispute caused by the meddling of his employer's wife, Gatchell took over the post of compounder. In 1799, when William Penrose died, a partnership of three was formed to continue the work, Jonathan Gatchell being one. This situation continued until 1811, when the partnership was dissolved and Gatchell carried on alone. When he died in 1823, his son George continued the business until it closed down in 1851.

The factory was originally sited on The Quay, near its junction with Penrose Lane. In 1802 a move was made to the Old Tan Yard at Anne Street, though a warehouse and a shop were retained on The Quay. Gerald McMullen, a Penrose descendant who wrote a history of the glassworks in 1946, commented that two features stand out in the troubled history of the Waterford glasshouse: the standard of manufacture was high and the rate of production was low. Carey & Co., china and glass merchants of Cork, had no doubts on quality: in 1813 they advertised that they sold Waterford glass and that it was "superior to that of any other factory in Ireland". Coming from a city with a glasshouse of her own, and soon to have another, this was praise indeed. However, the stream of bowls, cruets, decanters, jugs, tumblers, wine-glasses, etc. that flowed from the factory to the warehouse was never a river, though it contrived somehow to feed the markets of home and abroad, with North America always an insatiable customer.

The company's ledgers show that between 1830 and 1840 it employed sixty to seventy skilled workmen and produced about fifty tons of glass annually. It was not a big operation, nor was it by any means the only glassworks in Ireland. Why then did it establish such an astounding reputation? One reason was that it undoubtedly was good. Another is that the younger Gatchell just had a mania for exhibiting glass. Even in 1851, the year the factory closed, Waterford Glass was among the principal Irish items at the Great Exhibition, the stupendous world fair held in Hyde Park, London, in – appropriately enough – the Crystal Palace.

If Waterford glass was so good, why then did the factory close? One reason was that the company never had enough capital, and that was partly the result of unpaid bills, even from the Americans. Back in 1819 Jonathan Gatchell complained that he had received no payment for thirteen hogsheads of glass sold in Charlestown, and that he was still owed £1,000 from Philadelphia. But the main reason was that the government introduced in 1825 a crushing excise duty on all glass manufactured in Ireland. These two financial cancers gnawed away at the vital organs of the business, until at last George Gatchell advertised the entire stock of the Waterford Glass Works for sale without reserve at the Waterford Auction Mart in King St. (now O'Connell St.) - in 1851, on this day.

Photos: Waterford Museum of Treasures, Three Museums in the Viking Triangle

GENERAL ANDERSON AND THE BATTLE OF CORUNNA

|᛫᛫᛫᛫|᛫᛫᛫᛫|᛫᛫᛫᛫|᛫᛫᛫᛫|᛫᛫᛫᛫|᛫᛫᛫᛫|᛫᛫᛫᛫|᛫᛫᛫᛫|᛫᛫᛫᛫|᛫᛫᛫᛫|᛫᛫᛫᛫|᛫᛫᛫᛫|᛫᛫᛫᛫|᛫᛫᛫᛫|᛫᛫᛫᛫|

We buried him darkly at dead of night
The sods with our bayonets turning
By the struggling moonbeam's misty light
And the lantern dimly burning.

A couple of generations ago, these lines would have been familiar to most British schoolboys, and probably to many in Ireland as well. They are also inscribed on a monument in Christ Church Cathedral, Waterford. But why?

The Andersons of Gracedieu played a leading role in Waterford affairs for three hundred years. Their family seat was built in about 1870 and named Gracedieu after their former abode on Gracedieu townland. Like many Anglo-Irish families, they provided some distinguished officers to the British Army, in their case particularly to the medical services.

Their most colourful member was surely General Paul Anderson, born in the original Gracedieu House in 1767. He served as a colonel through the Napoleonic Wars and for some time was aide-de-camp to General Sir John Moore (no relation to the John Moore mentioned on page 96), whose close friend he became.

Moore was a remarkable commander, not only for his military ability but also for his humanity. In 1798 he served against the rebels in County Wexford, and in particular commanded the government forces at the battle of Goffsbridge. In his memoirs he records his horror at the undisciplined and bloodthirsty behaviour of

General Sir John Moore

the men he was supposed to lead. During the Peninsular Wars he would have had many Irish soldiers serving under him, including former Wexford insurgents.

In 1809 the little British force in Spain was hopelessly outnumbered, starved of resources, and on the brink of disaster. But thanks to Moore's masterly leadership they withdrew in good order as far as Corunna, where they were safely evacuated by the Royal Navy. It was all a bit like Dunkirk in 1940.

Moore himself never made it. Mortally wounded, he died at Corunna. It was up to Anderson and the other aides-de-camp to decide what to do with the body. The obvious thing was to bring it on board ship and preserve it for burial at a later date. But Moore had often told his staff that if he were killed in battle he would like to be buried where he fell, and they were deter-

The death of Sir John Moore

mined to carry out their friend's wish. There was no time to get a coffin, they simply wrapped Moore in his cloak. Impossible even to fire a volley over the grave, for it would attract the fire of the rapidly approaching enemy. Moore was buried secretly, by night, in haste, and left at Corunna in an unmarked grave.

Some years later, the story of the burial of Sir John Moore was read aloud from a magazine to a Trinity College student named Charles Wolfe. It moved him so deeply that he wrote a poem on the subject, which he eventually published anonymously in the *Newry Gazette*. Wolfe became a clergyman in Ulster, wrote nothing else of any consequences, and died young of TB while chaplain on Spike Island in Cork Harbour. But the chance discovery of his poem created a sensation, and Byron hailed it as "the most splendid ode in the English language". Its place in the school anthologies was assured - but how many of the thousands of readers realize that a Waterford man played a central part in the story?

Colonel (later General) Paul Anderson lived on for many years, dying eventually at Bath aged 84. He was obviously proud of his moment at the forefront of history, for in his will he directed that a marble slab be placed to his memory in Waterford Cathedral. The inscription gives a detailed account of his career, but whether through carelessness or because they were tired of hearing about his exploits, his family placed the monument so high up that the tiny lettering can hardly be read!

General Anderson died in 1851 – on this day.

CAPTAIN HENRY BOLTON, R.N.

The battle of Trafalgar in 1805, in which the British fleet under Admirals Nelson and Collingwood defeated the combined fleets of France and Spain, had a profound effect on public opinion in Ireland as well as Britain. It was a knockout blow to Napoleon's hopes of invading these islands, made all the more poignant by Nelson's death in the very hour of victory. Cornelius Bolton must have been redecorating Faithlegg House at the time, for he celebrated the battle by having a beautiful marble fireplace installed in one of the principal rooms, adorned with the heads and crests of the two victorious admirals carved by a sculptor named Sheppard. Alas, the heads were stolen some years ago when the house lay empty, but at least the crests remained.

Meanwhile, the war went on and Britain needed Irish officers. Cornelius had four sons. The eldest, being the heir, remained at home. Two others joined the army, and one was killed at the battle of Vitoria in 1813. The youngest, named Henry, was born at Faithlegg in July 1796. In March 1809 he enlisted in the Royal Navy as a First Class Volunteer, being assigned to the 74-gun ship of the line *Victorious*. Naval officers began their careers early in those days, as viewers of the movie *Master and Commader* will have noted. Henry was then aged twelve, and fought his first battle six months later.

This engagement was the disastrously messed-up amphibious assault on the Dutch port of Flushing. The town stands on the island of Walcheren at the mouth of the river Scheldt, and it had been heavily fortified by Napoleon. The British decided to take it in a surprise attack. Some surprise – the event was announced in the French newspapers before the fleet had even set sail.

The invading force was massive: 35 ships of the line and 200 other vessels under the command of Sir Richard Strachan (pronounced Strawn) transported 40,000 troops under the command of the Earl of Chatham. At first, all went well. The unfortunate islanders were subjected to a terrific bombardment, and the place was taken by storm. But having thus achieved his first objective, Chatham couldn't think what to do next. Eventually, after four months of dithering, he evacuated as many of his troops as disease and the unhealthy climate had spared (no wonder the place was called Flushing!), and they all sailed home in time for Christmas.

You've got to hand it to the Brits – they do have a sense of humour. While Chatham resigned his command with the reddest of faces, the whole country fell about laughing and the London mobs chanted:

> *Lord Chatham with his sabre drawn*
> *Stood waiting for Sir Richard Strachan [still pronounced Strawn],*
> *While just as eager to be at 'em*
> *Sir Richard waited there for Chatham.*

For little Henry Bolton the Walcheren campaign must have been a rather odd introduction to naval warfare. The lad performed his allotted tasks bravely, though his ship was frequently exposed to fire from the shore batteries.

Next year his ship was on patrol off Messina, where it was expected that Marshal Murat would invade Sicily. In February 1812, now a fourteen-year-old midshipman, he fought with distinction in a ferocious naval engagement between his ship, the *Victorious*, and a French ship of the line, the *Rivoli*, each of 74 guns. After four and a half hours of fighting the French struck their colours; they had lost 400 men, including most of their officers. Losses on the *Victorious* comprised 27 killed and 99 wounded, including young Henry Bolton.

After a long and distinguished career, Henry left the navy in 1830 with the rank of commander. For the next ten years he was Inspector of Coastguards at Donaghadee and Waterford. In his semi-retirement he lived at Ballinlaw on the River Barrow, just upstream of the present railway bridge. He was Sheriff of Waterford City in 1837 and again in 1850. In 1839 he married Annie, daughter and coheiress of William Kearney of Waterford. Their only son, a major in the 18th Hussars, died unmarried at Madeira in 1917, the last Bolton of the Faithlegg line.

Captain Henry Bolton, R.N., died in 1852 – on this day.

ANTHONY TROLLOPE AND THE POSTAL ENQUIRY

If you ever feel inclined to complain about the inadequacies of An Post, then just thank your lucky stars that we are not living in 1855.

In June of that year the House of Commons established a select committee to enquire into the postal arrangements for the south of Ireland. The chairman was Thomas Meagher, MP for Waterford and father of Thomas Francis Meagher. Before the House rose for the summer recess, the committee had examined 17 witnesses and a report running to 300 pages had been compiled, printed and presented. How's that for efficiency?

The most famous witness was Rowland Hill, who had set up the penny post fifteen years before, in 1840. But by far the greatest contributor was the Post Office Surveyor, Anthony Trollope, whose evidence occupies over 100 pages and displays an amazingly detailed knowledge of local conditions.

Trollope was an extraordinary man. Today he's remembered as the author of *The Barchester Novels,* based partly on his experiences in Clonmel and depicting life in an English country town. But Trollope's output was enormous, and even by the standards of Victorian England he was a workaholic. Every morning he was at his desk by 5.30; he wrote 250 words every quarter of an hour for three hours, and at 8.30, having completed ten pages of text, he would depart for a full day's work in the post office. His career was spectacularly successful. He reorganized the postal services first in Ireland and then in England. Among his innovations was that humble but useful object, the pillar-box. And when he felt that his superiors did not appreciate his work, he resigned.

Steam travel had now revolutionised the long-distance mail service; the problem was with the local deliveries. Devastating indictments of the slowness and inefficiency of the service were given by Joseph Malcomson, owner of the largest cotton factory in Ireland (at Portlaw) and principal shareholder of the Waterford Steamship Company. "To convey our mails from Portlaw," he wailed, "we have the worst type of one-horse car in the county, the worst horse that will go, and the most inferior driver of the car; the speed is not more than five Irish miles per hour."

The day mail was conveyed by messenger between Portlaw and Mullinavat on the Waterford-Kilkenny railway line, a distance of about ten miles, which took three hours. On the way the messenger picked up the bags for Piltown and Carrick as well. For this task he was paid five shillings a week, although he carried on his back letters and bankers' drafts that might well amount to £14,000. "What class of a man is this," a witness was asked, "who takes the work at five shillings a week while the ordinary wages of the district are seven shillings?" "Ach," replied the witness, "he's little more than an old woman, I believe."

John A. Blake, Mayor of Waterford, spoke of the problems of the captains of ships bringing grain from the Black Sea port of Odessa. They docked first at Cork and then proceeded to Passage East. But the mail was so slow that they couldn't book berths in advance, and if they had to wait for a berth there was the danger that the corn would overheat and catch fire.

James Delahunty, Coroner of Waterford Borough (an area of about thirty square miles), retailed the problem of trying to summon juries for inquests while the dead lay waiting for burial.

The report concluded with a list of the expenses claimed by witnesses. The largest sum was £27.18.0 (about €4,000 in today's money) claimed by the Mayor of Clonmel, Joseph Kenny. His evidence was also the briefest, consisting of his answers to four questions and comprising seven words: "I am" – "I have" – "Nothing" – and "I do". By the way, he was a solicitor.

The committee's recommendation was that the importance of the subject merited the continuation of the enquiry in the next parliamentary session. Yet no sequel to this report has yet been discovered. Perhaps … it's in the post?

Trollope's evidence to the postal enquiry concluded in 1855 – on this day.

Main source: Eileen Webster, "Report of a Select Committee on Postal Arrangements (Waterford etc.), 1855", Decies, no. 7 (1978), pp 16-19.

The pillar box as designed by Anthony Trollope but his would have been coloured red.

Photo: Donal Sheein

HOLY CROSS CHURCH, TRAMORE

The mid-19th century saw a rapid expansion in Irish church building. The Penal Laws had been repealed, a prosperous Catholic middle class was emerging, and the great symbols of their new-found pride and power were the large, solid, stone churches, designed by professional architects and often adorned with tall spires. Their style was almost invariably Gothic, in other words the style of the high Middle Ages. Gothic architecture became the obsession of the English architect Augustus Welby Pugin. For him, the Middle Ages were the climax of living Christianity, the period of the Crusades, the code of chivalry, the great monasteries, and so on. For him, a church without pointed arches, traceried windows, stained glass, and a dim mystical interior just wasn't a church.

The main Irish architect of this style was J.J. McCarthy, often stupidly called the Irish Pugin, as if he had no right to exist of himself. McCarthy's best known work is the splendid Armagh Cathedral, and he was also responsible for the cathedrals of Derry, Monaghan and Thurles, besides Maynooth College Chapel and about forty parish churches and monasteries. In this diocese he was the creator of four parish churches – those of Tramore, Clonea, Portlaw and the Nire. Holy Cross, Tramore, is one of the most striking churches in the country, dominating the town and the bay, and visible for many miles around.

In the 1850s, thanks largely to the arrival of the railway, Tramore was developing fast as a seaside resort and dormitory town for Waterford. The old thatched chapel was in no way adequate to serve the population, and a new church - more in keeping with the more prosperous image - was needed. The impetus for a new parish church was headed by the parish priest, Father Nicholas Cantwell, who summoned a committee to look into ways and means of financing it. The landowner, Lord Doneraile, was approached, and after some persuasion agreed to give the site free.

Fundraising now began in earnest. There were collections among the local shopkeepers and farmers, concerts in Waterford and Tramore, subscriptions from America, and of course the weekly contributions from parishioners. At last, enough funds had been raised, and in September 1856 the foundation stone was laid by Bishop Dominick O'Brien.

Within two years the walls had been built up to the top of the aisles. The stone used was the local trap-rock, with granite for the dressings. The church was dedicated in July 1860 and formally blessed two years later, but still the work of construction went on. The tower and spire were finally completed in 1871, after fifteen years and an expenditure of £18,000 – a large sum for those days. Wealthy donors helped to adorn the interior with high altars, side altars, communion rails, pulpit, crucifixion figures, and stained glass windows.

The Gothic style of the altars reflected on a smaller scale the building itself. However, in the 1920s a despotic parish priest with an obsessive hatred of sharp points had all the pinnacles lopped off, so that in my youth the altars looked very peculiar indeed. I wonder what his psychoanalyst would have said about that – if he had one! Far more drastic alteration followed in the wake of Vatican Two, with the removal of the church furnishings donated with caring pride by past generations.

Holy Cross Church, Tramore, has recently been beautifully restored. One of the most dramatic creations of J.J. McCarthy, it was founded in 1856 – on this day.

CARDINAL WISEMAN REVISITS WATERFORD

Nicholas Wiseman, Cardinal and Archbishop of Westminster, was born in 1802 in the beautiful city of Seville in southern Spain. His grandfather James Wiseman, a Waterford merchant, had migrated to Spain like many another because of the Penal Laws. His youngest son, also named James, was father of the future cardinal. James junior's first wife was the daughter of a general in the Spanish army. After her death he married Xaveria, daughter of Peter Strange of Aylwardstown near Glenmore. The Stranges were an old Catholic landowning family, with seats at Dunkitt

Xaveria Wiseman

and Drumdowney. Dispossessed under Cromwell, they acquired Aylwardstown through marriage with the Aylward family, and onto the side of the old Aylward tower-house they built a Georgian residence.

In 1805, when Nicholas was a mere three years old, his father died, and Xaveria returned home with her two little sons. So the cardinal, though born in Spain, spent most of his early childhood at Aylwardstown. His first schooling was in Waterford, then in 1810 he was sent to Ushaw College in Durham, and it was there that he decided to become a priest. On the reopening of the English College in Rome in 1818, Nicholas and five other students from Ushaw were sent there to continue their studies. His academic career was brilliant. In 1835 he returned to England, and in 1840 he was consecrated bishop.

Since the Reformation, the English bishoprics had been occupied by the Established Church. The best that Rome could do was to appoint a series of "vicars apostolic" who were given the titles of bishoprics in remote places. During the 19th century, English Catholics began to agitate for "real" bishops with English titles, and Wiseman became the natural leader of the movement.

There was vigorous opposition from bigoted elements in the British parliament and press, but Wiseman's tact and dignity steered the movement to success, and eventually the government agreed that Catholic bishops could have English titles, provided they were not those of existing Protestant sees.

Thus in 1850 Wiseman became the head of the Catholic Church in England, with the title of Archbishop of West-minster. He was also created a cardi-nal – the first English cardinal since the Reformation. There was great rejoicing among English Catholics, much weep-ing and wailing and gnashing of teeth by the Bigot Brigade, and Wiseman's prestige was enormous.

In August 1858 he was invited to Ireland by the Bishop of Clonfert to preach at the opening of a new church in Ballinasloe. From his arrival in King-stown he was greeted with rapturous enthusiasm wherever he went. In mid-September he arrived at Waterford Sta-

Cardinal Nicholas Wiseman,
Archbishop of Westminister

tion from Kilkenny and was greeted by the Mayor and a huge cheering crowd. Here he took his seat in the carriage of his kinsman Peter Strange and was conveyed to Aylwardstown. Crowds lined the route and followed the carriage all the way. On arrival he celebrated Mass, and spent the night in the house of his boyhood.

The following day the carriage returned to Waterford. Crowds waited all day on the bridge and quays for his arrival. A couple of miles outside the city he was met by a procession consisting of the trade guilds of the city bearing banners, and a vast concourse of people waving green boughs, while a band played patriotic airs. With difficulty the carriage made its way over the bridge and down The Quay to City Hall for a civic reception and banquet.

Nicholas Wiseman, Cardinal, Archbishop of Westminster, and local boy made good, revisited the city of his boyhood in 1858 – on this day.

Picture: Waterford Museum of Treasures, Three Museums in the Viking Triangle

THE MARRIAGE OF
(LORD) ROBERTS

St Patrick's Church in Patrick Street, Waterford, is undoubtedly the least known of our city's historic churches. It was built in the 1720s on the site of the medieval St Patrick's, and is one of the many churches throughout the diocese built by Bishop Thomas Milles. During the 18th and 19th centuries it was one of the three places of worship in Waterford of the Church of Ireland, the other two being Christ Church Cathedral and St Olaf's (which was also built by Bishop Milles, a few years later).

St Patrick's stood right next to the military barracks and close to Gandon's courthouse and to the later jail, and it played an important role in the life of these institutions. In the graveyard that surrounds the building lie the remains of thousands of Waterfordians, good and bad, great and small, Protestant and Catholic. The church building is plain and uninviting from the outside, but the interior is almost pure Georgian – though there are later features such as the 19th-century stained glass window. Since the 1960s St Patrick's has been the place of worship of the Presbyterians and Methodists and it is today the centre of a small but lively community.

In this church in May 1859 took place the wedding of one of Waterford's most celebrated sons. Frederick Sleigh Roberts was a 26-year-old lieutenant with a dazzlingly successful war record. He was a great-grandson of "Honest John" Roberts the architect. His father, General Sir Abraham Roberts, had a long and distinguished career in India. His mother, Isabella Bunbury, came from Kilfeacle in County Tipperary. Fred was born in 1832 at Cawnpore in India. As a small child he was sent to England to be educated, then at the age of twenty he returned to India to join his father's staff. Five years later the Indian Mutiny broke out, and in the fierce fighting that ensued he had some hairsbreadth escapes. At the siege of Delhi he was put out of action for a month by a bullet in the spine, which would have killed him had it not been for the leather pouch he was wearing. In January 1858, during a cavalry charge at the siege of Lucknow, he saved the life of a native soldier and captured one of the mutineers' flags, a feat for which he received the Victoria Cross, Britain's highest award for valour.

Later the same year, Roberts came home on sick leave, and he spent the winter of 1858-59 at Newtown Park, Waterford, the home of his parents and of his invalid sister Harriet. A plaque in the roadside wall commemorates his sojourn there. The young hero spent much of his time hunting with the Waterford hounds. His last hunt with them was an abysmal failure – not a fox was to be found. "We shall have better luck next time," Lord Waterford cheerfully assured him. It was not to be. The next time Lord Waterford appeared in the field, his horse stumbled at a ridiculously low wall, the Marquess was thrown to the ground, and his neck broke in the fall.

But Roberts was not there. He had other preoccupations. He had fallen in love. The lady who had won his heart was Norah Bewes, the daughter of a retired officer of the 73rd Regiment. She too lived in Newtown, not far from the Robertses, at a house called Landscape. The happy couple were married, not in the Cathedral as you might expect, but in St Patrick's Church, probably because of its military associations. The honeymoon was cut short by a summons to return to the flag, and to many more years of adventurous campaigning.

Their marriage was destined to be long and happy. Their only son was killed in the Boer War and was awarded a posthumous V.C. So when Field Marshal Earl Roberts died in 1914 there was no son to inherit the title. It was granted to his elder daughter Aileen, and on her death in 1944 passed to her sister Ada. Ada had married and had one son, a lieutenant in the Irish Guards who was killed in Norway in 1940. So when Ada Countess Roberts died in 1955, that was the end of the family of Frederick Roberts and Norah Bewes, who had been married in St Patrick's Church, Waterford, in 1859 - on this day.

WATERFORD'S PROTESTANT HALL

In the middle of the 19th century, the Protestant community in Waterford was declining in numbers and influence, but it was still full of vigour, and its bishop, Robert Daly, was a dynamic leader of his flock. One potent symbol of this energy was the erection of the Protestant Hall in 1859.

The site was a historic one, for it was part of the lands of the old St Catherine's Priory. The building was designed by Abraham Denny and built by John Fitzpatrick at a cost of £3,500. It's constructed of red brick and consists of twin three-storeyed towers flanking a wide pedimented centre, with a niche and statue, three-arched entrance, granite raised coigns, string courses, and heavy bracketed cornice. The wrought-iron railings that front the building have the crowned Bible as their motif. It's a good example of the Italianate style favoured by industrialists and merchants of the time – the Malcomson family, for instance, built all their houses in this showy style.

The foundation ceremony was also meant to impress. The proceedings began with a public breakfast at 10 a.m. in the new room of the Town Hall. The Rev. Richard Ryland gave a short sketch of the history of the Waterford Sunday School and presented the parchment scroll (which was to be placed under the first stone) for the signatures of the bishop, trustees and committee. Michael Dobbyn Hassard, MP for the city, on behalf of the Protestant freemen, presented the bishop with the silver trowel, and Abraham Denny presented the apron and other implements.

The company then adjourned to the Courthouse, where they joined the schoolchildren and their teachers who were already assembled there. The children were the first to move off to the gallery erected on the site of the new hall, accompanied by the band of the Waterford Young Men's Christian Association, who played the Sicilian Mariners' Hymn[1]. At noon the VIPs followed and the band played "St Patrick's Day". On arrival at the platform, the children sang the anthem "How gracious is the house divine" and the dean read the 127th Psalm – "Except the Lord build the house, their labour is but lost that build it." Then the scroll and coins were lodged, the bishop laid the stone and blessed the assembly, and the band played "God Save the Queen".

The hall was opened on 4 July 1861. Down the years it functioned mainly as a Sunday School Institute. Then in the early 1960s it underwent a major renovation, and when it reopened in 1964 the event was marked by a ceremony that

---

1 Ironically, this traditional tune is more familiar in Ireland as the air of a popular hymn to the Blessed Virgin – O Sanctissima, O piissima, dulcis virgo Maria ...!

resembled, and yet differed in important ways from, that which had marked the building's foundation over a hundred years before. It was now renamed St Catherine's Hall and was open to all denominations and creeds.

The proceedings began with supper in the hall, attended by descendants of the original founders, including James Denny. The bishop used the same prayer as in 1859. This time the Irish element was more marked – the meal was served by teenagers wearing traditional national costume, Lord William Beresford in his speech stressed the contribution of the Church of Ireland to the nation, the proceedings were recorded by Telefís Éireann, and the national anthem was of course the Irish one.

Finally, no public entertainment in Waterford at that time would have been complete without a contribution from Willie Watt, who brought the evening to a close with his inimitable rendering of "Bless this House" and "Oft in the Stilly Night".

St Catherine's Hall now houses a series of offices and Masonic Lodge V. It has served the community well since its foundation in 1859 – on this day.

THE IMPRISONMENT OF MARGARET AYLWARD

Thank God we live in an ecumenical age in which Catholics and Protestants can work together in the service of Christ rather than trying to poach members of each other's churches. In post-Famine Ireland, alas, things were very different. Mary Matthews was the child of a Catholic father by his estranged Protestant wife. On his deathbed Mr Matthews entrusted his daughter to a friend, a Mrs Jordan, begging her to place Mary in a Catholic orphanage. Mrs Jordan brought the little girl to St Brigid's Orphanage in Eccles St., Dublin which had been founded by Waterford-born Margaret Aylward. In due course she was boarded out in the countryside with a Mrs Kenny.

But now, having neglected her daughter for years, Mary's Protestant mother arrived in Dublin and claimed her back. St Brigid's refused to hand her over, and writs of Habeas Corpus were issued against Mrs Jordan and Margaret Aylward. At this stage a Catholic sympathizer, seeing which way things were going, abducted the little girl and placed her in a boarding school in Brussels. Margaret Aylward, brought to court, could not produce the child for the simple reason that she didn't know where she was. She was sentenced to six months in prison for contempt of court.

Her trial was long, complicated, and farcical. The judge, Thomas Lefroy, was a doddery old 84-year-old renowned for his strong Protestant opinions. He sentenced Margaret to serve her term, without hard labour, in Harrold's Cross Prison. When she arrived at the entrance, she would have seen carved above the gate the ominous injunction: "Cease to do evil and learn to do well." But the governor refused to admit her – it was a prison for males! Soon all Dublin, while sympathising with the prisoner, was laughing at the judge, in whose "honour" the following lines were composed:

|₁₁₁₁|₁₁₁₁|₁₁₁₁|₁₁₁₁|₁₁₁₁|₁₁₁₁|₁₁₁₁|₁₁₁₁|₁₁₁₁|₁₁₁₁|₁₁₁₁|₁₁₁₁|₁₁₁₁|₁₁₁₁|₁₁₁₁|₁₁₁₁|₁₁₁₁|₁₁₁₁|₁₁₁₁|₁₁₁₁|

In some courts in this land some injustice prevails
But the Court of Queen's Bench is both prudent and mild
It sentenced Miss Aylward to a prison for males
As the very best way of producing a child.
How she'll do it 'twill puzzle creation to tell
If she "cease to do evil and learn to do well".
And if in six months without labour confined
She produces a child, 'twill astonish mankind.

Margaret in fact served her sentence in Grangegorman. She was now in her sixtieth year and physically quite frail, and life in a Victorian prison was of course no picnic. Though psychologically as tough as old boots, she had several childish phobias, above all the darkness and being locked in a room. Each night she was locked in a stuffy cell in utter darkness. Only a partition separated her from the prison hospital, and all night she had to listen to the shrieks of two epileptics and the moans and lamenting of the other patients. Her health was affected: her teeth fell out, her arms became paralysed, and she began to suffer from varicose ulcers. Fortunately, her friends managed to have her moved to a room at the front of the prison, and her health improved.

Margaret's case aroused strong feelings in the world outside the prison. *The Times* of London denounced her as a kidnapper of Protestant children. But she had supporters in high places. Cardinal Cullen drove in state to see her, thereby drawing on himself some unworthy comments from *The Times*. A lady who had been in court when she was sentenced sent her a plaque representing Christ before Pilate "to console her for the scowl of the judge". Pope Pius IX declared her a Confessor of the Faith, and commissioned Archbishop Dixon of Armagh to visit her in prison and give her, with the papal compliments, a beautiful cameo depicting the head of St Peter cut in a precious stone and set in gold.

When her sentence expired, Margaret Aylward calmly walked out of the prison and back to Eccles St., where she resumed the management of her orphanage as if nothing had happened - in 1861, on this day.

For a modern appraisal of Margaret Aylward, see Jacinta Prunty, Margaret Aylward, 1810-1889: Lady of Charity, Sister of Faith (Dublin, 1999).

THE FIRE AT WHITE'S MILLS

In the middle of the 19th century, one of the largest business concerns in Waterford was that of the White Brothers, which occupied a very extensive block of buildings at Hanover Street, King Street (now part of O'Connell Street), and The Quay. Founded about 1847, by 1863 White's employed over fifty people. The tallest building was the steam mill, driven by a furnace in

Former White's Mills - now the Granary
Photo: Donal Sheerin

Hanover Street; the mighty engines were kept running day and night.

Sunday, of course, was a day of rest, and the practice was to shut down the mills before midnight on Saturday, check the premises carefully, and then lock them up until 12 o'clock the following night. During the night of Saturday to Sunday 28-29 November 1863, a passer-by – described by the local newspaper as an "unfortunate female", whatever that may mean – spotted smoke pouring from the windows of the screenroom at the very top of the mill. No mobile phones in those days! She at once gave the alarm to the quay and river watchmen, who ran to inform the police. Soon the staff and neighbours arrived and the mill doors were burst open with sledge-hammers (was this a good idea?), but by now the building was one mass of fire. The bells of Christ Church were rung to give warning of the danger, and soon great crowds of townspeople were converging on the scene of the disaster.

I wonder whether even today much could be done to save the mills. In 1863 there was no municipal fire service. Primitive fire engines were operated by the insurance companies and the military. The first to arrive was that of the National Insurance Company, to be followed by the West of England, the Sun Fire Office, and the barrack engine operated by the officers and men of the 10th Regiment.

But these engines needed water. The Corporation had recently installed a number of hydrants, but when the crew of the National engine tried to fix their hose to the nearest one (at the junction of King and Thomas Streets) they found that the plug had been taken up for repair a week before and not replaced. So water had to be carted to the engines from the next nearest plug (opposite the Chamber of Commerce) and the cistern at Cherry's Brewery. The obvious source of water was the river, but as luck would have it the tide was out, and the hose brought for the barrack engine could only be worked with difficulty.

|····|····|····|····|····|····|····|····|····|····|····|····|····|····|····|····|····|····|····|····|

So bright was the glare that in some parts of the city, as well as in Ferrybank and Newrath, even tiny objects were clearly visible. The blaze could be seen as far away as Hook Head by ships entering the estuary, one of which actually turned back to avoid being caught in what appeared to be a general conflagration. Next morning the passengers on the train leaving Carrick could also see the fire, as could the inhabitants of Tramore and Dunmore.

The damage to White's was enormous: the mill and most of the 1,700 barrels of corn in the stores were destroyed. Neighbouring premises were also destroyed. On the positive side, the demolition of adjoining walls prevented the spread of the fire. Although flaming brands threatened the shipping at The Quay, none caught fire, and these included several vessels laden with corn for White's. Above all, no lives were lost. By 7.30 on Sunday the fire had obviously done its worst and the crowds began to disperse.

Restored in recent years, White's Mills was the first home of Waterford Museum of Treasures; it now houses the Architecture Department of WIT and a restaurant.

The great fire at White's Mills took place in 1863 on this day.

Waterford would not have had fire fighting equipment such as that possessed by the Phoenix Insurance Company in London about that time.

MASTER MCGRATH AND
THE WATERLOO CUP

Whipper John Harney with Dicksy
as he was earlier called
Picture: Andrew Kelly

In the middle of the 19th century there lived at Colligan Lodge near Dungarvan a well-known owner and trainer of greyhounds named James Galwey. Around Christmas 1866 one of the bitches at Colligan gave birth to seven pups, the property of Lord Lurgan. Among them was a little black pup who was given the pet name of Dicksy. He grew up to be a friendly little lad who loved to play with the other dogs and to go for long walks with his handlers. He had a sleek black coat and was quite small, but he had powerful muscles and big feet, legs and shoulders.

Soon the time came for Dicksy to be given his first trial. It was a disaster. Dicksy did not seem to be greatly interested in the action. James Galwey, knew a loser when he saw one and ordered Dicksy's "slipper" – that's a man who lets a dog loose at the start of a race – to give him away as a pet.

Now the slipper, a man named McGrath, didn't like to see Dicksy spending the rest of his days as a fireside pet, and so although he pretended he had carried out the order he secretly kept the dog and continued to train him.

Soon afterwards there was a meeting at the Halfway not far from Dungarvan, and McGrath decided to enter Dicksy for it. He won – easily. His fame began to spread. Some time after that, Lord Lurgan held a big meeting at Brownlow House, his country seat in County Armagh, to which he invited all his friends to bring two of their best dogs. However, he lent his own two dogs out to friends, and McGrath the slipper was sent back to Dungarvan to fetch two more. He returned with a red dog and a black dog. The black dog took on all comers and won with ease. It was a sensational victory. James Galwey enquired who he was, and discovered to his astonishment that this was the once rejected Dicksy.

He now took him back Colligan and trained him in earnest. A week later, he was entered for another big race, and won easily. And in case you haven't already guessed, he had now been renamed after his slipper – Master McGrath.

| | | | | | | | | | | | | | |

The next big meeting of the year was the Waterloo Cup. This prestigious race had never been won by an Irish dog. Now Lord Lurgan pinned his hopes on the little black hound from Colligan. The best dogs in the world were against him, but he took them on. The whole of Ireland seemed to be there to cheer him. He won all his races, brought the Waterloo Cup back to Ireland, and Colligan celebrated for a week.

In the following year (1869) he won again. He ran again in 1870 and might have won, but when he was crossing a frozen stream the ice broke and he fell in. In 1871 he won the cup for the third time. He was now world famous, and was even invited to

Lord Lurgan and his great greyhound
Picture: Waterford County Museum

Buckingham Palace, where he was received by Queen Victoria and petted by all the royal family. The champion then returned to Brownlow, which was to be his home. But the following Christmas Eve he sickened and died at the age of five.

Two years after his death a limestone obelisk was erected to his memory at Colligan Lodge. It bears a marble plaque on which is a graceful sculpture in relief showing Master McGrath. In 1933 the monument was moved to its present site at the junction of the Clonmel and Cappoquin roads, where it is an eye-catcher for tourists. Today the morality or otherwise of open coursing is a matter of controversy. But a hundred years ago it was accepted without question, and the victories of Master McGrath brought lustre to the name of Ireland.

> *The hare she led on with a beautiful view*
> *And swift as the wind o'er the green field she flew*
> *But he jumped on her back and he held up his paw*
> *And "Three cheers for old Ireland!" says Master McGrath.*

He won the Waterloo Cup for the first time in 1868 – on this day.

JOHN EDWARD CAREW, SCULPTOR

Every day thousands of people pass through Trafalgar Square in London. Its monument to Lord Nelson is one of the most famous in the world. At the base of the column are four bronze bas-reliefs. The one on the side facing Whitehall depicts the death of Nelson on board *HMS Victory* in October 1805. This bronze is the work of County Waterford-born sculptor John Edward Carew.

It's virtually impossible to discover more than a few snippets of information about Carew's origins. When he died in 1868 he was said to be aged 86, and if this is correct then he must have been born about 1782. His birthplace is said to have been Tramore, but as the parish registers don't begin until the 1790s they can't help us. He is said to have been the son of a local stonecutter, and here at last we begin to strike lucky. For in the little country churchyard of Reisk is a beautifully carved headstone dated 1762, depicting the symbols of the Passion and signed "I. Carew fecit". And in St Patrick's graveyard in Waterford is the tomb of a John Carew who died in 1820 aged 76; the parish register confirms that he was a stonecutter. Could he have been the sculptor's father?

John Edward Carew is said to have trained in Dublin, but the RDS records don't mention him. A beautifully carved medallion in Fiddown Church, commemorating Rebecca Briscoe who died in 1798, *may* be his earliest work – it's too sophisticated to be the work of a local stonecutter. He was certainly in London by 1809, when he was a pupil of the sculptor Sir Richard Westmacott.

He must have been pretty talented. At first Westmacott paid him £5 or £6 a week, but by 1823 he was giving him £2,000 a year. By this time he had his own studio. He worked an eight hour day for Westmacott and in his spare time did private commissions which netted him a further £800 a year.

The turning point in his life came in 1823 when he was introduced to one of the great patrons of the arts, Lord Egremont, whose beautiful mansion at Petworth in Surrey was filled with the works of budding artists. For the next eight years Carew remained in London working for Egremont on a commission basis. He then moved his studio to Brighton.

|ıııı|ıııı|ıııı|ıııı|ıııı|ıııı|ıııı|ıııı|ıııı|ıııı|ıııı|ıııı|ıııı|ıııı|ıııı|ıııı|ıııı|ıııı|ıııı|ıııı|

In addition to churning out works to adorn the house, garden and parish church at Petworth, Carew worked for many other clients. In Chichester Cathedral you can see his statue of William Huskisson, famous as the first man to have been run over by a train. For two years he worked on the statue of Waterford-born Edmund Keane, whom he depicted as Hamlet contemplating the skull of Yorick; it took eleven horses to pull the block of marble down to Carew's studio in Brighton.

The year 1844 saw the production of his two best known works: the London Lord Mayor Sir Richard Whittington (that's Dick Whittington of cat fame) for a niche in the Royal Exchange, and the great Irish statesman Henry Grattan for St Stephen's Hall, Westminster. But his greatest work is surely his altar piece for the Catholic church of Our Lady and St Gregory in London, of which his biographer R.H.C. Finch wrote: "This is indeed a masterpiece. It seems to grow out of the very stone from which it is carved." It also brought him £1,100, a lot of money in 1853.

Carew's statue of Lord Mayor Dick Whittington at London's Royal Exchange

Carew's later years were troubled. After Lord Egremont's death he sued the estate for £50,000 which he said was due to him for commissions - he lost. Then in 1848 his eyesight began to fail and he no longer exhibited his work. Twenty years later he died a forgotten man – no obituary appeared in *The Times* or any art journal. "From obscurity he arose and to obscurity he returned." He died in 1868 – on this day.

Main source: R.H.C. Finch, "The Life and Work of J.E. Carew", Quarterly Bulletin of the Irish Georgian Society, IX, no. 3-4 (1966), pp 85-96.

JOHN WHEATLEY AND THE WHEATLEY HOUSES

Photo courtesy Copper Coast Geopark Limited

John Wheatley was born in Bunmahon in 1869, the eldest child of a labourer named Thomas Wheatley and his wife Johanna Ryan. The main source of employment locally was the copper mines, but their lifespan was rapidly coming to an end. The mines closed, and in 1876 the Wheatleys moved to Scotland in search of further mining work. Times were tough indeed. In his book *Mines, Miners and Misery* Wheatley described the grinding hardship of a childhood spent with his parents and seven siblings in a single-room miner's cottage without either drainage or its own water supply. At the age of eleven he joined his father in the local coal mine and worked underground for the next twelve years.

Meanwhile, he read, studied and deliberated. The first influence upon his development was his Irish Catholic background, and he became a local organiser for the Home Rule organisation, the United Irish League. His Catholic upbringing remained a lifelong influence, and as his political ideas developed he sought to fuse the Christian Socialist teachings of the time with involvement in the Independent Labour Party, which he joined in 1906.

|ıııı|ıııı|ıııı|ıııı|ıııı|ıııı|ıııı|ıııı|ıııı|ıııı|ıııı|ıııı|ıııı|ıııı|ıııı|ıııı|ıııı|ıııı|ıııı|ıııı|

Elected a local councillor in 1910, Wheatley played an active part in local politics. In 1914 he was one of only two of Glasgow's Labour councillors to oppose Britain's declaration of war on Germany. He also opposed conscription, and vigorously supported the more militant of Glasgow's socialist movements. At the end of the war, he failed by only 72 votes to obtain a seat at Westminster, but he was successful in 1922 and held the seat for Glasgow Shettleston until his death in 1930.

In January 1924 Britain's first Labour government took office under James Ramsay MacDonald. Wheatley was appointed Minister of Health. He immediately set about a major reform aimed at alleviating Britain's appalling housing shortage. This involved securing the co-operation of several vested interests – trade unions, building firms, local authorities – in a drive to secure for the poorer classes of society homes of a decent standard, built with adequate funding, and obtainable at a reasonable rent. For the next ten years a substantial proportion of all rented local authority housing in Britain was built under the terms of Wheatley's Housing (Financial Provisions) Act. Sixty years later, there were still people in Scotland who spoke of their "Wheatley houses".

The Labour government fell after only nine months in office; Wheatley's housing act was its only major achievement. In the years that followed, the Independent Labour Party became embroiled in bitter disputes with the official Labour Party, which moved further to the right under Ramsay MacDonald's leadership. Wheatley, controversial as always, never held office again, and died in 1930.

It's time he was honoured in Bunmahon, where he was born in 1869 – on this day.

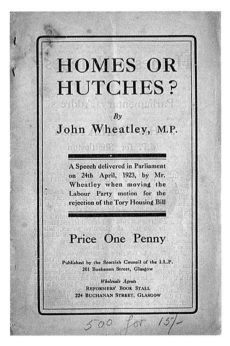

"LORD JOHN" POWER, CHAPLAIN AND BISHOP

John Power, future Bishop of Waterford and Lismore, was born in 1809 in the parish of Affane. He was educated in the diocesan seminary and was ordained priest in 1832. One of his early postings was to Clonmel, where as chaplain of the jail he found himself embroiled in a nasty incident that took place in 1848 - the execution of three murderers, the brothers Henry and Philip Cody for killing one Laurence Madden, and John Lonergan for shooting a landlord, Mr William Roe of Rockwell.

Hangings in those days were in public, and large crowds generally came to enjoy the horror of the occasion. The authorities seem to have expected trouble, for the scaffold was guarded by two companies of the 47th Regiment, while on the flank was a detachment of the 4th Light Dragoons.

The programme began with the appearance on the scaffold of the hangman, who proceeded (like any good workman) to test his equipment to see that it was functioning smoothly. First he examined the ropes, paying particular attention to the noose of each. Then he turned his attention to the trapdoors, and shot the bolts to make sure they were clear and free. When he proceeded to grease the ropes the crowd suddenly began to roar abuse, and he beat a hasty retreat back into the jail.

The next stage of the grisly ritual was the tolling of the prison bell, whereupon the spectators fell on their knees and began to pray. Through the doorway leading to the scaffold emerged the tall figure of Father John Power, clad in surplus and soutane and reciting in a loud voice the Office of the Dying. The prisoners and their escort came next, and the hangman began to prepare them for execution.

He first put the hood over Lonergan's head and the rope around his neck. Then came the elder Cody. He had just begun work on the younger Cody when the elder brother suddenly gave a scream of rage, leapt upon the hangman and began to beat him frantically with manacled hands. It was said afterwards that he thought (wrongly) that he was the informer who had betrayed them to the police. The younger brother tried to join in the fray but could not get the hood off his head, while the elder Cody tried to throw the hangman off the scaffold down into the crowd.

Father Power, appalled at the idea of launching into eternity two men whose hearts were filled with hate, attempted in vain to restrain them. Down below in the crowd, men shouted, women wept, and for several minutes the imposing ceremony designed to impress the lower orders was reduced to an undignified shambles. Eventually, however, the Codys were overpowered, the hangman rescued, the execution accomplished, and all returned home satisfied.

Father Power was deeply shaken by the event, which haunted him for the rest of his life. He was made Parish Priest of Powerstown in 1852 and of SS Peter and

|₁₁₁₁|₁₁₁₁|₁₁₁₁|₁₁₁₁|₁₁₁₁|₁₁₁₁|₁₁₁₁|₁₁₁₁|₁₁₁₁|₁₁₁₁|₁₁₁₁|₁₁₁₁|₁₁₁₁|₁₁₁₁|₁₁₁₁|₁₁₁₁|₁₁₁₁|₁₁₁₁|₁₁₁₁|₁₁₁₁|

Paul in 1866, and in 1873 became Bishop of Waterford and Lismore. He ruled the diocese for fourteen years, dying in 1887. Physically he was a remarkable man, the tallest priest in the diocese if not in all Ireland. He was also lean to the point of being skinny and his vestments hung off him as off a clothes-line. He spoke slowly and deliberately, choosing his words carefully. On account of his great height and impressive manner his priests nicknamed him "Lord John".

Bishop Power's most enduring legacy to the diocese was his beautification of the Cathedral. It was during his time that the present marble high altar and reredos were installed. Over the altar was built an elaborately decorated baldacchino – that's to say, a canopy of stone which is a giant version of the canopy borne over the Sacrament in religious processions. It was Bishop Power too who commissioned Goldie & Sons of London to design the magnificent baroque pulpit, chapter stalls and bishop's throne. The windows were reglazed with stained glass designed by the firms of Mayer of Munich and London. And, perhaps because he was nearer the ceiling than anyone else, Bishop Power had this

Photo: W Lawrence, Emerald Isle Album Series, Waterford City & County

elaborately decorated too. You can see the ornate painting on the ceiling in old photographs. Alas, it proved too costly to reproduce when the ceiling was given some urgently needed restoration in the 1930s.

John Power, the Lofty Lord, was consecrated Bishop in 1873 – on this day.

MICHAELANGELO HAYES AND THE GALLOPING HORSES

Bianconi's stagecoach network began at Clonmel and spread across the south of Ireland in the decades following the end of the Napoleonic Wars. The Waterford terminus was at what is now the Granville Hotel. In recent years there has been a great revival of interest in Bianconi, especially as a tourist plug. Over and over again you will see copies of four coloured aquatints depicting Bianconi's stagecoaches in different phases of operation. They are entitled "Car driving in the south of Ireland in the year 1836; Bianconi's establishment." The titles of the four pictures are: "Getting ready, Hearne's Hotel, Clonmel"; "Arriving at the end of a stage"; "On the road, at full pace"; and "Dropping a passenger." Not many people realize that they are the work of an important Waterford-born painter named Michaelangelo Hayes.

Hayes's father Edward was born in County Tipperary in 1797 and spent much of his early life in Waterford. Here he was taught drawing by Joseph Alpenny, whose water-colour portrait of him as a fifteen-year-old boy is in the National Gallery. In 1819 he married a local girl, and their first child was born in the following year. What more suitable name could be given to the son of a painter than – Michaelangelo? In 1830 Edward sent his first contributions to the Royal Hibernian Academy: a drawing of fruit, two landscapes in oil, and a self-portrait. Next year he and his family moved to Dublin, where he advertised in the newspapers as "Edward Hayes, miniature painter, late Professor of Drawing at the Abbeyleix Institute, the College of Kilkenny and the Ursuline College, Waterford". He died there in 1864 and was buried in Glasnevin.

Michaelangelo was taught to draw and paint by his father, and soon displayed an outstanding talent for depicting horses. His celebrated four aquatints of Bianconi's cars were done when he was only sixteen, and by the time he was seventeen he was exhibiting at the Royal Hibernian Academy. He painted races and fox-hunts, but 150 years ago horses were depicted at their most glamorous when thundering into battle, and Hayes made his reputation with military subjects that included cavalry – "The 16th Lancers breaking the square of Sikh infantry at the battle of Aliwal"; "The charge of the Light Dragoons at the battle of Moodkee"; "The heavy cavalry charge at Balaclava" – and so on.

Now, if you know anything about horses you'll realize that the traditional way of depicting them at full gallop is anatomically impossible. If horses really galloped with all four legs simultaneously extended, they'd fall flat on their bellies. Hayes understood this, and made a long study of how best to draw galloping horses. In 1876 he read a paper before the Royal Dublin Society entitled "The delineation of animals in rapid motion". When published as a pamphlet it achieved wide circulation and proved to be a landmark in the study of the subject.

Hayes became a full member of the Royal Hibernian Academy in 1854 and was elected its Secretary in 1856. At this time the poor old RHA was in quite a mess, its finances chaotic and its rules frequently ignored. Hayes set out to reform its ways, and within a short time he had made spectacular progress. But radical reforms generally produce a backlash from the die-hards, and within a year the RHA had performed a good old Irish split, resulting in two presidents, two secretaries (Hayes being one) and two committees. The undignified wrangling continued until 1860, when a new constitution was drawn up increasing the number of members from 14 to 20. Hayes was then re-elected secretary and held this post until he resigned in 1870.

On the last day of the year 1877 Hayes clambered up to the top of his house to investigate a fault in the water tank. He fell in and was drowned. He was buried, like his father, in Glasnevin.

Michaelangelo Hayes died in 1877 – on this day.

THE SHANBOGH AMBUSH

Thomas Boyd Esquire was Clerk of the Peace and Sessional Crown Solicitor of County Tipperary, through which he earned the comfortable salary of £900 a year, and he also had a large and lucrative private practice. In 1870 he purchased the estate of Shanbogh, in south-east Kilkenny, near Rosbercon, across the Barrow from New Ross. His seat was a house named Chilcomb Lodge. By 1880 he was proprietor of more than 1,800 acres, mostly in County Kilkenny but also in County Wexford (his brother was the doctor in Bannow).

Like many landlords who bought estates in the aftermath of the Famine, he was not prepared to stand idly by and let his tenants muddle along in time-honoured fashion, and his determination to bring a bit of efficiency to his affairs did not endear him to his tenants. It was a dangerous time to be an unpopular landlord, for the Land War was raging in the west of Ireland and agrarian outrages occurred all too frequently.

Boyd felt that some of his tenants were not paying enough rent, so he raised the rents accordingly. To offset the increase, he gave them an allowance of 25%, partly in lime and partly in seed. The predictable result was that he succeeded in antagonising simultaneously the tenants whose rents had been raised and those who hadn't got the allowance for lime and seed. The last straw was the eviction of a farmer named Holden, who owed 1½ years rent. Holden was allowed to remain in the house as caretaker, but Boyd put his own cattle on the farm.

It was Boyd's practice to drive out to this farm every Sunday after church. On Sunday 8 August he left Chilcomb Lodge later than usual, setting off in an outside car at about 4.15 p.m. He sat on the driving side of the car with his nephew Gladwell Boyd of Kilkenny, who was on a visit to Chilcomb. On the other side of the car sat his two sons, John Evans (who was in delicate health) and Charles.

The road from Ross to Waterford runs for some distance close by the side of the river and then branches off inland. As the party approached the farm at Shanbogh they noticed a woman standing on the ditch. As soon as she spotted them she waved a handkerchief, whereupon three men jumped over the fence and onto the road. They were masked and carried bayonet-mounted rifles. They had not, as you may have guessed, come to bid the family the time of day.

Two of them ran round to where Boyd's two sons were sitting and the third to the driving side of the car. The latter fired first at Boyd's nephew, but young Gladwell was quick off the mark and struck the rifle with his whip, diverting the attacker's aim. The effect of this deft manoeuvre was that the contents of the rifle were discharged into his uncle's side.

|᾿᾿᾿᾿|᾿᾿᾿᾿|᾿᾿᾿᾿|᾿᾿᾿᾿|᾿᾿᾿᾿|᾿᾿᾿᾿|᾿᾿᾿᾿|᾿᾿᾿᾿|᾿᾿᾿᾿|᾿᾿᾿᾿|᾿᾿᾿᾿|᾿᾿᾿᾿|᾿᾿᾿᾿|᾿᾿᾿᾿|᾿᾿᾿᾿|᾿᾿᾿᾿|᾿᾿᾿᾿|᾿᾿᾿᾿|᾿᾿᾿᾿|᾿᾿᾿᾿|᾿᾿᾿᾿|᾿᾿᾿᾿|

Meanwhile, the two assailants on the other side of the car had also fired. The one who had Evans Boyd as target was so determined not to miss that he practically stuck the bayonet into his victim's face. Evans, enterprising young man that he was, simply knocked it aside, receiving only a slight wound in the leg. Charles's attacker had better luck. When he fired, the bullet struck the youth a little below the heart, passed through the lung and out to the right of the spine, and hit his father lightly in the back.

Boyd seized the reins from Gladwell and drove off as fast as he could. Gladwell jumped down from the car and ran to the house for help. One of the attackers pursued him, hoping no doubt to make good use of his bayonet. But Gladwell had distinguished himself in many an athletic competition for his running powers and soon showed his assailant a clean pair of heels. As soon as the car arrived at Chilcomb, doctors were sent for, but they could do nothing for poor Charles Boyd, who died of his wound.

His murder shocked the south-east. However, the comment of the *Waterford News* is interesting: "If only Tom Boyd had adhered to his profession, and let land and tenants alone, this awful tragedy would have been averted, and he could have lived and died a happy and contented man. But he is not the first lawyer and townsman whose misfortunes sprang from mixing himself up with land."

The Shanbogh ambush took place in 1880 – on this day.

[Reported in Waterford News on Monday 9 August 1880]

THE *SOLITARY RAMBLES*
OF JOHN PALLISER

Life for the Victorian gentry was bound by a mass of stuffy conventions, and while most people fitted easily into the mould society had cast for them, some gentlemen – and ladies too – went to extraordinary lengths to assert their individuality. Exploration and big game hunting were two favourite methods of doing this, and among our local gentry few families could equal the exploits of the Pallisers of Derryluskan, County Tipperary, and Comeragh House, County Waterford.

Frederick Palliser emigrated to Ceylon, where he grew coffee and hunted big game. Wray Gledstanes (a relation) served in the Royal Navy and rescued a French lady from pirates in the China Seas. Edward joined the army and later worked on the Canadian Pacific Railway. Their sister married into the Fairholme family: her husband served in the Army and hunted on the prairies of the Missouri; one of his brothers travelled in Australia and another was lost on Sir John Franklin's expedition to find the North West Passage.

So it's hardly surprising that in 1847 we should find John Palliser of Comeragh House setting off on a long trip through the United States and the as yet unorganised Indian territory beyond the Mississippi. He found buffalo hunting "a noble sport" and had some exciting encounters with grizzly bears. He returned home by way of New Orleans, whence he dispatched to Ireland a menagerie consisting of two buffalo cows and two calves (which died of TB in the damp Irish climate), a brown bear, two Virginia deer, an antelope, and a half-wolf sleigh dog named Ishmah who had saved his master's life by huddling up to him one icy night so that man and beast kept each other from freezing by their body-heat. Alas, he took to harrying sheep and had to be sent off to a private zoo.

Palliser recorded his adventures in *Solitary Rambles and Adventures of a Hunter in the Prairies*. It became a best-seller.

His adventures served to whet his appetite. A few years later he suggested to the Royal Geographical Society that he should lead an expedition to explore the passes and plains on the Canadian side of the boundary between the British and American possessions. This boundary existed only as a long straight line on the map, and had never been surveyed or marked out. The Society was in favour of his plan, but felt that the expedition should be a scientific one and include observers and equipment. To this Palliser agreed, and the expedition set off across the Atlantic in 1857.

It was a resounding success. Palliser and/or his comrades travelled by canoe from Lake Superior to the site of modern Winnipeg, by boat from Hudson Bay to the North Saskatchewan River, from Winnipeg south to the 49th Parallel, and so westwards, zigzagging across the prairies and parklands of modern Manitoba,

Palliser in his Wild West hunting attire

Picture: Waterford County Museum

Saskatchewan and Alberta. They studied the semi-arid short-grass prairies which are now known as Palliser's Triangle. They reported on the Fertile Belt that lay between the triangle and the boreal forest to the north. They examined six hitherto unrecorded passes through the Rocky Mountains and two between the headwaters of the North and South Saskatchewan Rivers. They returned to Britain by the Pacific coast and the Panama isthmus.

In recognition of his exploits the Royal Geographical Society awarded Palliser its Patron's Gold Medal. He had many more adventures in different parts of the world, which he managed somehow to combine with his duties as a landlord at Comeragh House, where his household was increased by the addition of his widowed sister Grace Fairholme and her daughters, and by the wife and children of his brother Frederick, who had eloped with a ballet dancer. In later years he contented himself with striding over the Comeragh Mountains.

John Palliser – hunter, explorer, landowner and surrogate father – died in 1887 aged seventy and was buried in the little Church of Ireland Church nearby at Briska. Unfortunately, most of his family papers were destroyed when Comeragh House was burned by the IRA in 1923. He has been paid greater honour in North America, where he is credited with having opened up a new era of settlement and development. However, his warnings that "Palliser's Triangle" was unsuitable for agricultural development went unheeded, and the area was settled for farming; it took the storms and drought that led to the formation of the Dust Bowl in the 1930s to prove him right.

He died in 1887 – on this day.

Main source: Irene Spry, The Palliser expedition: an account of John Palliser's British and North American exploring expedition, 1857-1860. Toronto, Macmillan, 1973 (reissued 1995, 1999).

JASPER PYNE AND THE SIEGE OF LISFINNY

The ruined tower of Lisfinny Castle near Tallow was the scene in the late 19th century of an extraordinary siege. Its defender was Jasper Douglas Pyne, maverick member of a Protestant gentry family that had held lands in the Castlelyons area for 300 years. His father was the Rector of Oxted in Surrey; his brother was the squire of Ballyvolane House. But Jasper threw himself enthusiastically into the cause of radical Irish politics, and his great chance came with the inauguration of the Plan of Campaign in 1885.

In that year he refused to pay the rate levied by the Grand Jury. As a result his cattle were seized and brought for auction. They were accompanied by a large crowd, headed by Jasper, and by a band playing "See the conquering hero comes". Just before the auction he made a provocative speech, then paid the rate, and the cattle – now decked out with green ribbons – were driven back to Pyne's home at Lisfinny, still accompanied by the band.

The following October he was adopted as parliamentary candidate for West Waterford. At the general election which followed, he was returned with a large majority, and at the next election (the following year) he was returned unopposed. He proved to be an active member of the House of Commons, joining with gusto in the campaign of obstruction conducted by Parnell and his companions. Jasper contributed by tabling questions on such vital national issues as whether the safety matches supplied in the smoking-room of the House were the same as those supplied to other government departments.

Then in October 1887 came the eviction of tenants of Lord Waterford at Scrahan near Kilmacthomas. Jasper Pyne's speech on that occasion was so inflammatory that he was charged with incitement. Ignoring a summons to attend court, he withdrew in early November to Lisfinny Castle where, with supplies to last six months, he prepared himself for a siege.

The event was a source of great entertainment for the local populace and great embarrassment for the government. The police had been issued with a warrant for his arrest, but not for entry into his dwelling-house, and they wandered disconsolately beneath the castle walls. Jasper would chat to them jovially from the upper storeys. He received visits from friends who "not without trepidation" had to be hoisted up seventy feet by a windlass to reach the opening in the tower. About 5,000 electors presented him with 200 sovereigns as a token of their esteem.

Dublin Castle received many suggestions as to how Jasper could be got out of the castle. One disgruntled Londoner suggested using steam engines to flood the building. In the end, however, Jasper made his own arrangements. One Friday evening a herd of two hundred cattle was stampeded in the vicinity of the castle. The police rushed to deal with the bovine diversion, then suddenly spotted the figure of Jasper Pyne being lowered from one of the windows. Before he even reached the ground, the police overpowered him. However, it was not Jasper Pyne – only a dummy. Jasper had let himself down the other side of the tower and leapt into a waiting car that made off at a fast gallop for Cork. The telegraph wires at Tallow were cut, so the police could not raise

Jasper Pyne being lowered from his castle
inset shows delivery of daily paper
Picture: Waterford County Museum

the alarm. By the time the hue and cry had been raised, he had disappeared. Ah, politics just isn't the same these days.

The dramatic escape of Jasper Pyne was a gift to the media, and it was widely reported. A full account, complete with "authentic" illustration, appeared in the *Irish Penny Magazine,* to the amusement of the general public and the further embarrassment of the government. Local ballads were composed in his honour:

Where the Bride goes winding by
Pointing upwards to the sky
Stands Lisfinny Castle, ivied, grim and tall;
And within its storied tower
Pyne, the hero of the hour
Greets the friends or foes upon him that may call.

The following November, Jasper Pyne went on the Dublin mailboat to England but was not on board when the ship docked. Nor was he ever seen again.

Jasper Pyne made his escape from Lisfinny Castle in 1888 - on this day.

LOUISA, MARCHIONESS OF WATERFORD

Louisa Stuart was born in 1818 in Paris, where her father was the British Ambassador. She was the younger daughter of Sir Charles Stuart (Lord Stuart de Rothesay). When she was twelve years old the French had another revolution and she returned to England. Their home was at Highcliffe Castle on the south coast of Dorset, which Lord Stuart virtually rebuilt with the aid of his two talented young daughters. In 1835 the elder girl, Charlotte, was married to Charles Canning, who was later to become the first Viceroy of India. In the same year Louisa was presented at Court, where her stunning good looks attracted many admirers. Soon her beauty was the talk of London society, but Louisa just didn't seem to be fired by any of her suitors.

Then, in the autumn of 1839, she travelled to Scotland with her mother to attend the Eglinton Tournament. This extraordinary spectacle was a serious attempt by some young bloods of the day to revive the medieval sport of jousting. The first day's events were witnessed by a vast crowd of 100,000 spectators, despite a heavy and continuous downpour of rain and a thunderstorm.

Among the contestants was "the Knight of the Dragon", in real life Henry third Marquess of Waterford, then aged twenty-eight, immensely rich, a superb horseman and well known for his wild exploits. The moment he met Louisa, he lost his heart to her. And now an extraordinary thing happened. For the mad marquess, the man who had jumped his horse over a five-barred gate in the middle of a drawing-room, was too shy to propose for the hand of Louisa Stuart.

Eventually he persuaded his sister to write to Louisa's mother. "I have had the most extraordinary letter from Lady Sarah Ingestre," said Lady Stuart one day. "It is a proposal for you from her brother, and of course I must lose no time in writing a refusal." But to her utter astonishment, Louisa replied: "Oh, but – wait a little. I should like to think about it first." Three years later Henry and Louisa were married in the Royal Chapel of Whitehall by the Archbishop of Armagh, who conveniently happened to be Lord Waterford's uncle.

Ten days after the wedding the happy couple arrived at Curraghmore, where they were given a tumultuous welcome by the tenantry and employees. Their period of married bliss was all too short. Just one week after their arrival, Louisa was being driven by her husband in a phaeton[2] pulled by two horses, when they took fright and turned the carriage over. She was unconscious for three days, and although she made a complete recovery she was never able to bear children.

Curraghmore must have been quite a shambles after years of rule by the "mad marquess", and Louisa soon threw all her energies into reorganising the house, gardens and estate. Over 600 people were employed at Curraghmore, and Louisa devoted herself to their welfare. New cottages were built and old ones improved, trees were planted, schools were built and a clothing factory established. During the Famine Henry and Louisa worked tirelessly to alleviate the sufferings of the local people. A woman of great piety, Louisa built two new Church of Ireland churches (at Portlaw and Guilcagh), and did her best to cheer up the dreary Protestant services of the time by designing stained glass windows and training the congregations to sing hymns.

In 1859 Louisa's husband was tragically killed in a hunting accident. Curraghmore passed to his brother, but Louisa received as her jointure the huge estate of Ford in Northumberland which the Beresfords had inherited through their marriage with the Delaval family. Curraghmore's loss was Ford's gain. For over thirty years Louisa devoted herself to beautifying and improving the castle and village. Inevitably she built a new school, and she decorated the walls with huge panels depicting stories from the Bible. She herself was the artist, and the models were the schoolchildren and the people of the village and estate. Today that school is the Lady Waterford Hall; it is a veritable portrait gallery of the villagers of Ford in the 1860s and '70s.

Louisa Waterford died in 1891 – on this day.

---

2 A fast and rather dangerous open carriage with four large wheels. It is named after Phaeton, who in ancient Greek mythology drove the chariot of the sun so recklessly that he nearly set fire to the earth!

HARRY POWER, BUSHRANGER

Harry Power was born in Waterford. He grew up to be a tall, well-built fellow, almost six feet in height. In 1841 he was convicted of an appalling crime – the theft of a pair of shoes. His punishment was to be transported to Australia for seven years. He served out his sentence in Van Diemen's Land, and in 1848 obtained his certificate of freedom. With a convict's record, it was hard to make a fresh start, so he moved to another district and assumed the surname of Johnson. For a time he worked as a horse-dealer, but soon he was enticed by the lure of the goldfields. Those who struck it rich were the lucky few, and Harry was not one of them. For the many who failed, life had little to offer but to take to the bush and live by plundering and murdering.

In March 1855 Harry was stopped by the police on suspicion of being a horse thief. There was little love lost between the ex-convicts and the police, and when impertinent questions were asked about the ownership of the horse he was riding Harry's response was less than polite. In the ensuing scuffle one of the police was wounded. Harry's penalty was 14 years hard labour on the roads. After two and a half years of this work he was transferred to the Pentridge stockade, where conditions were even grimmer. This was too much to endure, and Harry managed to escape. Resuming his old name of Power, he took to the life of a bushranger, robbing coaches and homesteads. Soon there was a price on his head of £500, dead or alive.

A few years later, several of Harry's victims reported that he was now working with a partner, a well-built youth who spied out the land, held his horse, covered his back, and so on. Obviously Harry, who by now was no spring chicken, had decided to train an apprentice. In May 1859 the police arrested a young man and charged him with two counts of robbery under arms. He was identified as Harry Power's partner. He was all of fourteen years old, and he was destined to become the most notorious bushranger of all. His name was Ned Kelly.

Meanwhile, Harry's nefarious activities continued unabated. As many as six hundred robberies per year were attributed to him, and the reward of £500 continued unclaimed. His conduct towards his victims was invariably courteous, and he prided himself on never aiming a gun at them. For a time he operated in New South Wales, but then returned to Victoria, judging that this state offered a more acceptable combination of secure conditions of employment and favourable opportunities for expanding his commercial activities. He felt safe, too, in the vicinity of Ned Kelly's home. His confidence was mistaken. On the night of 5 June 1870 he was surprised in his hideout by Sergeant Monford of the State

Police, aided by a native tracker, and arrested. The reward for his capture was collected by a certain Jack Lloyd, uncle of Ned Kelly.

Harry was again returned to the Pentridge stockade, this time with a sentence of fifteen years hard labour ahead of him. However, his daredevil exploits and chivalrous behaviour had brought him widespread fame through the columns of the *Argus* newspaper, and when after a few years his health broke down there were hundreds of appeals to the governor for his release. In 1877 Harry was a free man once again.

Harry Power, Waterford-born bushranger *extraordinaire*, died by accidentally drowning in the Murray River in 1891 – on this day.

Dave Moore

WILLIAM CHARLES BONAPARTE-WYSE

William Charles Bonaparte-Wyse was born in Waterford in 1826. He was the younger son of a couple whose married life was the talk of the town. His father, Sir Thomas Wyse of the Manor of St John's, was the election agent of Henry Villiers-Stuart in the famous Beresford-Stuart contest of that year. He had a prominent career as a politician ahead of him, but he really deserves to be remembered for his role in setting up the national school system. William Charles's mother, the tempestuous Princess Letitia Bonaparte, was Napoleon's niece.

When he was only two his parents separated, Letitia departing dramatically and leaving the children to the custody of their father. They were brought up by their aunt Mrs George Wyse in company with her own children, and were then sent to boarding school in England.

William Charles's childhood continued to be stormy. His first school, Prior Park near Bath, burned down. At the age of eleven he joined his elder brother Napoleon at Oscott College near Birmingham. Nappo ran away more than once and William Charles was frequently in trouble. On one occasion he and another boy kidnapped some of the sheep that grazed in the college grounds and drove them up the steep and twisty stairs of the building onto the flat roof. The astonished staff gazed up at the woolly faces staring over the parapet, and the sheep looked down in equal bewilderment. You can imagine the difficulty of getting them down the stairs again.

But that was not the end of the matter. Many years later, William Charles told the story to the French writer Alphonse Daudet, who used it as the basis for "La mule du Pape" (the Pope's mule), one of the stories in his most famous work *Lettres de mon Moulin*.

At the age of eighteen William Charles left Oscott with the reputation of being an enthusiastic debater, a writer of excruciatingly bad poetry, and the perpetrator of some unusual practical jokes. He spent the next fifteen years travelling in England, Ireland and on the continent, and writing more poetry. Then in 1859 he visited for the first time the district of Provence in the south of France. Immediately he felt a deep affection for the place, its people, and its culture – above all, its language.

Provençal had been the language of the medieval troubadours, but it had now sunk to the status of a despised peasant *patois*. However, a dynamic literary group, the *Félibrige*, led by the poet Frédéric Mistral, aimed at the preservation and purification of the language and the renaissance of its literature. When William Charles arrived at Avignon he read Mistral's work and met the author at his home of Maillane on Christmas Day 1859. It changed his life. He now immersed himself in Provençal culture and began to write poetry in the language himself.

And the incredible happened. The man whose verses in English were at best mediocre proved to be a gifted poet in his adopted language. He became a member of the *Félibrige* and a close friend of Mistral. He visited Spain and encouraged the revival of the Catalan language. He was also a friend of one of the finest French poets of the time, Stéphane Mallarmé.

William Charles spent much time in England, and also in Waterford, where he stayed with his eccentric brother Nappo in the Manor of St John's. His detailed impressions of people and places are recorded in the raciest terms in his journals. In 1864 he married Ellen Linzee Prout, a member of a Cornish family. They had four sons, three of whom died childless. The fourth was Andrew Bonaparte-Wyse, Permanent Secretary of the Minister of Education in Northern Ireland during the 1920s and 1930s. Not many people know that in its formative years the head of the department of Education in the Six Counties was a Catholic – indeed, a Knight of Malta, forsooth.

His father, William Charles Bonaparte-Wyse, died in Cannes in 1892 – on this day.

THE FIRE AT BALLINAMONA

|␣␣␣|␣␣␣|␣␣␣|␣␣␣|␣␣␣|␣␣␣|␣␣␣|␣␣␣|␣␣␣|␣␣␣|␣␣␣|␣␣␣|␣␣␣|␣␣␣|␣␣␣|␣␣␣|␣␣␣|␣␣␣|␣␣␣|␣␣␣|␣␣␣|␣␣␣|␣␣␣|

For 300 years, down to the death of Major Robin Carew in 1982, Ballinamona Park was the seat of the Carew family. The founder of the family acquired it through marriage with one of the three daughters and co-heiresses of a land speculator named Andrew Lynn. His descendants divided into two main branches, one at Ballinamona and the other at Castle Boro in County Wexford. The head of the Wexford branch was created Lord Carew in 1834. Throughout the 18th century the Carews controlled one of the gentlemanly local factions that passed for political parties in Georgian Ireland. They, the Congreves, Christmases, Alcocks, Boltons and Newports jockeyed to control Waterford Corporation and to nominate those who would represent it in the Dublin parliament. The Municipal Reform Act of 1840 eventually swept the whole lot of them from power for ever.

Ballinamona Park was a fitting base for a family that aspired to political power. Our first county historian, Charles Smith, described it in 1746 as a well-built house, adding: "The improvements which are carrying on are designed in a good taste. On the east side of the house is a handsome canal, and about it are considerable plantations, gardens etc. On a commanding hill in the deerpark is a handsome turret, that affords a prospect of part of Tramore Bay."

Ballinamona Park before the fire of 1894. When it was rebuilt, it had just two storeys.

The house comprised a three-story block over a basement. The farm buildings, a discreet distance away, include barns with massive stone pillars carrying their roofs. In 1866 two wings were added to the central block, one containing the billiard room and office, the other the men-servants' quarters.

The worst enemy of such old country houses is fire. On 10 November 1894 the Waterford News reported in the colourful style of the time: "We deeply regret to record that a destructive fire broke out at an early hour this morning at Ballinamona, the residence of Captain R.T. Carew. The entire mansion, with the exception of the wings, was completely destroyed, together with a large quantity of furniture, as well as the jewellery of Mrs Carew and other valuable property.

"The alarm was first given at the Manor Barrack between four and five o'clock, when that energetic police officer, Head Constable Clear, at once dispatched the intelligence to the District Inspector, Mr Somerville, and the police at the other stations, as well as the military. In a very short time all the available police and the military, to the number of about fifty, were on the spot, and through their exertions, energetically assisted by the villagers and neighbours, the fire was got under, but not till the mansion, which has existed for several centuries, was almost completely destroyed. The amount of the damage, which is very considerable, cannot be correctly estimated at present. Much sympathy is felt for Captain Carew and his estimable lady, who are deservedly esteemed by all who know them."

Actually, it was only the central block that was consumed; the wings survived. Robert Dobbyn the solicitor, who did not like the Carews, wrote in his diary: "Ballinamona House, the residence of Robert Thomas Carew, burned down accidentally. Insured with Alliance Co., but no one cared bar a few of the flunkey brigade. [i.e., hangers-on of the aristocracy]. Mr and Mrs Carew a hungry pair and very snuffy."

However, the house was rebuilt on a smaller and more manageable scale, and soon recovered from the fire that devastated it in 1894 – on this day.

THE BATTLE OF COLENSO

In December 1899 the British public, fed for years on imperialistic jingoism, was shocked out of its complacency by news of a series of dramatic defeats inflicted on their mighty army by the amateur forces of the tiny Boer republics in South Africa. The government needed to send out some great leader who would rally morale and save the day. They chose a tiny 67-year-old man with a white moustache, who was living in virtual retirement as Governor of the Royal Hospital, Kilmainham. His military record was impressive, his prestige enormous. He belonged to the old Waterford family of Roberts, and was known affectionately to the public as Bobs. Field Marshal Lord Roberts set out to assume overall command in South Africa amid tumultuous acclaim, but also under a deep personal cloud. For the news had arrived that his only son had been killed at the battle of Colenso.

Fred Roberts was a 26-year-old lieutenant in the King's Royal Rifle Corps who had distinguished himself in action on the North-West Frontier of India. At Colenso, two horse-drawn gun batteries foolishly dashed forward far in advance of their flank supports to open fire on a strongly entrenched and virtually invisible enemy. Running short of ammunition and without shelter of any kind, they soon found themselves the object of a fearful storm of bullets and shells from the expert Boer marksmen. The horses were torn to pieces, the gunners strewn on the ground around the guns. One was later found with 64 wounds in his body. The few survivors abandoned the guns, while their nearest comrades, including Fred Roberts, watched helplessly from their position 500 yards to the rear. However, as Colonel Long was being removed from the gun beside which he had fallen, he shouted: "Abandon be damned – we don't abandon guns!" General Buller called for volunteers to go out and rescue the guns. Roberts was one of those who stepped forward. He was mortally wounded in trying to save one of the guns.

"I have never seen," wrote one survivor, "even at field firing, the bullets fly thicker. All one could see was little tufts of dust all over the ground, a whistling noise – phux! – where they hit – and an increasing rattle of musketry some-where in front." Captain Walter Congreve, another volunteer who lived to tell the tale, went forward with a team of horses and a limber (the part of a gun carriage used for ammunition boxes), and succeeded in hooking them to one of the guns. Being wounded, he took shelter, but on seeing Roberts fall badly wounded he went out and brought him in. In the process he was shot through the leg and the toe of his boot and grazed on the elbow and shoulder, while his horse shot in three places.

Four Victoria Crosses, Britain's highest medal for bravery, were awarded for this action. Congreve got one, and so did Roberts, but in his case it was posthumous, for he died of his wounds two days after the battle. The old field marshal must have been very proud of his son, especially as he too had won the VC back in 1858 as a lieutenant during the Indian Mutiny. By a strange coincidence, all three cases of a father and son both winning the VC (Roberts, Congreve and Gough) have Waterford connections. Walter Congreve was a cousin of our Mount Con-greve family, and the Goughs came from Rathronan near Clonmel.

Two VCs were awarded for the same action during the battle of Colenso, which took place in 1899 – on this day.

OSCAR WILDE: THE DUNGARVAN LINK

On this day in 1900 the civilized world celebrated the 150th anniversary of the birth of Oscar Wilde. One of the striking features of his first court appearance in 1895 was the vigour with which he was attacked by Lord Queensberry's counsel Edward Carson, subsequently the great Unionist leader. It need not have been so. Wilde and Carson were fellow Dubliners who had been students together at Portora and Trinity College. Wilde's friends suggested that he should enlist the able Carson as his lawyer, but Wilde airily declined, choosing instead a chivalrous old incompetent who knew nothing of the sexual underworld in which Wilde dabbled. Carson was promptly snapped up by Queensberry, "college loyalty faded before Protestant morality", and Wilde was summarily demolished in the witness-box.

But there was more to the Carson-Wilde relationship than that. In 1954, at the centenary of Wilde's birth, an elderly solicitor named Morroe FitzGerald wrote a letter to *The Irish Times* from Westpark on Church Road, Tramore (I knew the house well just before that time – it was then owned by the Doupe family, and Bob Doupe taught Art at Newtown; I often played there as a small boy). The writer recalled that in 1919 he had prepared an old-age pension claim for a 75-year-old woman from Dungarvan, "a little wizened creature, but very alert ..... The only sign of advanced age was an extraordinary network of fine wrinkles which covered the skin of her face like a crackling on old china".

As evidence of her age, this lady announced that in 1859, when she was fifteen, she had been employed as children's nurse by Oscar Wilde's mother. For in that year the Wilde family began coming to Dungarvan for several months' holiday every summer. Oscar was then about five years old and was accompanied by his little playmate – Edward Carson.

When Mícheál Mac Liammóir read this letter in *The Irish Times*, he commented: "Ah yes, dear boy, that would explain it all. Oscar probably upset Edward's sandcastle."

The old lady, incidentally, "survived the close cross-questioning of the Waterford Old Age Pension Committee" and got her pension.

Oscar Wilde died in 1900 – on this day.

Sources: Richard Ellmann, Oscar Wilde (London, 1987), esp. pp 18, 414-15, 557. Letter to Irish Times, 28 Aug. 1954.

THE 1900s

IOMPAR A MHÁLA –
THE BAG CARRIER

There's an old fence in the parish of Dunhill, a boundary between three townlands – Dunhill, Ballyphilip and the High Place of the River. There is a stream running by the side of it, and there is terrible damage when this stream floods. It was during a flood that the "Bag Carrier" – Iompar a' Mhála - was drowned. His ghost used to be seen there at night, and fear prevented anyone from travelling there after nightfall.

Now, there was a farmer in the area and a scoláire bocht – a poor student - would come to his house at various times to teach his children. He used come to the house by crossing the haunted river. One night the farmer bet the poor student a pound that he would not go back across that river. "It's a bet," said the student.

It was a beautiful moonlit night. Down went the poor student to the fence of the three boundaries, while the farmer and his sons watched from afar. The student crossed the river, but who was standing on a stone in front of him but the Bag Carrier. The farmer and his sons saw the spirit and off they took as fast as their legs could move the earth underneath them.

"In ainm Dé," said the student to the Carrier, "cad an bhfuil tú ag déanamh annso?"[1]

"It is a long time I'm here," said the spirit, "and no one has ever had the courage to speak to me, but there's an end to the penance. Come with me now and I'll show you something that will do you good."

The Carrier brought him to a stile in the fence. Up they went onto the path at the top of the fence and in they went to Ballyphilip hill.

"Put a stick in there," said the Carrier to him, and his finger pointing at a certain sod on the side of the hill. "Dig that place and you'll find a crock of gold. But you don't need to spend any of it on me because I'm damned. When I was drowning and the stone went from under my foot, what I said was 'M'anam ag an diabhal' instead of 'M'anam ón diabhal':[2] that's a mistake I made and I'm paying for it dearly."

That same night the student got a pike and a shovel and started to dig where he was shown. And sure enough the crock of gold was there. The following day, what he did was go to the parish priest in Dunhill to say Mass on a certain Sunday for the soul of the Bag Carrier. After that he went around to every priest in the area and gave them money for the same cause. All the Masses were to be said on the same Sunday. He stayed going around from priest to priest until all the money was spent.

---

1 "In the Name of God, what are you doing here?"
2 "My soul *to* the Devil" instead of "My soul *from* the Devil."

|ᴵᴵᴵᴵ|ᴵᴵᴵᴵ|ᴵᴵᴵᴵ|ᴵᴵᴵᴵ|ᴵᴵᴵᴵ|ᴵᴵᴵᴵ|ᴵᴵᴵᴵ|ᴵᴵᴵᴵ|ᴵᴵᴵᴵ|ᴵᴵᴵᴵ|ᴵᴵᴵᴵ|ᴵᴵᴵᴵ|ᴵᴵᴵᴵ|ᴵᴵᴵᴵ|ᴵᴵᴵᴵ|ᴵᴵᴵᴵ|ᴵᴵᴵᴵ|ᴵᴵᴵᴵ|ᴵᴵᴵᴵ|ᴵᴵᴵᴵ|

When that was done, he made his way back home. It was a stormy night and he crossing the path where there is a bridge on the road between Fenor and Bally-adam. There was no bridge there that time but a path. Going over the path, what did he see under the fence but a man and a poor appearance on him.

"In ainm Dé," said the scoláire bocht, "what brought you out on such a night?"

"Six children I've left at home behind me," said the man, "and they shouting with the hunger. I could get no patience in listening to them. I had to go and see if I could get them something to eat some way or another."

"I only have one sovereign left," said the student. "Here, you take it, and say a prayer for the man who drowned in the stream at the fence of the three bounda-ries. And another thing, there will be Mass said for him in every church in the diocese tomorrow morning."

The poor man went down on his knees in the water on the path and said a prayer to God for the dead.

There was an old thatched roof church in Fenor at the time, situated where Mrs. Cheasty has the little wood today. When the priest turned to the congrega-tion at the final prayer, he announced that Mass that morning was for the soul of the Bag Carrier. While he was talking, a white crow flew in the door and up on the altar he went.

"Are you the soul of the Bag Carrier?" asked the priest.

"I am," said the white crow.

"Did I free you?" asked the priest.

"You did not," said the crow.

"Then who was it freed you?" asked the priest.

"It was the man that went down on his knees in the water on the path in Fenor last night," said the crow. "From his heart came the prayer that saved me."

Main source: Based on a story in the collection of the Folklore Department of University College, Dublin. It was written in Irish by Maurice Lacy, school teacher, Fenor, who had heard it from Martin Farrell of Fenor. My thanks to Máiréad Murphy of Dunhill, from whom I heard the story and who translated it for me.

WATERFORD AND THE ULSTER BANK

Premises leased by Ulster Bank in 1902
Photo: W Lawrence, Emerald Isle Album Series, Waterford City & County

The Ulster Banking Co. was founded by local merchants in Belfast in 1836. From the outset it issued its own banknotes and embarked upon a strategy of opening branches in the principal towns throughout Ulster. A number of branches began trading over the next two decades, and from 1850 the bank's first offices were opened beyond the province of Ulster, including a branch in Dublin in 1862.

A conviction that the establishment of new branch banks held out the promise of ever expanding profitability soon prompted Ulster Bank to extend its presence not only into the suburbs of Belfast and into Leinster but also further south. Most notably, the Bank made a determined push into the province of Munster by opening, in close succession, branches in Waterford, Cork and Limerick. Four other major banks were already trading in Waterford when Ulster Bank opened for business on 9 July 1902, having leased premises on the corner of the Mall and Lombard Street, next to the Imperial Hotel.

By the end of 1920 Ulster Bank had a grand total of 120 branches in operation, making it a powerful force in Irish banking. The years that followed, however, were a time of great instability all over Ireland due to the struggle for independence. The establishment of the Irish Free State brought tremendous political and civil unrest in its wake. The boycott in the state of banks and other businesses with head offices in Belfast caused problems, and many of Ulster Bank's branches were also subject to armed raids. The Waterford branch was itself raided in 1922. Gradually, however, the country returned to normal conditions.

In 1917 the Bank purchased three dwelling-houses and shops at 97, 98 and 99 The Quay with a view to erecting, in time, a purpose-built banking house to accommodate the expanding business. Appropriately, this had been the site of the City Exchange, erected in 1715. Plans for the new building were well in hand by 1927, although expenditure on it was cut back due to the prevailing economic depression. Nonetheless, the new branch, occupying a corner site overlooking the river Suir, was a handsome red-brick structure with a stone-faced ground floor frontage and some stone detailing on the upper stories. The business of the branch transferred to the new premises on 8 November 1932. The prestigious new building reflected the bank's rising profile within the local community. It is now protected by a listed status.

Ulster Bank arrived in Waterford in 1902 – on this day.

Buildings that were demolished to make way for new bank offices that opened in 1932
Photo: Poole Collection, National Library

LITTLE NELLIE OF HOLY GOD

"Dat ol'-time religion" as practised in this country undoubtedly had much of which we should be ashamed – bigotry, intolerance, blind adherence to a myriad trivial rules at the cost of neglecting the really important spiritual and moral issues. But there was also a simple faith that kept people in touch with the divine in their everyday lives.

In the early years of the last century William Organ or Arrigan, a native of Dungarvan, was a soldier in the Royal Artillery, then stationed at Waterford. He was married to a Portlaw girl named Mary Aherne, and they already had three children. Then in August 1903 Mary gave birth to a fourth child, Nellie Organ, born in one of the houses belonging to the Artillery Barracks. The infant was baptized in Ballybricken Church.

Regiments in the British Army were frequently transferred to different parts of the United Kingdom and its empire, and when Nellie was two years old the Royal Artillery was posted to Spike Island in Cork Harbour. Here her mother's health rapidly deteriorated, and in January 1907 she was carried off by the scourge of Ireland – tuberculosis. What was Nellie's father to do? His duties as a soldier would allow him but little time to care for his children, and the eldest child was still too young to be put in charge of them. A widowed father in those days often had little choice in the matter: if he couldn't look after his children himself, they must be sent to an orphanage.

Nellie and her sister were sent to the Industrial School at Sunday's Well in Cork run by the Good Shepherd Sisters. Soon it was discovered that she too was suffering from TB and also from curvature of the spine; obviously, she had not long to live. However, as her frail body wasted away, an astonishing change took place in her mental and spiritual development. When she entered the orphanage she was only 3 ½, yet her understanding of the nature of God and her sense of a divine presence surpassed that of most adults. As she lay on her sickbed she spent long hours talking, as she insisted, to Holy God, and with a child's cheerful innocence she told the nuns all about the conversations they had between them. The attitude of the sisters changed from irritation and scorn to curiosity and then awe. All who visited her left with the impression that they had been in the presence of unusual sanctity. Soon Nellie's reputation began to spread beyond the convent walls.

|᠁|᠁|᠁|᠁|᠁|᠁|᠁|᠁|᠁|᠁|᠁|᠁|᠁|᠁|᠁|᠁|

Nellie longed for her communion with God to be a physical one, but at that time even children far older than Nellie were discouraged from receiving the Sacrament, and it was unheard of for a child as young as her to be given the Host. However, her continual begging, and the fact that she had obviously not long to live, had the desired effect. Permission had to be sought from the Bishop of Cork, but it was obtained, and Nellie received her first Holy Communion at the age of 4½.

Nellie died on 2 February 1908 and was buried in the public cemetery of St Joseph, where her grave became a shrine visited by many, who found there peace and consolation. About a year and a half later, her body was transferred to the convent cemetery at Sunday's Well. When disinterred, it was found to be intact, her fingers quite flexible and her clothes exactly as they were on the day of her death. You can believe it or not, as you will; those who witnessed it have stated what they saw.

The Pope, Pius X, was then in the middle of a misguided crusade to crack down on intellectuals within the Church. But he was also a man of intense piety with a love of children and a special devotion to the Eucharist. The brief career of Nellie Organ profoundly moved him, and was a strong influence on his decision to encourage children to make their Communion early and often.

On the Feast of the Immaculate Conception in 1984 a memorial to Nellie in Ballybricken Church, where she had been baptized, was blessed by Bishop Russell.

At the centenary of her birth in 2003, an exhibition of artifacts associated with her life was mounted in Dungarvan Museum. Visitors came by the coachload to wonder and to pray. So perhaps modern Ireland has not entirely (so to speak) thrown out the toddler with the bath-water.

Little Nellie of Holy God was born in Waterford in 1903 - on this day.

E.T.S. WALTON AND
THE SPLITTING OF THE ATOM

Ernest Walton (no relation of mine, though by coincidence my father was also named Ernest) was born on 6 October 1903 in a thatched house named Epworth Cottage at Strandside South, Abbeyside, Dungarvan. His father, the Rev. Arthur John Walton, came from Cloughjordan in Tipperary and was an ardent home ruler. His mother, Anna Elizabeth Sinton, came from Richill in Armagh. At that time Dungarvan had a sizeable Methodist community, with its own church in Friary St. (subsequently part of Shaw's) and Walton senior had come to the town as its minister. It was the custom for ministers not to remain long in any one place, and in July 1904, after three years in Dungarvan, Rev. John Walton moved to Rathkeale in Limerick, and thence to Ulster, where he remained.

As was to be expected, Ernest went to school at "Methody" – the Methodist College, Belfast. He was a bright lad, and in 1922 won an Armagh County Scholarship to Trinity College, Dublin. He arrived at a troubled time – on the day of the entrance exam there were no trains to Dublin owing to the outbreak of the Civil War. He graduated in Physics and Maths in 1926, and in 1927 transferred to Cambridge to work on his Ph.D. For the next seven years he studied with Ernest Rutherford, the father of nuclear science, who had won the Nobel Prize for Chemistry in 1908.

For ten years Rutherford had been furiously engaged on a project to split the atom. He used streams of fast alpha particles from radioactive radium to bombard nitrogen atoms, and succeeded in producing transmutation into oxygen. The problem was that only one particle in 100,000 hit the target, and no other type of bombarding particle was available.

Walton and his colleague John Cockcroft set out to make a particle accelerator. Their equipment was somewhat primitive, to put it mildly. It included bicycle crossbars, plasticine, biscuit tins, sugar crates and other junk. The accelerator consisted of two glass towers made from petrol pump cylinders. One tower produced some 400,000 electron volts to speed up the hydrogen protons which were shot down the other tube. The equipment was set up in a disused lecture hall, where scraps of lead nailed to a packing crate served to protect the scientists from electrocution or radiation.

At Cavendish Laboratory, Cambridge, on 14 April 1932 the scientists sent an electrical charge down the accelerator to hit a piece of lithium. A fluorescent screen under a microscope monitored the debris thrown out. The particles hitting the screen, Walton said, were "like stars suddenly appearing and disappearing". They were in fact alpha particles from disintegrating atoms. The world would never be the same again.

|ɪ ɪ ɪ ɪ|ɪ ɪ ɪ ɪ|ɪ ɪ ɪ ɪ|ɪ ɪ ɪ ɪ|ɪ ɪ ɪ ɪ|ɪ ɪ ɪ ɪ|ɪ ɪ ɪ ɪ|ɪ ɪ ɪ ɪ|ɪ ɪ ɪ ɪ|ɪ ɪ ɪ ɪ|ɪ ɪ ɪ ɪ|ɪ ɪ ɪ ɪ|ɪ ɪ ɪ ɪ|

During World War Two, Cockcroft organized atomic energy research in Canada. Walton returned to Ireland and became Professor of Physics at Trinity College, Dublin. Towards the end of the war he received a pressing invitation from a senior British scientist to join an unidentified military project. The college said he could not be spared. The work in which he had been asked to join turned out to be the Manhattan Project – the making of the atom bomb. Walton, a peace-loving and religious man, was later relieved that he had not had to make that decision.

In November 1951 the Swedish Royal Academy of Sciences awarded the Nobel Prize for Physics jointly to Walton and Cockcroft. So far, it has been the only occasion on which a Nobel Prize in a scientific subject has been won by an Irishman. In 1957 he was a co-founder, and later President, of the Pugwash Conference, a group of distinguished scientists whose aim is to put pressure on governments to avoid using nuclear power for warlike purposes. Named after the town in Nova Scotia where they first met, they took as their motto the words of Bertrand Russell and Albert Einstein: "Here then is the problem which we present to you – stark and dreadful and inescapable. Shall we put an end to the human race – or shall mankind renounce war?" In 1995, the fiftieth anniversary of the dropping of the first atom bombs and the year in which Walton died, the Pugwash Conference was awarded the Nobel Peace Prize.

In his old age Walton lived in retirement in Dublin. In November 1989 he was given a civic reception in his native town, and the Causeway Park was named in his honour.

In 2004 a plaque was erected on the house in Abbeyside where Ernest Walton was born in 1903 – on this day.

Ernest Walton in Dungarvan 1989
Photo: Waterford County Museum

Because the knowledge of how to construct nuclear weapons cannot be erased from human memory, and because, in the extremity of war, nations that previously forswore them may race to produce them anew, it will be necessary to eliminate war itself as a means of resolving disputes among nations.
Hiroshima Declaration, Pugwash Conference, 1995

PATRICK LAFCADIO HEARN

One of the few historic links between this country and Japan is provided by the career of Patrick Lafcadio Hearn. This extraordinary man was half Irish (hence Patrick) and half Greek (born on the isle of Lefkada - hence Lafcadio). His father was a Surgeon-Major in the British Army which was then occupying the Greek Islands; he was of Protestant Anglo-Irish stock and his family was unconnected to the Waterford Hearns. His Greek mother was a devout member of the Orthodox Church; she was illiterate and spoke no English. It was a love match of which neither family approved.

Hearn's early years were chaotic and miserable. He was dumped on his father's people in Dublin; his parents split up and both remarried, his father died soon after, and his mother was committed to a mental asylum. At boarding school in England, the solitary boy lost an eye playing a game called Giant's Stride. His only source of adult affection came from his aunt Sarah Brenane, a widow who lived in Dublin and had converted to Catholicism.

So thoroughly did Lafcadio hate his Irish background that he symbolically rejected the name Patrick. And reminiscing in later years, he recast the few happy memories of his childhood, setting them in Wales instead.

Only in two places was Lafcadio happy in Ireland. The first was near Cong in County Mayo, where he spent blissful holidays with his cousins, one of whom was his great boyhood chum. The second was Tramore. Here too he spent happy holidays, Mrs Brenane having rented Sweetbriar Lodge. Despite her narrow Catholic pietism, the old lady became in effect his adopted mother. Here in Tramore he roamed at will along shore and cliffs, befriending the local farmers and fishermen and greedily absorbing the local folklore.

Lafcadio deeply resented the interference in his aunt's affairs of another nephew, Henry Molyneux, whom he accused of mismanaging her financial affairs. In 1869 Molyneux managed to get rid of Hearn by giving him a one-way ticket to America: "I was dropped moneyless on the pavement of an American city to begin life." But he wandered more or less by chance into journalism and found that he had a natural talent as a writer. Some restless years followed in Cincinatti, New Orleans and Martinique. Then in 1890 his newspaper, *Harper's Weekly*, sent him to report on Japan. It was to prove the turning-point in his life.

Hearn fell in love with Japan, became a Japanese citizen, married a Japanese lady, and spent the rest of his life lecturing and writing on his adopted country. Japan was then a remote, exotic country for most Europeans, but Hearn's writings on its folklore and traditions did much to popularize Japanese culture in Europe. His home in Matsue is today a place of pilgrimage. Alas, by the time he died the country was changing rapidly into a modern, industrialized, military power, and his work became an elegy for a lost medieval oriental way of life.

Hearn's connection with Tramore was forgotten for many years, except by his descendants who occasionally came to visit the graves of Mrs Brenane and Henry Molyneux outside the main door of the Catholic church. The centenary of his death in 2004 was marked by a ceremony in the local library. Since then the closer relations between Ireland and Japan have created a better awareness of his importance. And a Japanese garden is to be created in his memory in the grounds of Tramore House.

Patrick Lafcadio Hearn died in 1904 – on this day.

Bust of Lafcadio Hearn at Tramore library
Photo: Donal Sheerin

THE WRECK OF THE *ANNETTA*

Photo: Waterford County Museum

Even in these days of sophisticated tracking equipment and rescue services, the storms off our coasts can wreak havoc and bring tragedy. In the days when sailing ships were the predominant craft trading in and out of our ports, the hazards were infinitely greater, for they were completely at the mercy of winds, tides and currents. A shipwreck is all the more poignant when it occurs just before Christmas.

Such was the case with the *Annetta* of Dungarvan. She was a two-masted schooner built at Bideford in Devon in 1849; her port of registry was Waterford. In December 1905, now nearly sixty years old, she was bound for Youghal with a cargo of coal. Aboard were Captain Kirby of Dungarvan, Jackie Smith of Youghal, John Kiely, and two other seamen. On the night of Sunday 17th, as she approached her destination she found herself running before a ferocious south-south-easterly gale which caused mountainous waves. The story is told by Dungarvan's maritime historian, John Young.

As the *Annetta* neared the port of Youghal she had to negotiate the sand-bar opposite the railway station. Even in calmer weather this could be a daunting procedure, but in such a storm it was a terrifying prospect. The despairing crew took to the rigging and trusted to their ship to do her best.

Luckily, their plight had been spotted from the shore. A crew was mustered for the Youghal lifeboat, the *Mary Luckombe*, and she put out into the icy waves. The coastguard rocket crew fired several rockets over the *Annetta* but such was

|ıııı|ıııı|ıııı|ıııı|ıııı|ıııı|ıııı|ıııı|ıııı|ıııı|ıııı|ıııı|ıııı|ıııı|ıııı|ıııı|ıııı|ıııı|ıııı|ıııı|ıııı|ıııı|ıııı|ıııı|

the cold that the crew were unable to grasp the cords. At last the crew of the lifeboat succeeded in manoeuvring their craft alongside the stricken vessel, but again the seamen were unable to save themselves. The lifeboatmen had to board the *Annetta* and drag her crew down from the rigging of the now foundering craft.

One man was abandoned three times owing to the breaking seas and the large amount of wreckage. At the third attempt he was got on board the *Mary Luckombe*, but by this stage the lifeboat itself had been damaged and its rudder had been smashed to pieces. One of the lifeboatmen, Dan Troy, was washed over-board but managed to get back on board without injury.

Eventually, three of the *Annetta's* crew had been saved. For Captain Kirby and Jackie Smith, however, rescue came too late: they were washed overboard and disappeared. It was time for the *Mary Luckombe* to head for the shore and safety. At last daylight came to reveal what was left of the *Annetta* and the storm began to abate. Captain Kirby's body was found washed ashore on Youghal Strand, but it was another week before Jackie Smith's body was discovered in the Blackwater.

In their courageous boarding of the *Annetta* and taking off the crew in heavy seas, the men of the Youghal lifeboat *Mary Luckombe* distinguished themselves, not for the first time. The coxswain, Michael Hannigan, was awarded the RNLI's silver medal for courage above and beyond the call of duty.

The wreck of the *Annetta* took place in 1905 – on this day.

The lifeboat endeavouring to rescue the crew
Photo: Horgan Brothers, Youghal

NOEL BROWNE:
SWIMMING AGAINST THE TIDE

AGAINST THE TIDE

NOEL BROWNE

Noel Browne, stormy petrel of Irish politics in the mid-20th century, was born in Bath St., Waterford, on 20 December 1915. His father, Joseph Browne, a sergeant in the Royal Irish Constabulary, came of small farming stock in County Galway. His mother, Mary Teresa Cooney, was a native of Ballinrobe.

While Noel was still a baby his father abruptly resigned from the force and re-emerged firstly as a shirt factory worker in Derry and then in 1920 as an NSPCC official in Athlone; it was here that Noel's formative years were spent.

"His boyhood and youth were a mixture of night-mare and fairytale – for the family was stalked by that great killer of the Irish at that time, Tuberculosis. His father, worn out by cycling in all weathers to visit the homes of the poor, died of it. His mother contracted it and, spurned by her relations, used up her last remaining energy to bring her brood of young children to England, where she dumped them on her eldest daughter and died. TB ran its swathes through the Browne children, and eventually Noel contracted it too. He went through a horrifying and quite futile operation to cure it – he was lucky to survive both."

But there was the fairytale element too. Taken up by a teacher in the private school where his sister worked, he was coached for a scholarship to the Jesuit college of Beaumont, one of England's top public schools. More was to follow. Asked to befriend a lonely Irish schoolfellow, he found that his new pal came from a wealthy background, and the reward for his friendship was provision for further education at Trinity College. He qualified as a doctor and worked among the poor of Dublin.

"In 1948 he was elected to Dáil Éireann as a member of Clann na Poblachta, and on his first day in the Dáil he was appointed Minister for Health in the first inter-party government. A mere youngster of 32 in a government composed mainly of wrinklies left over from the Civil War, he lost no time in getting to work with the zeal of a crusader. His career of less than three years as minister is remembered mainly for one spectacular success – the virtual eradication of TB – and one dramatic controversy – the Mother and Child Scheme."

His personal contribution to the campaign against TB is beyond question – undoubtedly many Irish people lived who would have died but for him. Yet he could have done little had it not been for the happy combination of a number of factors – the achievement (which he generously acknowledged) of his Fianna Fáil predecessor in radically overhauling the crumbling Victorian shambles that passed for an Irish health service and introducing a campaign of mass X-ray and vaccination; the discovery of new methods of treatment, the introduction of BCG and the use of streptomycin; and the capital accumulated by the Hospitals Sweepstake, which enabled Browne to build a number of brand new TB sanatoria (including Ardkeen).

In the Mother and Child Scheme, Browne took on simultaneously two hostile powers, either of which could have defeated him – the medical profession and the Catholic hierarchy. Politics is the art of the possible, and that means a readiness to compromise – not a quality with which crusaders are associated. Arrogant and tactless, in retrospect it seems almost as though he had sought a confrontation in order to show up the narrow-minded intransigence of his opponents. Here is the comment of Brian Inglis, an Anglo-Irish Protestant left-winger whom you'd expect to have been Browne's natural ally. In his memoirs *West Briton* Inglis comments:

I had met him once, when a small deputation of the Civil Liberties Association went to the ministry to try to obtain reforms in the Dundrum Criminal Lunatic Asylum ... Barely troubling to disguise his impatience, Browne treated us as if we were cranks, wasting his own time and our own. The reforms were later made, but the interview had left our deputation with no illusions about the difficulties Browne's colleagues must have faced in dealing with him.

And here is the comment of his chief civil servant. James Deeny, a good friend to Waterford, was Chief Medical Officer in the Department of Health and spearheaded the campaign against TB under three ministers – James Ryan, Sean MacEntee and Noel Browne. He clashed with Browne, and resigned. In his autobiography, *To Cure and to Care*, he comments:

A foolish and unnecessary confrontation ... Between the lot of them they made a right mess of the Mother and Child Scheme. The real tragedy of the debacle was that it set back public health in the country for years ..."

In later years the fearless champion of minority causes such as gay rights, Browne became a cult figure for progressives, thanks partly to his inspiring autobiography *Against the Tide*. But read it in conjunction with John Horgan's more objective work *Noel Browne: Passionate Outsider,* published in 2000.

Noel Browne was born in Waterford in 1915 – on this day.

THE COLLAPSE OF ABBEYSIDE CASTLE

Waterford County Museum has some dramatic photographs of Abbeyside Castle, Dungarvan, showing it to have been a tall 15th century tower-house six storeys high. The ruin is completely roofless and the scant remains of its parapet reach into the sky like gigantic claws. But the most striking aspect of the tower is that its east wall, generally the one facing the photographer, has completely fallen away, exposing the whole interior with its two great stone-vaulted ceilings, as if in some primitive X-ray. Most of these photographs were taken round the turn of the 19th century by Richard Edward Brenan.

The building, known as MacGrath's Castle, stood a couple of fields away from the Catholic church with its medieval tower (formerly that of the Augustinian monastery that gave Abbeyside its name). The MacGraths who built this castle were a warlike clan who arrived in the Déise from Clare in the late Middle Ages and settled in the Sliabh gCua area to the east of Cappoquin. Their headquarters were at Mountain Castle (now called Castle Farm and home of the Nugent family) and later at Sleady in Modeligo parish, and they played an exciting role in the wars of the 16th century.

The earliest on record is a Donal MacGrath, whose tomb may still be seen at Abbeyside Church. The barely decipherable Latin inscription records that he died in 1470-something (unfortunately the end of the date is obliterated). Perhaps he was the builder of the adjacent castle.

We know remarkably little of its history. During the rebellion of 1641 it formed part of the defences of Dungarvan and was garrisoned by the Irish. In

March 1642 Dungarvan was attacked by the ferocious Lord President of Munster, Sir William St Leger. His troops burned the houses in Abbeyside and forced the little garrison to surrender, allowing them to march out with their lives and their clothes but nothing else.

An engraving in Smith's history, published in 1746, shows that the castle was still intact at that time and probably inhabited, but a century later it was well and truly ruined. The local lads, however, still found it useful whenever some grand celebrations were taking place. In 1854, when the Pope proclaimed the dogma of the Immaculate Conception of the Blessed Virgin Mary, there were illuminations all over the town, and barrels of tar were dragged to the summit of the building and then set alight. This feat of daring was repeated in 1877, when an exciting by-election resulted in the victory of the Home Rule candidate, Frank Hugh O'Donnell.

It's a wonder such pyromaniac episodes didn't bring down the whole castle, and in fact one night in January 1916 the local inhabitants heard an ominous rumbling, and when they awoke in the morning they found that two of the remaining walls had fallen down. The south wall, amazingly, still stood to its full height, and some intrepid climbers flew a tricolour from the top during the War of Independence.

Fragments of the walls remained as late as the 1960s, but nothing now remains above ground of this once striking landmark of Dungarvan Harbour. Two of the walls of MacGrath's Castle, Abbeyside, collapsed in 1916 – on this day.

This chap seems to be on his mobile phone requesting a horse
Photos: Waterford County Museum

SERGEANT MICHAEL HEALY

Photo: Waterford County Museum

The Albert Medal was instituted in 1866 in memory of Prince Albert, to be awarded to persons who had carried out acts of heroism at sea that had resulted in the saving of life. In later years it was extended to cover acts of bravery on land as well. It was abolished in 1971, the surviving recipients being asked to accept the George Medal instead.

Inevitably, some awards of the Albert Medal were made posthumously. One of the most famous of the recipients was Sergeant Michael Healy. Healy was born in Dungarvan in 1890, and like many other young men of the time emigrated to Wales, where he worked in the Pontardawe steel works. On the outbreak of the Great War he joined the Munster Fusiliers, rising to the rank of sergeant. He was awarded the Distinguished Conduct Medal for capturing a machine-gun and five prisoners. He was later awarded the Military Medal, and then the bar to the Military Medal.

On 1 March 1917 his battalion was fighting in the trenches at Chuignolles in northern France. The enemy lines were close by, and there was a lively exchange of grenades. Suddenly a grenade which had been thrown by a soldier, instead of going over the parapet, struck the top and rolled back into the trench. "With a total disregard for his own personal safety and solely prompted by the desire to save his comrades," Healy rushed forward and seized the grenade, attempting to hurl it out of the trench. He was too late: it exploded in his hands, wounding him mortally. He was buried in the military cemetery at Bray-sur-Somme.

Healy's mother travelled over from Dungarvan to receive the Albert Medal from the King in person. "It was quite easy to talk to the King," she told the press, "he put me at my ease and conversed in homely fashion with me. He expressed deep sympathy with me in my loss, and congratulated me on having had such a son. He also talked about the food situation, and hoped that I did not have to wait in queues."

Sergeant Michael Healy was one of the most highly decorated Irish soldiers of the First World War. He won his Albert Medal in 1917 – on this day.

Main sources: Website of Waterford County Museum, Dungarvan;
Albert Medal (Wikipedia).

THE SALVAGE OF UC44

On the night of Saturday 4 August 1917 the sea off Dunmore East was calm as a millpond when suddenly a massive explosion was heard out at sea. The noise had barely died away when faint cries were heard. Quickly three fishing boats were rowed out in their direction and Captain Tebbenjohanns, the only survivor from a German submarine, the UC44, was found floundering in the water and was rescued.

The campaign of unrestricted submarine warfare launched by Germany earlier that year had exacted a terrible toll, for the Germans had also perfected a type of submarine ideal for laying mines. These operated by night, and before radar they were virtually impossible to detect. The main enemy target was the ships carrying Irish cattle to feed the hungry English.

The UC44 was happily laying mines off Dunmore when, as the ninth mine was being launched, she struck the eighth mine. How the captain survived the resulting explosion is a mystery. More to the point, the submarine, though now lying on the ocean floor, survived too.

When this news reached the Admiralty, they were desperately anxious to salvage her and study the strong and weak points of a mine-laying submarine. There was also a strong chance that the captain's orders had not been destroyed.

The task was given to Commander Davis, an experienced salvage officer. His method was ingenious. A number of cables were worked under the U-boat, forming a kind of cradle. The ends of the cables were attached to huge flat-bottomed steel barges with inflatable tanks. At low tide their tanks were filled with water and the cables tightened. The incoming tide lifted the cables off the bottom and it was then possible to tow the U-boat inshore for a few hundred yards until the fall of the tide made her touch bottom again. With the next tide, the process would be repeated.

The whole operation was hazardous in the extreme. It took nine days to fit the cables round the submarine. Then a 24 day storm mixed up all the cables. The surrounding sea had to be kept clear of other U-boats by a small fleet of minesweepers. Commander Davis and his men were pretty sure that there were some unexploded mines left on board (there were in fact nine), and one bump too many could blow them all into the next world. At one stage the submarine slipped out of her cable and dropped on the seabed, and they held their breath, but all was well.

Their patience and bravery were at last rewarded. On 25 September, after twenty lifting operations, UC44 was safely beached and provided priceless information that saved many lives, British and Irish. Commander Davis was awarded the DSO.

UC44 was wrecked off Dunmore East in 1917 – on this day.

Main source: Clarence Winchester (ed.), "Raising a Submarine Minelayer",
Shipping Wonders of the World, I (1936), pp 578-581.

SIR WILLIAM GOFF AND HIS FAMILY

Sir William at the wheel of WI 1 on The Mall
Photo: National Library of Ireland

One of the best known figures in Waterford at the turn of the last century was Sir William Goff Davis-Goff of Glenville, baronet – politician, sportsman, and benefactor of the city. He had a pedigree as long as your arm and the family had been based in Waterford since the mid-17th century. At that time they seem to have gone in for extremes of behaviour. One brother was chaplain to King Charles I, converted to the Roman Catholic Church and became an Oratorian monk. Another became an Anglican vicar and was imprisoned for "delinquency" (whatever that means) in 1645. The third became a major-general in the parliamentary army, married a cousin of Oliver Cromwell, was one of the judges at the trial of Charles I and signed the King's death warrant. I'm afraid he's the one the Irish Goffs are descended from.

The family seat was at Horetown near New Ross, where until the passing of the land acts they had an estate of about 2,500 acres. On the eve of the Famine this estate was inherited from an uncle by Strangman Davis, the son of Francis Davis of Waterford and Rebecca Goff. He adopted the extra surname of Goff to mark the occasion. On his death in 1883 he was succeeded by his son, our Sir William.

He was born in Cathedral Square, Waterford, in 1838. He was educated at Trinity College Dublin, joined the army and became a captain in the 2nd Dragoon Guards. Returning to civilian life, he settled in Waterford and married in 1866 Anne, daughter of one of the city's most prominent personages, Michael Dobbyn Hassard, M.P., of Glenville. That's how Glenville came into the family.

William was a wealthy man, for his father had inherited not only the Goff estate at Horetown but Strangman's Brewery as well. He played an active part in local affairs. He was a member of the corporation for over forty years, was Sheriff of the city in 1869 and 1899, and High Sheriff of the county in 1892, and a Deputy Lieutenant of the county.

Photo: Waterford County Museum

When King Edward VII and Queen Alexandra visited Waterford in 1904, Alderman Goff was instrumental in making their visit a success. His reward came in the following year's birthday honours, when he was made a baronet. Like most of his class, Sir William was a staunch unionist, and held an anti-home rule rally in the grounds of Glenville in 1912, Captain De la Poer presiding.

However, it's as a sportsman that Sir William was most highly regarded. As an undergraduate he was a crack oarsman at Trinity. He was a keen yachtsman. He was a pioneer of the motor industry, and owned the first officially registered car in Waterford. Its number WI 1, was inherited by a whole succession of Goff cars for several generations. He was the first man to *officially* drive a car over Redmond Bridge when it opened in 1913 (Captain Jack Carew – later Major Carew of Ballinamona – who whisked over in front of him with a carload of young ladies, was the real first). He actively promoted the development of the Dunlop Tyre Company in this country and was its chairman for some years. A keen cyclist, he claimed to be the first man in Waterford and the second in Ireland to ride the high-wheeled bike. When cycling became fashionable he erected at his own expense a splendid cycle track in the People's Park. The Goff Track was destined to play an illustrious part in Irish cycling history.

Sir William and Lady Goff had two sons. The younger was killed in action during the Boer War. The elder, Sir Herbert, succeeded his father and was in turn the father of the late Sir Ernest Goff, who will be remembered by many who knew him when he resided at Glenville in Waterford, then at Ballinaparka near Aglish, and then at Kinsale. His eldest child, Annabel Davis Goff, rocketed to fame both locally and in the United States with the publication in 1989 of her nostalgic memoir, *Walled Gardens: Scenes from an Anglo-Irish Childhood*.

Annabel's great-grandfather, Sir William Goff Davis-Goff, died at Glenville in his eightieth year in 1918 – on this day.

THE *FORMBY*, THE *CONINGBEG*, AND THE LOCAL DISASTER FUND

Brian Cleare's painting of the dredger *Portlairge* (called the mud boat in Waterford) acting as tug to the schooner *Antelope* with the *Coningbeg* and *Formby* at the Clyde wharf

SS Formby
Photos: Andrew Kelly

War, as General Sherman observed, is all hell. World War One was more hellish than most, for it affected millions of people, civilians as well as soldiers. Both the great naval powers, Britain and Germany, were determined to starve the other into surrender. The Royal Navy blockaded the German ports to prevent food imports. By December 1917 the war was in its fourth year. German civilians, especially children and the elderly, were dying in their thousands; there were food riots in the leading cities, and a nice legacy of hate was building up against perfidious Albion.

Meanwhile, the German High Command had declared unrestricted submarine warfare against all shipping headed for the United Kingdom. British propaganda portrayed the U-boats and their crews as monsters of particularly loathsome depravity; their bravery in taking to the sea in what were virtually tin coffins was ignored. But the German sailors were, after all, only obeying orders. The real heroes were the merchant seamen who kept the vital supplies of food and materials coming in despite the ever-present threat of instant destruction from the unseen foe beneath the waves. But for their oft-repeated courage Britain and Ireland might well have been forced to surrender.

One of the main trade routes between Britain and Ireland was the Waterford to Liverpool run operated by the Clyde Shipping Company. Its ships brought Irish cattle to Britain and returned to Ireland laden with food and general provisions.

The *Formby*, flagship of the Clyde fleet, was built in 1914 mainly as a cattle boat, though she had passenger accommodation as well. On the morning of 15 December 1917 she left Liverpool for Waterford under her captain, Charles Minards. The crew no doubt were looking forward to spending Christmas with their families in Waterford and brought with them the presents they had bought in Liverpool. At six o'clock that evening they were spotted by Captain Hashagen of U.62, and at two minutes to eight he fired one torpedo right into her engine-room. There was a massive simultaneous explosion of both boilers and the torpedo, wrecking the ship from bow to stern. The only surviving relic is the name-plate of one of her lifeboats. One body was washed ashore, that of the stewardess.

The *Coningbeg* was built in 1903 for the Waterford Steamship Company and was originally named the *Clodiagh*. In 1912 she was taken over by the Clyde and thoroughly modernized. Like the *Formby* she was principally a cattle boat but had passenger accommodation as well. On the morning after the sinking of the *Formby* the Irish Sea was hit by a ferocious blizzard. The following day the storm abated, and at 1 p.m. the *Coningbeg* cast off and headed off down the Mersey under her captain, Joseph Lumley. At eight o'clock that evening she was spotted by Captain Hashagen in the U.62, and for four hours he stalked her down the

SS Coningbeg

Irish Sea, waiting for the opportunity to attack. A humane man, he later wrote in his memoirs: "It is dreadful to be steaming thus alongside one's victim, knowing that she has ten or perhaps twenty minutes to live, till fiery death leaps from the sea and blows her to pieces. A solemn mood possesses the few upon the bridge. The horror of war silences us."

Then, at 11.45, he fired his torpedo. "Hit amidships," he wrote in his logbook. "Vessel in flames, breaks in two and sinks immediately. A few seconds after the explosion only the burning stern is over the water. Three minutes after the hit the vessel is sunk with all hands." No identifiable bodies or wreckage were found.

Of the 83 crew members lost on the two ships, 67 were from Waterford City and environs. The plight of the families who waited for news on the Clyde Wharf, numb with misery, in those cold wet days, may be imagined. For many of them, too, the loss of a breadwinner meant destitution – and this within a week of Christmas.

A few days after the disaster, a public meeting was held in City Hall and an appeal fund was launched. It raised nearly £8,000, a large sum for those days. Thanks to the generosity of the public, the committee was able to provide financial assistance on a weekly basis to the dependants of the victims until their conditions were eased by the granting of Board of Trade pensions. Even so, some continued to need help for years after, until eventually the fund was wound up in 1927. The lion's share of the work in this arduous and delicate undertaking fell to its devoted secretary, Gerald Hart Kelly of Gladstone Street.

Eighty years after the catastrophe, a monument to the victims was erected at Adelphi Wharf and unveiled by President Robinson. Its existence was largely due to the untiring efforts of the late Renee Lumley – the victims had included her grandfather-in-law Joseph Lumley, master of the *Coningbeg*, and his son William, Second Engineer on the *Formby*.

The Waterford Local Disaster Fund was set up in 1917 – on this day.

See Richard McElwee, The Last Voyages of the Waterford Steamers
(Waterford, n.d.).

The monument on Waterford Quay to all those lost on both ships
Photo: Donal Sheerin

RICHARD BAGWELL,
PATRIOT - AND UNIONIST

Anyone studying the history of Ireland in the 16th and 17th centuries will sooner or later come across the name of Richard Bagwell. He was the author of two learned works, *Ireland under the Tudors* and *Ireland under the Stuarts,* each consisting of three volumes. Though written many years ago, they have never been surpassed.

Bagwell was born in Clonmel in 1840. He came of Protestant Unionist landowning stock. From his father he inherited an estate of over five thousand acres, mainly in Counties Waterford and Tipperary, with a fine house and well-ordered demesne at Marlfield.

He also inherited a love of Ireland and a long tradition of service to her. His father, John Bagwell, was MP for Clonmel from 1857 to 1874. During one debate in the House of Commons an Ulster MP declared that Ireland was in such a lawless condition that the life of a man of property, or indeed any man with a good coat, was not safe there. Bagwell replied that he too lived in Ireland and had considerable property there, and that he would go at any time through the most disturbed district fortified with no other weapon than his umbrella. He then became known in Parliament as "Umbrella Bagwell".

Young Richard was given the best of education. He was sent to Harrow, one of the top schools in England, and to Christ Church, Oxford. He became a barrister. He worked for many years in the Irish civil service as a Commissioner of National Education.

He published *Ireland under the Tudors* between 1885 and 1890. It's a bit short on analysis, but there have been plenty of historians since then to attend to that. However, if you want to know what actually happened, Bagwell is still your only man. Moreover, his research was done mainly on original sources in the Irish State Papers at the Public Record Office in London. These he studied in depth, and he really knew what he was talking about. But the most remarkable feature of his work is its objectivity. Although he writes from the standpoint of a landlord, Bagwell is always fair, and when he feels the government deserves to be attacked he does so. His sections on religion in 16th-century Ireland compare with anything written since his time.

His second major work, *Ireland under the Stuarts,* appeared in 1909-1910. Like its predecessor, it's still the best narrative account of the period. But gone, alas, is the objectivity. Bagwell now recites exclusively from the government side, and God knows the government of this country in the 17th century deserved to be criticized. What had happened between the publication of the two books to cloud his scholarly judgement?

The answer is the Home Rule question. When Gladstone's first Home Rule Bill was debated in the House of Commons in 1886, Bagwell proposed a resolution to the Select Vestry of the Church of Ireland in Clonmel professing unswerving loyalty to the Crown and uncompromising hostility to any question of legislative independence. His study of Irish history had convinced him that the country had never been united, except for a brief period under Brian Boru, and that in every battle on Irish soil from Clontarf to Ballingarry the Irish had fought one another. Home Rule, he was convinced, would be a recipe for civil war.

Bagwell was genuinely patriotic. He had in fact written a popular ballad that concluded with the lines:

From youth to age, from age till death
To me of greatest worth
Must be the land that gave me breath
Our own dear Irish earth.

But as the years went by he became more and more convinced that the best way of governing our own dear Irish earth was from Westminster. His family's experiences during Easter Week 1916 did nothing to change his mind: his son and daughter-in-law were fired on while innocently driving through Dublin, and Mrs Bagwell was wounded in the shoulder.

Two years later, when the Irish Convention summoned by Lloyd George dispersed in disarray, a group of diehard Southern Unionists formed a committee to oppose any dilution of the Union, and Bagwell was elected its chairman. But he was now in his 79th year, and his tenure of office was cut short by his death.

At least he did not live to see the destruction of his beloved library, including all his papers, when Marlfield was partially burned by anti-Treaty forces in 1923 as his son was a member of the Irish Free State Senate.

Richard Bagwell, historian, patriot - and Unionist, died in 1918 – on this day.

MICHAEL COLLINS IN DUNGARVAN

The six months that elapsed between the signing of the Anglo-Irish Treaty on 6 December 1921 and the outbreak of the Civil War surely make up one of the most complicated periods in Irish history. As the British began to withdraw their forces, the republican movement split into those who supported the Treaty and those who opposed it, while many remained neutral and a bewildered public just longed for a return to normality.

In March 1922 the RIC evacuated their barracks in Dungarvan Castle, their place being taken by anti-Treaty IRA. As a general election loomed, both sides made frantic efforts to enlist support. On St Patrick's Day de Valera addressed a huge crowd in Dungarvan Square. There were tricolours everywhere as the Long Fellow stood up in a motor-car, harangued his audience on the inadequacies of the Treaty and warned ominously of trouble ahead.

Nine days later it was the turn of Michael Collins. His opponents made every effort to stop him even reaching Dungarvan by felling trees and trenching the roads along his route. At length, by dint of much sawing, chopping and planking, the little procession reached Dungarvan by means of byroads and boreens.

The plan was for the Big Fellow to address the crowd in the square from a lorry. This was soon filled by the platform party, which included many journalists. Mr Michael Brennock, chairman of the UDC, opened the proceedings. He had barely begun his address when he was disconcerted to find that the lorry's engine was actually running. Worse was to follow. The lorry began to move, IRA men cleared a path through the crowd as if by magic, and soon it was heading off at an alarming speed, taking with it Michael Collins, his associates, the journalists, and of course the chairman, who was just beginning to warm up to his speech. Down Bridge Street and across the bridge the lorry sped, shedding journalists on its way. At one stage it headed straight for the graving bank, then ran along the footpath – then off into Abbeyside.

Photo: Waterford County Museum

Everyone jumped off and the driver ran for his life with bullets zinging round his ears. The platform party dusted themselves off and returned to the town on foot, minus their tricolours which had been taken by the IRA. Michael Collins made his speech from the balcony of the Devonshire Arms Hotel (now Lawlor's). His fine figure, striking good looks and forceful manner created a strong impression. He silenced his many hecklers by answering their jibes with bitter sarcasm. It took more than a hijacked lorry to silence the Big Fellow, and he was still a long way from Béal na mBláth.

Michael Collins paid his eventful visit to Dungarvan in 1922 – on this day.

Main source: Edmund Keohan, Illustrated History of Dungarvan (1924), pp 55-57.

DEATH OF LIAM LYNCH

Liam Lynch was one of the most vigorous, efficient and successful republican leaders of the War of Independence, impressing his superiors in GHQ by his organisational talents, attention to detail, leadership qualities, and impatience with time-wasters. In appearance and manner, however, he was hardly the typical paramilitary leader – tall, bespectacled and austere, more like de Valera (for whom he was sometimes mistaken) than Michael Collins.

Lynch made his name as Commandant of Cork No. 2 Brigade, with headquarters in Fermoy. But his ambition was for greater co-operation between the different brigades, an aim that was achieved when he was elected to command the First Southern Division, which brought together eight Munster brigades. During the uncertain period of the Truce he sought to keep the division in close contact with GHQ in Dublin.

The Treaty he rejected out of hand, declaring famously: "We have declared for an Irish republic and will not live under any other law." He dismissed the obvious popularity of the Treaty by remarking contemptuously that "the people were merely sheep to be driven anywhere at will". But he worked hard to hold the republican movement together and avoid a civil war at all costs.

The fall of the Four Courts left him as commander of the anti-Treaty forces. He decided to fight a defensive war, trusting that if the "Munster Republic" south of a line between Limerick and Waterford could be held then the new Irish Free State would collapse. It was a disastrous strategy, ending after only six weeks with the capture of Fermoy in August 1922.

The fighting, however, continued, becoming more bitter and pointless as the weeks turned into months, with atrocities mounting on both sides.

In March 1923 the Army Executive met in a remote location in the Nire valley, at which Lynch narrowly carried a vote to continue the war. A month later another meeting was held at a farmhouse in the Knockmealdown Mountains. Surprised by the sudden approach of Free State troops, the republican leaders fled. Lynch was shot in the abdomen and died that evening. With his death the way was open to end the Civil War. And by a strange coincidence the Good Friday Agreement was signed on the 75th anniversary of his death in 1998.

Liam Lynch died in 1923 – on this day.

Liam Lynch
Photo: Waterford County Museum

JOHN HEARNE
AND THE CONSTITUTION

All over Europe in the 1930s, democratic governments were tumbling and dictatorships were in fashion. And what about little old Ireland? The Economic War was reducing the country to a shambles, the Blueshirts and the IRA were happily re-living the Civil War, and de Valera must surely have mused whether a continental-style dictatorship was the only way to bring order back to our streets and get the trains to run on time. There was little to stop him. Fianna Fáil had a strong majority in the Dáil, the Senate had been abolished, the Governor General was ignored, and Britain was in the throes of the Abdication Crisis. And what did the Chief do? He did not establish a dictatorship – he put before the people a new constitution. And who did he get to draw it up for him but a Waterford man.

John Joseph Hearne was born in Manor Street in 1893 (a plaque marks the spot today) and educated at Waterpark and UCD. He went on to study for the priesthood at Maynooth, but decided that the law was the career for him. The Treaty of 1921 kept Ireland within the British Commonwealth, but it was a priority of the Cosgrave government to justify their position by ensuring the maximum degree of independence for Ireland as a dominion. Our delegates participated impressively in the various imperial conferences of the twenties, and Hearne was their legal adviser. In 1929 he was appointed legal adviser to the Department of External Affairs, and by the mid-thirties he had gained international recognition as an authority on constitutional law.

The Constitution of 1937 was largely Dev's brainchild, but it was Hearne who drafted the document on which Dev worked. Dev was determined to accommodate the aspirations of as many interest groups as possible, so he invited their comments on the first draft, and it was Hearne too who had to read their reports and co-ordinate them as best he could.

This was no easy task. Take the thorny issue of religion. The Catholic hierarchy wanted a Catholic constitution for a Catholic people, but Dev was determined to be fair to the minorities. His solution to the dilemma was masterly. He included a clause acknowledging the "special position" of the Catholic Church (whatever that meant), and went on to acknowledge the special positions of the other churches as well, including the Jewish congregations. Incidentally, how

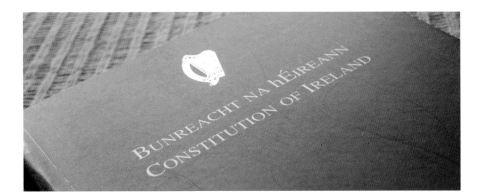

many other countries can you think of in the thirties whose constitutions guaranteed the civil rights of the Jews?

The Vatican was not pleased with the result, the Pope remarking enigmatically: "Ni approvo – ni non disapprovo. Taceremo." [I do not approve – neither do I not disapprove. We shall remain silent.] But Dev stuck to his guns.

The final draft of the constitution was approved by the Dáil and put to the people by referendum on 1 July 1937. The result was amazing. Just over one-third voted for it and just under one-third against it – while the remaining third never bothered to vote at all!

Dev sent a special copy to Hearne, dedicated to him as "architect in chief and draftsman ... in testimony of the fundamental part he took in framing this the first free constitution of the Irish people".

Hearne continued to play a distinguished part in Irish affairs. He was our High Commissioner in Canada from 1937 to 1950 and our Ambassador to the USA from 1950 to 1960. He died in 1969. The constitution by which we are governed today, and in which he played so significant a part, came into effect in 1937 – on this day.

[See Eugene Broderick, "John Hearne and the making of the 1937 Constitution", Decies no. 69 (2013), pp 171-206.]

A GERMAN BOMBER CRASH LANDS AT CARRIGLONG

On Sunday 23 August 1942 a Junkers Ju-88 twin-engined bomber of Aufklärungsgruppe 123 headed north on a reconnaissance mission over the Irish Sea and Northern Ireland. Its approach was spotted by look-out posts at Carnsore Point and Clogher Head, who duly reported to Central Control at Clondalkin. But it was not only the Irish forces that were aware of the German bomber's presence: its progress was also tracked by radar stations along the Welsh coast. Three fighter planes stationed at Valley near Holyhead were ordered up to intercept and destroy it. They were Supermarine Spitfires of the Deblinski Squadron, a unit of the Free Polish Forces serving with the RAF.

The Spitfires attacked the Junkers, damaging one of its engines and slightly wounding one of the crew, Oberfeldwebel Karl Hund, who had two of his fingers injured. To get away from its pursuers the Junkers headed westwards over neutral Éire. One of the Spitfires was also damaged and its pilot, Flying Officer Sawaik, was badly wounded in the chest. He managed to land his plane in a field near the Meath village of Ratoath, but then his luck finally ran out, for on landing the plane hit some hidden rocks and was wrecked. He was removed to a hospital in Dublin, where he died of his wounds later that evening.

Meanwhile, the Junkers headed south, with smoke pouring from its damaged engine. When it reached the south coast it found the other two Spitfires waiting for it. Again the German desperately took evasive action, heading back inland with the Spitfires in hot pursuit, their machine-guns firing. When the damaged engine caught fire the pilot, Hauptmann Gottfried, knew that his only hope now was to try to bring his aircraft down in a field. He landed the Junkers in the field of Owen Power at Carriglong, north of Tramore. On impact with the ground the plane burst into flames, but luckily the four crew members managed to scramble free of their blazing craft. The triumphant Spitfires performed a series of victory rolls over Tramore, to the consternation of the crowds emerging from Mass or walking along the Prom. They then headed back to Wales.

Meanwhile, members of the Tramore LDF had arrived at Carriglong. They took charge of the four German airmen and what was left of their plane. They waited with them until the arrival of Irish Army personnel from the military barracks in Waterford. The Germans, no doubt feeling they were lucky to be alive, were removed to the internment camp at the Curragh, where they remained for the rest of the war.

The crash-landing at Carriglong was the fourth of five incidents in which foreign aircraft were forced down in the Waterford area during World War II. It took place in 1942 – on this day.

A DÉISE HERO OF
WORLD WAR TWO

Should Pope Pius XII have publicly denounced the Nazi atrocities? The question is far more complicated than silly people on both sides of the issue will admit. My own view is that on balance, alas, he should have, even though it would probably have cost him and his entourage their lives. What is beyond dispute is that Pius secretly supported the private efforts of brave men and women who of their own initiative set up escape routes through the Vatican.

One such was Monsignor Hugh O'Flaherty, whose exploits have been commemorated in several books, films and TV programmes. Another was the Rosminian priest Father Tom Lenane. He was born at Newport in Wales in 1903, the son of a coal trimmer from Aglish in County Waterford. When in 1940 Italy entered the war, he was stationed at the Rosminian headquarters in Rome. To disguise his Welsh nationality, he assumed the identity of a dead Irish priest, "Éire" being of course neutral. He even faked his Irish passport, complete with rubber stamps he had carved from the heel of a boot.

Father Lenane's skill in forgery drew the attention of the Italian underground, and soon his talents were enlisted in securing the escape of captured allied servicemen. One of his favoured methods was to disguise his subject as a Catholic priest, coaching him carefully in the ways of the Church. There were some hairsbreadth escapes. On one occasion the Gestapo raided the Rosminian house and forced him to accompany them as they searched the premises; luckily they did not get as far as the loft, where "Uncle Tom" (as he was known) had several allied airmen hidden. On another, as it was All Souls Day he took a British officer disguised as a priest with him to pray at a cemetery; when they got there they found scores of German soldiers also there praying for their dead comrades, but they noticed nothing amiss.

Father Lenane was in charge of supplying food to the Rosminian house, and on one occasion he had just taken in a consignment of piglets when he got word of a Gestapo raid. The intruders were bound to requisition the juicy piglets if they found them, but luckily they did not think of looking for them under the cassocks of the priests!

After the war Father Tom Lenane was decorated for his bravery by King George VI. He returned to Britain, where he worked tirelessly until his death in 1979. I hope that his memory is preserved still in Eaglais na nDéise, his father's native village.

Main source: David Jones, "The priest who defied the Gestapo", article in Ireland's Own and in The Platernian Newsletter, Winter 1011, issue 1, pp 4-5.

THE *KERLOGUE* RESCUE

The *Kerlogue* painted by Brian Cleare

The *Kerlogue* was a 350-ton motor vessel built in Holland in 1938 and owned by the Wexford Steamship Company. Her master was Tom Donoghue from Abbeyside, Dungarvan. On 27 December 1943 she set off from Lisbon bound for Dublin with a cargo of oranges.

World War Two had been in progress for four years, and by now the Battle of the Atlantic was being won by the Allies, but it was far from over. As a vessel belonging to a neutral country, the *Kerlogue* had been granted a Navicert by the British, and one of the conditions was that she must call at a designated UK port (in this case Fishguard) for examination and clearance on both the outward and homeward legs of the voyage.

At first light on 29 December the *Kerlogue* was some 360 miles south of the Fastnet and west of Brest when two German bombers circled the ship signalling "SOS – lifeboats – follow". They then flew off to the south firing Verey flares. Captain Donoghue altered course, and after two hours steaming a number of rafts were observed ahead of them. Recalling the scene years later, the first mate said: "As the rafts rose in view on the crests of the giant waves, we could see men on them and others clinging to their sides, and one did not know if they were Allied or Axis until somebody noticed long ribbons from a sailor's cap, which denoted that these were German navymen."

What had happened was this. Five German merchant vessels were on their way from Japan to occupied France with a cargo of rubber and other strategic materials. They hoped to run the Allied naval blockade in the long December nights when detection would be difficult. But the British Admiralty learned from decoded Ultra signals of their approach, and also that an escort flotilla was on its way to meet them.

One of the merchant vessels got through, but a second was sunk. A battle then developed between the German escort flotilla and the two British cruisers sent to intercept them. The British were outnumbered, but in the heavy seas their longer range guns and steadier gun platforms gave them the advantage. After an hour's fighting, the German force divided under cover of a smokescreen, three of their ships heading west. The cruisers followed them and sank each in turn. When the *Kerlogue* arrived, the survivors were fighting for their lives in the icy water.

For the next ten hours the *Kerlogue* moved from group to group, hauling the exhausted men on board. She continued after dark, and by nine that night she had taken aboard 168 sailors, some of whom had been in the water for over twenty-four hours. The crew did what they could to dry them out, warm them, feed them, and tend the wounded, but the facilities on board the overcrowded ship were hopelessly inadequate for the task. Three Germans died and were buried at sea. The senior German officer requested that they be landed at Brest or La Rochelle, but Captain Donoghue refused. He decided instead to head for Cork, the nearest Irish port. The Germans made no attempt to seize the ship, nor did the Luftwaffe flying overhead intervene.

The *Kerlogue* berthed at Cobh in the early hours of New Year's Day and the Germans were handed over to the Irish authorities. Captain Donoghue then headed for Fishguard to obtain his clearance. On arrival he was roasted by the senior British officer for having broken the terms of his Navicert. He angrily retorted that his only concern had been to save life. The *Kerlogue* eventually arrived in Dublin – with the uneaten oranges – on 5 January. Captain Donoghue received the thanks of the German Ambassador for his errand of mercy.

The *Kerlogue* turning in Waterford
Photo: Andrew Kelly

Some years ago, following a programme I did on the *Kerlogue* rescue, I received a letter from an elderly policeman in Berlin. In December 1943 he had been a seventeen-year-old sailor, struggling for his life amid the huge waves. "I will never forget," he wrote to me, "the sight of that wonderful Irish ship and the bravery of our rescuers, who plucked us at the last moment from certain death."

The *Kerlogue* rescue took place in 1943 – on this day.

ARCHBISHOP SHEEHAN AND THE FOUNDING OF RING COLLEGE

One summer's evening in the year 1906, two men named Patrick Kiely and Michael Sheehan went to the fishing village of Baile na nGall near Ring. The day's work was over, the fishermen had returned from the sea and the farmers from the fields. The two men put up a blackboard against a window and began to give an Irish class.

It's hard for us today to visualize the impact caused by such a simple gesture. In 1906 Irish was not the first official language of an Irish state – it was a badge of poverty in a remote and neglected part of the United Kingdom. For generations, teachers and parents had been trying to beat it out of their children. To address a priest in Irish was regarded as an insult. Yet here were two teachers calmly giving a lesson in reading and writing Irish to fishermen and farmers who were illiterate in their own tongue. Moreover, one of them was not only a priest but also a doctor of philosophy and a professor at Maynooth.

Michael Sheehan was born at Newtown in Waterford City in 1870. When he was ten years old his family moved to Dungarvan. He was educated by the Christian Brothers there, then privately, and later at the Augustinian College. A brilliant scholar, he was destined for the priesthood. After only a year at St John's College he was sent to Maynooth, and by the time he was 23 he had completed his studies and was back in St John's as professor. He was still too young to be ordained priest! In 1895 he was ordained by his namesake Bishop Sheehan of Waterford. Further studies followed at Maynooth, Oxford, Greifswald, Bonn and Rome, and by the time the 20th century dawned he had a string of academic qualifications, including two doctorates.

He still did not know one word of Irish. However, at Greifswald University in Germany one of his friends and fellow-students was Richard Henebry of Portlaw. They both studied under Professor Zimmer; all three were ardent students of the classics, but Henebry and Zimmer were also Celtic scholars. It seems never to have dawned on Sheehan that modern Irish might be worth studying. One day he asked Zimmer. The great German simply opened his arms enthusiastically and exclaimed: "In the modern Irish language there is an unlimited field for the scholar!"

Back at home, from now on Sheehan spent his vacations in Ring learning Irish from the local people. At first he was met with suspicion and hostility. Anyone who actually wanted to learn Irish, they reckoned, must surely be at best cracked and at worst dangerous, and anyone who tried to help him could be letting himself in for a heap of trouble. However, Sheehan found an old woman who agreed to

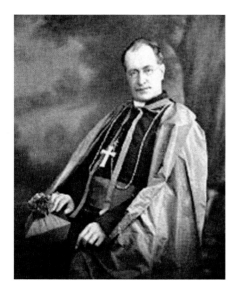

be his teacher, and he immersed himself in the language. Soon he was able to preach in Irish. He would watch his congregation closely, trying to learn from their expression – respect, boredom, amusement, bewilderment, nausea – whether he had got the pronunciation and grammar right.

When Sheehan and Ó Cadhla set up their blackboard in Baile na nGall that summer's evening, they began a movement that led in a short time to the foundation of Ring College. Three years later a large residential building was erected.

Further honours poured on Sheehan. He became Vice-President of Maynooth, a Commissioner of Intermediate Education, and in 1922 Coadjutor Archbishop of Sydney, Australia. But he never lost his vision of a restored Déise Gaeltacht - and it was in Ring that he was buried when he died, in 1945 - on this day.

Coláirce na Rinne 7 an Cuan

Postcard from Waterford County Museum

Photos: Andrew Kelly

Power, it has been truly said, corrupts. Indeed, the greater the power the greater the corruption. Undoubtedly there was a great deal wrong with the Irish Catholic Church in the years before the reforms of Vatican II. But it seems to me that those reforms, while they rid the Church of much that got in the way of the Gospel message, also washed down the plug-hole practices which did no harm and gave fulfillment to many people whose lives became the poorer in the post-Vatican II world. Among these were the great public non-liturgical manifestations of the Faith. And in Waterford the most magnificent of these was surely the great Rosary Rally held in St John's College in 1954.

It's hard for young people today to realize the tremendous hold that the Rosary had on people sixty years ago. The prayers were simple and you had heard them from your cradle days onwards. Reciting them was second nature, and you needed no priest, no book, not even a set of beads – all you needed was to be able to count up to ten, and if you had ten fingers or even ten toes to help you, so much the better. No matter what your poverty or pain or sickness, the Rosary was there in your head, and the rhythmic recital of the most familiar of prayers put you straight in touch with the stories that lie at the heart of the Christian faith – the birth, passion and resurrection of the Saviour. Above all, the Rosary was a family prayer, and for many people now well into middle age one of their most intimate childhood memories is of kneeling on the kitchen floor – preferably a very hard, very cold, stone floor – while turns were taken to recite the decades under the leadership of a watchful parent.

In the 1950s the great apostle of the Rosary was Father Patrick Peyton. A native of County Mayo, he had left home at the age of nineteen to go to America. Shortly before ordination he had been afflicted with the traditional Irish scourge of TB. His recovery seemed miraculous, he joined the Congregation of the Holy Cross, and he made the Rosary Crusade his special mission.

His great rally in St John's College was attended by upwards of forty thousand people. They came on foot from all parts of the city, by bicycle from further afield, and by train and bus from all parts of the south-east. The streets were spanned by streamers; windows of shops and houses were decorated with altars and holy pictures; papal and national flags flew everywhere. Throughout the evening crowds poured into the college grounds. The scene was dominated by an altar placed high up in a window of the college. On it was a huge statue of the Blessed Virgin, surrounded by vases of multi-coloured flowers. Above it, stretching along the wall of the building, was a gigantic inscription, ninety feet long and four feet high – a credit to the technical skills of Messrs John Hearne the builders. It announced in great red wooden lettering the motto of the Rosary Crusade: "The family that prays together stays together."

At 7.45 p.m. the proceedings began with a procession from the Bishop's Palace, led by 140 De la Salle brothers from all over Ireland, followed by the students from the order's college at Faithlegg, then eighty priests of the diocese, the cathedral chapter, and finally Bishop Cohalan and Father Peyton. During the procession recordings were played of John McCormack singing "Panis Angelicus" and Father Sidney McEwan singing "Bring flowers of the rarest" and "Mother of Christ".

The highlight of the evening was of course the homily by Father Peyton, at the end of which the slogan "Ave Maria" suddenly appeared illuminated at the top of the building (compliments of Messrs John Gaule & Sons, electrical engineers). This was the signal for the people to sing the Lourdes Hymn, accompanied inevitably by the Barrack Street Band. The ceremony concluded with the imparting of Benediction by the Bishop.

Ah, whatever happened to the Family Rosary? And how "together" are today's families?

Waterford's great Rosary Rally was held in 1954 – on this day.

WATERFORD'S SECOND ALL-IRELAND HURLING VICTORY

During the 1940s and 1950s All-Ireland hurling was dominated by three counties – Cork, Tipperary and Kilkenny. As two of these counties are in Munster, it followed inevitably that for Waterford to reach the All-Ireland final she must beat one and possibly both of them. Kilkenny, on the other hand, could expect a much easier run, and when the two counties clashed in the 1959 final the black and amber men were looking forward to their fifteenth All-Ireland title. Waterford had reached the All-Ireland Final for the first time in 1938 and had been beaten by Dublin. Ten years later she won her first All-Ireland title, defeating Dublin decisively. It was not until 1957 that the two Suirside counties, rivals for so long in league and tournament games, clashed at an All-Ireland final.

The main characteristic of the Waterford players was their speed and skill. The forwards were small and light, with the notable exception of Tom Cheasty of Ballyduff, whose muscular attacks had caused him to be compared to a charging rhinoceros. Waterford's strength was in the lightning attacks that could easily take their opponents off guard and were a joy to watch. On the other hand, their defence was vulnerable, despite valiant work by goalkeeper Ned Power of Tallow. Kilkenny's strength lay in the players' sheer hurling skill, and in Ollie Walsh they had one of the greatest hurling goalkeepers of all time. Moreover, their long experience in playing All-Irelands gave them enormous self-confidence and unflappability. They never panicked, however many points they were down, and had established the reputation of snatching victory from defeat and scraping home by a single point time after time. In the 1957 final, a magnificent match, Waterford were leading by six points ten minutes before full time, and yet when the final whistle blew Kilkenny were the winners by one point.

In 1959 Waterford trounced the previous year's champions, Tipperary, in the Munster Semi-Final, and eventually met Kilkenny at Croke Park once again. 74,000 spectators witnessed one of the great hurling classics of all time. It was also the first All-Ireland to be televised, for the BBC sent over a camera crew to record it, and an edited version appeared on a sports programme some days later. The commentator, Kenneth Wolstenholme, gasped in amazement at the skill and speed of the players. The Waterford coach, John Keane, had prepared his team well. The captain was Frankie Walsh of Mount Sion and among the forwards was the late Donal "Duck" Whelan of Abbeyside. He was to experience many a tussle with Jim "the Link" Walsh of Tullaroan. Kilkenny was captained by Sean Clohosey of Tullaroan, and goalkeeper Ollie Walsh of Thomastown was to give one of his most impressive performances.

|ııı|ııı|ııı|ııı|ııı|ııı|ııı|ııı|ııı|ııı|ııı|ııı|ııı|ııı|ııı|ııı|ııı|ııı|ııı|ııı|ııı|ııı|ııı|ııı|

The standard of play was dazzling, and yet the match had an ironic end. Almost on the call of time a dramatic goal by Seamus Power of Mount Sion brought Waterford level, with the score at 1.17 to 5.5 (twenty points each). Then suddenly Power had possession once again, and the Kilkenny defences were down. But Power was under the impression that Waterford were in the lead by one point, and knowing that the match was almost over, instead of aiming for a point he just took an "almighty flake" and missed. The score remained a draw.

The replay was another spine-tingling contest, but the result was never in doubt. Waterford had learned valuable lessons: their forwards were just as fast, but their backs were much tighter now. The Kilkenny play was as skilful as ever, but lacked its usual sense of urgency, and in the second half they just seemed to run out of steam. The final score was 3.12 to 1.10.

Waterford won its second All-Ireland Hurling Final in 1959 – on this day.

Main source: Norman Freeman, Classic Hurling Matches 1956-1975
(Dublin, 1993), pp 18-36.

THE MIGHTY MEN OF 1959

The winning Waterford team of 1959: Back l to r – Freddie O'Brien, John Barron, Ned Power, Jackie Condon, Martin Og Morrissey, Joe Harney, Austin Flynn, Phil Grimes, Mick Lacey and Joe Coady; Front l to r – Paudie Casey, Tom Cheasty, Larry Guinan, Mick Flannelly, Frank Walsh (Captain), John Kiely, Tom Cunningham, Seamus Power, Mick O'Connor, Charlie Ware and Donal Whelan
Connolly Collection/SPORTSFILE

COUNTY WATERFORD, THE N25, AND THE BOWEN FAMILY

A car zigzags across the pre-1963 Youghal Bridge
Photo: Waterford County Museum

The N25 runs through practically the whole of County Waterford. From Waterford City it heads straight for Dungarvan, then winds its way up into the Drum Hills, descends to the banks of the Blackwater, crosses the river at Youghal Bridge and finally enters County Cork when it crosses the little river Tourig.

Driving along this road, you are never far from the unseen hand of the Bowen family. John Kingston Bowen was appointed County Surveyor in 1915, the second person to hold that post since county councils were established in 1899. He was then only 27, and he was destined to remain in office for nearly thirty years, until his untimely death from cancer in 1944. He was a man of energy and foresight. Realising that the future of national transport lay with the roads rather than the railways, he set about ensuring the highest quality of roads for this county. Road-making gangs were established, mechanical equipment bought (especially steam-rollers), quarries opened up. During the lean years of the war, J.K. Bowen realised that, once the war did eventually end, the destruction in Europe was such that there would be intense competition for road-building equipment – therefore Ireland should get in ahead of other countries without waiting for peace to come. Thus, during my boyhood in the 1950s, Waterford was known for having better roads than any other Irish county.

Passengers head for the other side of old Youghal Bridge to board a different bus
Photo: Donal Sheerin courtesy of Aherne's Townhouse & Seafood Bar, Youghal

In maintaining the N25, J.K. Bowen ensured the preservation of such stone depots as survived. These were little lay-bys built every few hundred yards, in which rocks were collected from the fields, to be broken down until they were small enough to be used for resurfacing the roads. And our iron mileposts were re-erected inside these stone depots – you can see a whole succession of them as you proceed along the road. These are special features of County Waterford – long may they continue to be appreciated.

One of the great obstacles faced by County Waterford's road builders of the early 19th century was how to get the road across the mouth of the Blackwater above Youghal. This was eventually accomplished thanks to the genius of the Scots engineer Alexander Nimmo, who was also the creator of Dunmore East harbour. The cost was £30,000 – a huge sum of money in those days. An act of parliament, passed in 1828, gave permission for work to start. The bridge, made of Munich fir, was 1787 feet long and 22 feet wide; Nimmo died in 1832 before it was complete.

In 1882 Nimmo's bridge was taken down and replaced by a new structure; only the toll cottage remains today. The new bridge was a joint venture by Cork and Waterford counties, operating (apparently) independently of one another. It was an extraordinary-looking structure, for the two parts appeared quite different and seemed to meet in the middle only by accident. In 1922, during the Civil War, the bridge was severely damaged by retreating Republicans as they tried to disrupt communications ahead of the advancing Free State Army. Post-war repairs never quite restored the bridge to its original condition, and as the years went by floods and storms contributed their share of damage.

By the 1950s the bridge was downright dangerous, but the cost of replacing it was prohibitive. An Irish solution was found to an Irish problem: barrels filled with concrete were placed along the bridge, and motor traffic had to slalom between them. This caused great hilarity among foreign visitors, and Youghal Bridge became quite a tourist attraction. But it was also a cause of great inconvenience to the locals. The Cork-Waterford bus was a case in point. After leaving Youghal, the bus would deposit its passengers at the start of the bridge, and they would then have to walk across, carrying whatever belongings they had with them – heavy luggage was conveyed by taxi and trailer - and then board another bus waiting on the Waterford side.

Not until 1963 was a new bridge opened for traffic. It's much further upriver, at Rincrew, and lies entirely within County Waterford. It was the work of J.G. Murphy & Sons of Cork, whose managing director was Vincent Bowen, son of the aforesaid J.K. Bowen. It included the longest sections of pre-stressed concrete so far used anywhere in the world, and eminent engineers came from all over to view it.

Youghal Bridge was opened for traffic in 1963 – on this day.

Sorting out the bags for the walk across
Photo: Donal Sheerin courtesy of Aherne's Townhouse & Seafood Bar, Youghal

GREAT WESTERN'S LAST VOYAGE, 1966

Brian Cleare's painting of the *Great Western* battling across the Irish Sea

Knock, knock. "Slater here, sir. Your early morning cup of tea, Just rounding the Hook, sir." The door opens and through bleary eyes I see the genial figure of little Mr Slater, the cabin steward on the *Great Western*. Ten minutes later I am dressed and leaving my little deck cabin, for which last night I had paid the princely sum of five shillings. I stand by the ship's rails and look out on the finest view ever seen by any voyager – the hills of home.

Day is just breaking and I see that the sky will be clear, so that our journey up the estuary to Waterford during the next hour or so will take place in the chilly rays of the early morning sun. Snatches of "Dawn on the Hills of Ireland" run through my brain. Already the view is magnificent. To the starboard I see Hook Head, crowned with its Norman tower which houses the oldest working lighthouse in these islands. On the port side I see in the distance the lights of Dunmore, and further along the coast the dim silhouettes of the pillars at Brownstown Head and the Metal Man. As the estuary narrows and the morning brightens I see the long finger of Creaden Head and the dumpy outline of Duncannon Fort.

We steam on upstream, carefully following the marker buoys, and each bend of the river reveals another much loved sight. The villages of Passage East and Ballyhack. The tall shadow of the Hurt Hill. The junction with the Ross river, the sleepy village of Cheekpoint, the Barrow Bridge, with Great Island still unsullied by its monster of a power station. We have now turned westwards and pass great houses (some in ruins) and demesnes – Faithlegg, Woodlands, Snowhill, Belle-vue. On our left is the guide bank of Little Island, and through a gap in the trees we catch a fleeting glimpse of its wondrous castle.

By now my fellow passengers are on their feet, and some of them are enjoy-ing a hot breakfast below decks, confident that however rough the crossing of St George's Channel has been (and boy, could it be rough!), the voyage can do no further harm to their bellies. But I will live with my hunger for a while longer. At last we see the spires of Waterford, and soon we are turning carefully in mid-river before putting in at Adelphi Wharf. I see my parents waiting on the quayside, and I know that soon I will be whisked off to a hearty breakfast of real Irish eggs, bacon and sausages – at home.

The yellow-funnelled *Great Western*, a familiar sight to any Waterfordian aged forty or so, was the last inheritor of a long tradition of passenger service between Waterford and Pembrokeshire. For centuries the Welsh port of embar-kation had been Milford Haven. Then in 1906, over a million tons of rock having been blasted from the cliffs to make a clearing for quays and railway station and to provide material for a half-mile-long breakwater, the terminal was transferred to Fishguard – or, more correctly, Goodwick.

The *Great Western*, named after the rail company that owned and operated her, was a twin-screw steamer built at Birkenhead in 1933. Her hull was of steel, she was 283 feet long and 40 feet broad. She came into service in 1934 and spent almost all her peacetime career working between Waterford and Fishguard.

Photos: Andrew Kelly

Her main function was to convey live cattle from Ireland to Britain, and her few equally live passengers definitely took second place. I remember the astonished faces of returning English tourists who were forced to queue while the precious bovines filed on board wearing the smug expressions normally borne by VIPs.

But though her passengers were few, they felt themselves to be an honoured bunch. For the *Great Western* was a thorough lady. She departed and arrived at civilized hours and she took you straight to destination, unlike the wretched *St David,* which dumped you on the quayside at Rosslare in the freezing dark and left you to fight for a train seat.

Staff and regular passengers knew each other well. My friends the Anderson children persuaded the captain to sound the ship's siren when passing their house (Ballycar in Newtown) so that their mother would know it was time to head for town to collect them.

But alas, the passenger traffic ran at a loss, and in 1959 the little cabins were removed. The cattle continued for a while longer. Then in 1966 British Railways closed the route. Our faithful *Great Western* was taken to Heysham and then to Belgium, where she was broken up in 1967. But she will always live on in my memory, and doubtless in other people's as well.

She left Waterford for the last time in 1966 – on this day.

EPILOGUE

|᠁|᠁|᠁|᠁|᠁|᠁|᠁|᠁|᠁|᠁|᠁|᠁|᠁|᠁|᠁|᠁|᠁|᠁|᠁|᠁|

As the 21st century unfolds, our lives continue to change with bewildering speed. The revolution in communications has led to a greater openness in many ways, but it also seems to have imposed a ruthless pressure to conform, while we are in danger of losing our sense of ourselves in an alarmingly monocultural world. Meanwhile, the problems we inherited from the previous century have not gone away, and have in some cases become substantially worse, while the "war to end all wars" that we are busy commemorating at present turns out to have been all too obviously misnamed.

Before we lose ourselves in the present, however, we must anchor ourselves securely in what we have inherited from our past, for that is what really makes us what we are. That is why it is so important to understand our history. This summer Waterford has played host to many visitors, who have come to admire our scenery and monuments, our customs and festivities. We need to know what we are presenting to them.

I hope that this selection of stories will help hosts and visitors alike to appreciate and enjoy our very diverse heritage.

Julian C. Walton

ACKNOWLEDGEMENTS

|··········|··········|··········|··········|··········|··········|··········|··········|··········|··········|··········|··········|

GRATEFUL ACKNOWLEDGEMENT IS MADE FOR ALL ASSISTANCE GIVEN BY THE FOLLOWING:

Aherne's Townhouse & Seafood Bar, Youghal

Wayne Brown (recording of CD items)

Brian Cleare (wonderful paintings of ships)

Copper Coast Geopark Limited

Crawford College of Art & Design, Cork

Duncannon Military Fort & Fortifications (Marion Coady & Lorraine English especially)

Dunhill Multi-Education Centre staff

Erica Fay (who chairs the Waterford Archaeological and Historical Society)

William Fraher (always on hand to give of his knowledge)

Barbara Grubb (Dromana)

The Honourable Society of King's Inns

Horgan Brothers, Youghal

Bill Irish (great collection of pictures)

Andrew Kelly (things would have been so difficult without Andy's assistance)

Des Manahan (music for the CD)

Dave Moore (those very good cartoons pre-date photography)

Máiréad Murphy (Dunhill)

National Library of Ireland (photographs)

Noreen Nugent at Waterford County Museum (untiring in her archival searches)

Ivan Power (photo)

Donal Sheerin (who would go to any lengths to get a photograph)

Andy Taylor (Tramore's special historian)

The Ulster Folk and Transport Museum

Waterford Museum of Treasures, Three Museums in the Viking Triangle

Mark White (of Antidote, one of the most patient people on earth)

Eddie Wymberry (nothing is too much for that man)

*If we have inadvertently omitted from the list somebody
who rendered assistance, we apologise profusely.*

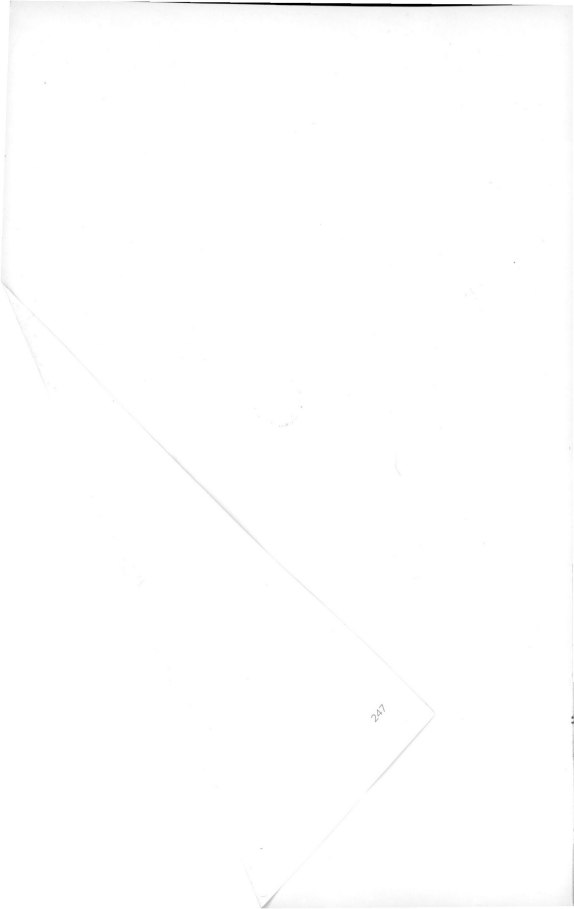

247